more...
Group®
RETREATS

Compiled by Cindy S. Hansen

Group Books
Loveland, Colorado

More...Group Retreats

Copyright © 1987 by Thom Schultz Publications, Inc.

All rights reserved. No part of this book may be reproduced in any manner whatsoever without prior written permission from the publisher except where noted in the text and in the case of brief quotations embodied in critical articles and reviews. For information write Permissions, Group Publishing, Inc., Dept. BK, Box 481, Loveland, CO 80539.

Designed by Judy Atwood Bienick
Cover illustration by Steve McInturff

Scripture quotations are from the Holy Bible, New International Version. Copyright © 1973, 1978, 1984 International Bible Society. Used by permission of Zondervan Bible Publishers.

"The Grace of God" is adapted and expanded from original material written by Larry Norton, Resources for Youth Ministry, 74.2. "This I Believe" is revised from an earlier retreat by Dean Dammann, Resources for Youth Ministry, 77.3. Reprinted with permission from the Board for Youth Services, Lutheran Church—Missouri Synod, St. Louis, MO.

Library of Congress Cataloging-in-Publication Data
More—group retreats.

    Continues: The group retreat book / by Arlo Reichter & dozens of contributors. c1983.
    1. Retreats for youth—Handbooks, manuals, etc.
I. Hansen, Cindy S. II. Reichter, Arlo, Group retreat book.
BV4531.2.M63 1987 259'.23 87-11961
ISBN 0-931529-12-3 (pbk.)

15 14 13 12 11 10 9 8 7   04 03 02 01 00 99 98 97 96

Printed in the United States of America.

Contents

Section Four: Bible Study

Section Five: Faith

Introduction

This resource is second in a series of Group retreat books. The back cover of *The Group Retreat Book* advertised that it was "the only retreat book you'll ever need." Well, this is the only OTHER retreat book you'll ever need. There are several reasons why:

● A recent Gallup poll asked both Christian and non-Christian young people whether they liked the ideas of retreats. Over half said yes.

● In a poll of 600 kids at a denominational national gathering, 66 percent of the young people said they wanted *more* retreats.

● A recent GROUP Magazine survey found that the second-most-common youth group activity is a retreat.

● *And*, we've been deluged with requests for more retreats.

So, we've responded enthusiastically with *More . . . Group Retreats*. Like *The Group Retreat Book*, this resource contains retreats written by youth workers from across the country—people actually in the field of youth ministry. It contains tried-and-true ideas that meet the needs of your young people.

More . . . Group Retreats includes 30 retreats on a variety of topics such as self-image, spiritual growth, popularity, back-to-school concerns, reaching out to others, power struggles within a family, discipleship, grace, leadership, Bible study, tough times, Christian views on sexuality, the blahs, and more. Each retreat includes an introduction, objectives, guidelines for preparation, step-by-step ideas for the main ingredients, and reproducible handouts that help your young people dig into the topics.

Consult *The Group Retreat Book* for "retreat basics" such as:
● getting started with retreats;
● writing a retreat purpose and goals;
● planning retreats;
● choosing the best location;
● tips for transportation;
● setting budgets;
● fund raising;

- publicity;
- leadership tips;
- retreat rules, themes, formats, checklists and outlines;
- food and snack ideas; and
- post-retreat follow-up.

Retreats are a valuable part of any youth ministry. They offer opportunities to help kids get to know one another better; structure to discuss important topics; a chance to break away from daily pressures; and a chance for renewing and re-energizing enthusiasm for life.

Jesus often used retreats as a method of renewal for his disciples. He took Peter, James and John and led them to a high mountain by themselves (Matthew 17:1-8).

Give your youth group members exciting mountaintop experiences. Help them get away to renew their faith and grow closer together. Best wishes and God's blessings as you experience the powerful world of retreats.

Section One
Self-Image

1

Being Up, Being Down

By Kristine Tomasik

Self-confidence, or nagging insecurity? This retreat builds members' inner core of confidence based on God's love. Being Up, Being Down is outlined for a weekend setting with meeting segments plus lots of time for fun and relaxation. It can be used just with youth—or as a morale-booster for the whole church!

During this retreat, participants will:

● increase their sense of confidence and their zest for life;

● learn positive ways of "talking to themselves"; and

● discover new ways of looking at themselves—with God's eyes of love.

Before the Retreat—Gather a roll of butcher paper; newsprint; markers; several cans of different-colored spray paint; poster paint; brushes; chalk; construction paper; scissors; glue; tape; string; candles; matches; incense; quiet music; dime; and, for each person, a Bible, several sheets of paper and a pencil.

On a sheet of newsprint, print the words found in Freeze Sculptures.

—————— Retreat Ingredients ——————

FRIDAY

Freeze Sculptures—Greet the participants and launch immediately into a rousing time of enthusiastic group singing. If possible, include a few of those fun little-kid songs that have motions. They will get the teenagers' circulation going!

Introduce the retreat theme by saying: "Self-confidence! Even the word makes you stand up a little prouder. Self-confidence is something everyone wants. Our goal this weekend is to help you replace uncertainty, fear, criticism and worry with enthusiasm, motivation, joy and self-confidence.

Retreat Schedule

Friday
8:00 p.m. Arrive at retreat site
8:30 p.m. Freeze Sculptures
9:00 p.m. Make a Mural
10:30 p.m. Snack time
11:30 p.m. Sack time

Saturday
8:00 a.m. Breakfast
9:00 a.m. Busting the Kick-
Yourself Habit
11:00 a.m. Free Time
Noon Lunch
1:30 p.m. Double Mask-Making
3:30 p.m. Free time for volleyball,
tug of war, flag football
or basketball

5:30 p.m. Dinner
6:30 p.m. Group hike—burn off
the calories from dinner
8:00 p.m. Revelation and Blessing
9:30 p.m. Quiet time for personal
devotions
10:30 p.m. Refreshments
11:30 p.m. Lights out

Sunday
8:00 a.m. Breakfast
9:00 a.m. Scripture Search and
Affirmation
10:30 a.m. Clean up, pack and
depart

"I'm going to read a list of words about self-confidence—interspersed with words about the opposite attitude, no confidence. As I read each word, express that attitude in a freeze sculpture—a pantomime. Really ham it up."

Here are some words to read. Switch from list to list as you go.

unsure of yourself	confident
fearful	happy
critical	enthusiastic
don't care	motivated
anxious	energetic
depressed	joyful

Discuss briefly by asking these questions:

● How did these postures feel? Which ones did you enjoy? Which ones felt uncomfortable?

● Why do you think we have these feelings?

Make a Mural—Display the list of words (which you have printed on newsprint before the retreat). Tape a long, continuous sheet of butcher paper—as long as you can manage—around the walls of your room. Give teenagers art supplies such as spray paint, poster paint, brushes and chalk and turn them loose to illustrate the words. They can simply make abstract drawings or they can use stick figures to draw scenes. One catch: They should make the mural a continuum, one end depicting extreme lack of confidence, the other end depicting buoyant energy. Provide teenagers adequate time to do this art-expression mural, and make sure everyone participates—including you! Leave the mural up for the remainder of the retreat.

When the mural is completed, ask kids to take a "visual vote." They should give their answers to the next questions by standing in front of the spot on the mural that most closely represents their answer.

● Where do you see yourself most often on this mural?

● Where on this mural would you like to move to?

Make no comments on the visual voting, but thank the group and ask them to sit down. Discuss briefly:

● What are some dangers of lack of self-confidence?

● Do you think it's possible to go too far off the confidence end of the scale? Why or why not? What are some dangers of over-confidence and egotism?

● Do you think it's a good idea to make a huge leap on the continuum overnight—from very low confidence to very high confidence? Why or why not?

● Do you think it's possible—or even desirable—to "arrive" totally in self-confidence land?

● Is there anything good about some self-doubt? Explain.

Conclude this discussion by saying: "It's important to have a balanced, grounded kind of self-confidence. We probably all know people who are overly optimistic. For these people, eveything's always fine. That's just not realistic! We all have our blue moods. But just as unrealistic is the person who's always moping around feeling uncertain.

"Nor is it a very good idea to expect ourselves to take a huge leap from one end of the scale to the other. We can begin to achieve a balanced, grounded confidence by realizing several important things."

Pause, and write on the "confidence" side of the mural, "I love myself." On the opposite end write, "I hate myself." Continue by saying: "Loving ourselves—or disliking ourselves—that's what's really going on here. This weekend, we'll learn some practical ways of being kind to ourselves. As you practice these ways, your self-confidence, motivation and energy will rise!

"But I wouldn't be telling you the whole story if I didn't share with you the best motivator of all. God really loves you! And he wants you to love yourself, too."

Ask the kids to relax, shut their eyes and take part in the following guided prayer. Tell them to try and see, feel and imagine what you describe. Read the following slowly, pausing to allow participants time to visualize: "God loves you. Really accepting this—letting it under your skin—makes all the difference in your confidence level. Right now, visualize God's love as warm, fragrant, healing oil . . . Feel it creeping in under your skin . . . Feel it begin to seep further and further into your body, seeping into all your cells . . . Let it reach into any sad places . . . Let it reach into any uncertain places . . . Let it reach into any anxious places . . . Let yourself feel God's warming, healing love . . . "

Dismiss the group quietly when you are through.

SATURDAY

Busting the Kick-Yourself Habit—Welcome the group back and sing another song or two to help them wake up. Explain that you're *sure* since this group is full of confident people, you'll have no trouble getting volunteers for this test of coordination. Take a dime, wet it and stick it to the first volunteer's forehead. Ask him or her to try to shake it off. The dime will really stick, but the volunteer will be able to shake it off after a few tries. Call for a few more volunteers and let them each shake the dime off. Then, select an adult sponsor (or somebody you know won't mind being laughed at) for the final part of this game. After you stick the wet dime to his forehead, quickly take it off again. He will be trying to shake a non-existent dime off his forehead, because he'll feel that it's still there.

Once he catches on and you all have a few good laughs, make the following point: "It would be easy for this sponsor to kick himself for falling for this trick. But that would be pointless. Anyone else in his situation would have done the same thing! But believe it or not, every day many of us go around kicking ourselves for things that are just as unavoidable. One person is angry with himself because he made a stupid remark in class. Someone else screams at herself because she didn't make the track team, even though she tried her hardest. Someone else feels badly about himself because he just isn't as well-liked as his brother."

Post a large sheet of butcher paper lengthwise and ask participants to brainstorm the rotten kinds of things teenagers say to themselves to kick themselves. Write these responses on the left half of the paper. Discuss briefly:

● Why do we sometimes talk to ourselves like this?

● Is it ever okay to mentally kick ourselves?

Say: "Talking bad to yourself is just one more way of hating yourself. When you have this kind of negative drone playing in your mind, it's easy to lose motivation, enthusiasm and joy. So instead of talking bad to yourself, be kind! Talk nice to yourself!"

Ask participants to brainstorm encouraging, positive messages which they could give themselves to replace negative criticisms. For instance, instead of saying, "I did awful at my tuba recital!" they might tell themselves, "I did better than I did last time!" or "I made three mistakes in one song, but I played the other songs straight through without error." Write their suggestions on the right side of the butcher paper.

Explain that you are now going to give participants a chance to practice "talking nice" to themselves! Have them choose a partner—preferably someone they know and trust fairly well. Partner A should think of the last time he or she was angry with himself or herself and tell Partner B about it. Together, they should think up encouraging (and truthful) things that A could have said instead. Then, A should actually verbalize those encouraging things with B listening. Switch roles.

Close this session by having participants share (in the large group) the nicest thing God has ever said to them. It could be a Bible verse, or it could be something the Holy Spirit brought personally to their minds.

Double Mask-Making—Begin by reviewing the lists of "confident" and "not-so-confident" feelings from the first activity. Ask:

● Do you think it's possible for someone to have an outer appearance of confidence while all the time feeling insecure on the inside? Explain.

● What are some dangers of trying too hard to cover up what's inside?

Say: "Having our outer self match up to our inner self is called congruence. Congruence is emotionally healthy.

"If we are always trying to cover up what we really feel, that's incongruent. Incongruence makes us phony."

Give participants basic mask-making materials such as construction paper, scissors, glue, tape and string. Invite them to make a set of masks. One should represent their "outer face"—this is the face they show to the world. What do they let others readily see about them? The other mask should represent their "inner face"—this is their inner self. What do they most fear others will see? What "flaws" do they work hardest to hide?

To make their masks unique, participants may go outside to collect specific materials such as sticks, leaves, feathers, shells, "garbage" or any other materials that they feel will help them express their outer and inner faces. Allow enough time to work. Then have them save their masks for the evening session.

Revelation and Blessing—Gather participants for a solemn ceremony. Explain that they are all priests and priestesses in Christ Jesus. This means that they have the power to "hear confession"—to see someone's inner face if he or she will show it. They also have the power to "bless"—to heal, minister to and accept each other. Dim the lights and light some candles. (You also can play quiet music and burn incense to enhance the solemn atmosphere.) Invite everyone to feel a holy, reverential mood. Ask participants to find a partner and, maintaining this holy mood of awe, show each other their outer face (mask)—then their inner face. Have them explain as much of each mask as they like. After a person has shown his or her inner face, the partner is to bless the mask in some way. For example, a person could hold the mask and make a sign of the cross over it.

Let the ceremony begin, and continue as long as need be. Dismiss the group quietly.

SUNDAY

Scripture Search and Affirmation—Welcome participants to the closing session of your retreat. Tell them they will be searching the scriptures to find references to God's love and acceptance of them—both their outer face and their inner face.

Give everybody a God Loves Me handout, pencil and Bible. Ask participants to read each passage, then jot notes about the positive things God is saying about them and their lives. Now invite participants to convert this biblical data into affirmations. Explain: "An affirmation is a positive, short, clear message of hope and love that you can believe about yourself. It should always be phrased in the present; it should always be stated positively—what you do have or want—not what you don't."

Read the following sample affirmations so participants get the idea. Then have them complete their own scriptural affirmations on their handout.

Romans 8:15-17—I am inheriting tremendous wealth and blessing as the beloved child of God.

Romans 8:28—All things are now working together for good in my life.

John 10:10b—Abundance is being freely given to me. I accept it!

Matthew 22:39—The more I love myself, the more love I can give to others.

Proverbs 2:10—God's perfect wisdom is in my heart.

Philippians 4:6-7—God's wonderful, gentle, consoling peace lives within me.

Divide into pairs and discuss the handouts. Then, on the opposite side of their handouts, invite each participant to write several affirma-

God Loves Me		
Bible Verse	**Positive things God says about me**	**Affirmation: short, clear message of hope**
Romans 8:15-17		
Romans 8:28		
John 10:10b		
Matthew 22:39		
Proverbs 2:10		
Philippians 4:6-7		

tions describing their particular gifts and strengths. Partners can help by naming strengths they see. For example, "I am a gifted, energetic artist." Or, "I have a wonderful ability to care for and nurture others."

End the session by repeating the visual vote you took at the beginning of the retreat. Ask participants to stand in front of the spot on the mural that best represents their feelings now. Affirm everyone's stance with this prayer: "God of our ups and God of our downs, teach us, we pray, to love ourselves as you love us. Help us to love our inner face and our outer face. Let us truly take your love like healing oil into our deepest selves, that we may pass it on to others. Amen."

2

Courage to Be a Christian

By Julie Sevig

I t takes courage to be a Christian today. Teenagers need to recognize not only the faith and courage of those who have gone before us, but the courage they can have in their own daily lives. Participants will look at the lives of courageous people of faith such as Daniel and the Apostle Paul, as well as contemporary Christians. Young people will also reflect on their own faith and how far they will go to stand up for their beliefs under peer pressure.

A main part of this overnight retreat is the Underground Worship experience. This activity provides a good way to imagine the boldness some people need today to proclaim their faith. It also offers the group a chance to reflect on the religious freedom we have, which includes sharing our faith openly.

This retreat is designed as an overnight lock-in experience, but it can be lengthened. It follows a tight schedule, which includes sleep and a variety of activities—Bible study, small group interaction and recreation.

All experiences are intended to help teenagers realize:
● how much courage it takes to be a Christian;
● how much courage it took for others to preserve our Christian heritage;
● the impact of one person's courage in sharing his or her faith;
● how much courage they have and how much they need to profess their Christian faith; and
● that their personal response to their faith can make a difference not only to themselves but to others.

Before the Retreat—Several months in advance, select a committee of young people to decide on the date, times and location of the retreat. The church building works well, but this retreat can also be used in a camp setting. Research several opportunities for recreation like swimming or ice-skating. You might want to rent a gymnasium for volleyball, basketball or other planned activities. Preview movies or other video programs you are interested in using.

Spend some time brainstorming about guest speakers or worship leaders in whom you would be interested. Visit with these individuals about your plans for the type of retreat you have in mind and get their responses. Once you have decided on these plans, contact your leaders, explain your program and confirm their response in writing. Make all reservations and then begin promoting your retreat.

In preparation for the Underground Worship session, read your newspaper and news periodicals for stories of Christians in other countries who must courageously struggle for the opportunity to practice their faith. Research some histories of Christian persecution like the influence of Thea Ronning, a missionary in China prior to the Boxer Rebellion. Select portions of these articles to read as background information for this meaningful experience.

Select young people to prepare and perform a role play to introduce the theme of courage. Use characters from *The Wizard of Oz* with particular emphasis on the Lion, who wanted courage. You will need five people and a dog (unless someone wants to be Toto!)—the Wizard, Dorothy, Tin Man, Lion and Scarecrow. Each character needs to ask the Wizard for his or her needs (to get back to Kansas, for a heart, for a brain and for courage). The Wizard can assure the group that they already have those things. He should point out each person's gifts, ending with the Lion who already has courage.

At least one month in advance, recruit your chaperones or sponsors and make sure they are committed for the whole retreat. Reconfirm your plans with your worship leaders and guest speakers. Double-check the videos or films you have reserved or ordered and make sure you have the proper equipment to use them (VCR, projector, screen, etc.).

Ask participants to bring wacky clothes for the Freedom Banquet. Purchase food that teenagers enjoy like pizza and pop and decorations like streamers and balloons. Record festive music on a cassette tape, and don't forget to take your tape player!

Gather Bibles; paper; pencils; candles; offering trays; and one piece of clay in a plastic bag for *each* participant. Prepare the handouts for I Want CCCCCourage! and First Word. You might want to prepare your list of items for German Football plus the 10 rounds of words and titles for Pencil Charades since these activities are at the beginning of your retreat.

Use group singing throughout your retreat. If you're not comfortable leading the singing, find someone who is. Pick songs ahead of time, but be open for requests. All of the songs used in this retreat are in *Songs* (Songs and Creations, Inc.).

Retreat Schedule

Friday

6:30 p.m. Introductions and orientation

6:45 p.m. Community-Building Activities

7:30 p.m. Group singing

8:00 p.m. I Want CCCCCourage!

9:00 p.m. Recreation

10:15 p.m. Freedom Banquet

11:00 p.m. Underground Worship

Midnight Thank God for Courageous Christians

1:00 a.m. Movies, popcorn, sleep

Saturday

9:00 a.m. Breakfast

10:00 a.m. First Word

11:30 a.m. We Are Free!

Noon Lunch and departure

Retreat Ingredients

FRIDAY

Community-Building Activities—Ask the group to line up in alphabetical order, according to their first names. This is a good way to mix the group and help them get to know each other. Once everyone is lined up, divide the line into teams of three to eight people, depending on the size of your group. Have them line up as in a relay with each team behind its designated runner. These teams may be used for any type of relay game. Two fun choices are German Football and Pencil Charades.

In German Football, the leader stands a good distance away from the teams that are lined up. When he or she calls out an item like a Nike tennis shoe, an earring, a 10th-grade boy or one smelly sock, the designated runner rushes the item to the leader. The leader will award points to the team whose runner arrives first with the correct item. The leader can also award points for second place, if you wish. This is a good game because it takes no preparation and no materials, other than what the participants have on them. It also forces the team members to work together and get to know one another better.

Pencil Charades is much like regular charades, except participants *draw* instead of act out words or titles. Using a list prepared in advance, the leader brings one person from each team to the center and shows the top word. The teenagers run back to their groups and draw the item without talking or gesturing. They can speak only when someone guesses the item and they must acknowledge the correct answer. The person who guesses the item or title then rushes to the center, whispers the answer to the leader, gets the next word and then returns to the group to draw, and so on.

Play several rounds with 10 words or titles making up a round. Use simple words at the beginning like guitar, television or church. Then progress to names of movies, TV shows and religious terms like baptism, sermon and salvation.

I Want CCCCCourage!—Introduce the theme of your retreat with *The Wizard of Oz* role play worked out in advance. Point out to the group: "We are like that, too. God has given us gifts, and we need to recognize and use them. During this Bible study we'll pay special attention to the need of the lion who wanted 'cccccourage.' "

If you have arranged for a guest speaker or another worship leader, that person will want to build on the introduction presented by these young people. Allow about 20 minutes for his or her presentation and then proceed to the handout for I Want CCCCCourage! (If you were unable to get a speaker, move directly to the handout immediately after the role play.) In either case tell the group: "In this Bible study session we will examine the lives of two Bible characters, Daniel and the Apostle Paul. We'll look at our own lives of courage. We will also talk about what prevents us from being Christian in our everyday world and what we can do about it." Divide into small groups. Give each group a Bible and an I Want CCCCCourage! handout.

Freedom Banquet—When the group returns from their recreation, arrange to celebrate our freedom as Christians with a banquet. Make it extra-special by decorating while the group is away. Hang streamers and balloons. Turn down the lights and use candles. Play festive music.

You may even suggest banquet attire for the participants—hats, sweatsuits, inside-out clothing or anything weird. If the banquet is to be a surprise, adults and youth leaders could dress in a weird way and be waiters! Serve pizza and pop or other fun foods that kids enjoy.

Underground Worship—This is a simulation of living in a country in which people do not have the freedom to worship openly. Read portions of recent newspaper articles or tell stories of how Christianity has survived despite persecution.

Tell the young people that for one hour they will pretend they are living in such a country. Ask young people to regroup themselves into the small groups they had during their relays. The people in each small group will be a family. Assign each family to a particular room which they should consider home. Choose adults and older teenagers to act as guards and the cruel interrogator. Tell the kids they are free

I Want CCCCCourage!

This Bible study deals with two people who had to go against peer pressure and stand up for what they believed in: Daniel and the Apostle Paul.

In your small group spend some time getting to know each other by answering the following questions:

- What is the name or nickname you like to be called?
- How do you feel about your name?
- Why did you come to this retreat?
- What is your favorite thing to do on a Saturday?
- What is your favorite "pig-out" food?
- What is something you have the courage to do or something courageous you have done?

After sharing the answers to these questions, spend some time in the group reading Daniel 6:1-23 and discuss these questions:

- Why do you think Daniel prayed in front of the windows?
- How do you think he felt before being thrown into the pit of lions?
- Can you think of a time you stood up for what is right? Explain.
- Can you think of a time you felt unashamed to share your faith? Explain.

Read Philippians 1:12-30.

- What do you think a typical day in prison was like for Paul?
- How would you have reacted to Paul if you'd been a fellow prisoner?
- In verse 20 what were those times when Paul needed extra courage?
- In verse 28 Paul talks about enemies. According to Paul, who or what are your enemies?
- In verse 29 he mentions suffering for Christ. According to Paul, how do we suffer, or how should we suffer, for the cause of Jesus Christ?

After your group has finished discussing this handout, close the Bible study with sentence prayers, asking God for courage in some specific area of your life.

to move about, but the guards are free to stop and question them at any time. Guards may also search their homes and bring them to the interrogator with no explanation. Individuals or groups can also be placed in jail or executed immediately.

The goal of this exercise is for at least 50 percent of the group to succeed in worshiping together. Worship may be just saying the Lord's Prayer or reading a scripture passage together without being caught or stopped.

Quietly pull a few kids to the side and tell them they are spies for the guards. Give them the password and let them know they are responsible for telling the guards where their families are trying to meet.

Because Underground Worship is most meaningful and fun when the families succeed in getting together, have the guards let up on their role if the group is having little success. There's nothing like hearing victorious applause and screams from a far-off location after the families have succeeded in having the courage and boldness to worship together!

After the hour bring the group together to spend some time talking about their experience:

● How did it feel to be questioned?

● How did it feel when family members were taken away by guards?

● How did you answer when the guards asked if you were a Christian?

● How did it feel to be a guard or an interrogator?

Thank God for Courageous Christians—After the debriefing session, spend some time celebrating the privilege we have to worship together and share our faith with one another. Turn off the lights and use only candlelight. Ask participants to read scripture passages, offer prayers and sing songs that are meaningful to them. This type of unstructured sharing would be typical of the type of worship experienced by many people in oppressed countries.

If you have scheduled a guest speaker for this time, ask him or her to give a short message (five to 10 minutes) about courage with a personal story of boldness, if possible. Close your worship with prayer remembering those who must be courageous every time they worship. Sing a song like "In Christ There Is No East or West" to remind us of our relationship to others who seek to serve God throughout the world.

SATURDAY

First Word—Begin the day by singing some songs young people enjoy. Include some action songs that get the blood flowing and the mind working. Close the singing with a song like "Spirit of the Living God" that leads into today's theme of self-value.

Have a young person or an adult share the First Word of the day from Romans 12:2. This scripture passage will tie together yesterday's thoughts on peer pressure and today's Bible study on self-image.

Begin this session by passing out the bags of clay to each participant. Introduce the morning session by saying something like: "All of us need to know we are okay. This Bible study deals with the freedom we have to be ourselves. Because our self-image determines how courageous we are in our faith, it is important to recognize just how special and unique each one of us is.''

After this brief introduction, ask the group to make individual sculptures out of the clay in their bags. Have them pass their sculptures to the person on their right. These people may do anything they wish with the sculpture. After a few minutes ask the group how they felt about:

- making a sculpture out of their clay.
- giving up the sculpture they had created.
- what the other person did to their sculpture.

Explain to the group: "We are very similar to the clay sculpture. We are created by God, yet we let the views and ideas of others alter or change us. We need to celebrate our freedom—the freedom to be ourselves because Christ died for us. It *really* doesn't matter what others say or think. It's God's opinion that counts!''

Distribute the Self-Image Survey and pencils to everyone in the group. After participants have completed the survey, divide into small groups (you may want to use the small groups from the previous day).

Self-Image Survey

Below is a list of words that may or may not describe you. Check the first blank if *others* have ever described you in that way. Check the second blank if *you* believe that word describes you.

SURVEY

Others	You		Others	You	
_____	_____	cautious	_____	_____	proud
_____	_____	open-minded	_____	_____	gifted
_____	_____	shy	_____	_____	selfish
_____	_____	funny	_____	_____	friendly
_____	_____	afraid	_____	_____	aggressive
_____	_____	daring	_____	_____	polite
_____	_____	bighearted	_____	_____	disrespectful
_____	_____	sensitive	_____	_____	egotistical
_____	_____	rude	_____	_____	kind
_____	_____	arrogant	_____	_____	faithful

Ask them to talk about their surveys and answer the following questions:

● Do others think of you in a positive or negative way? Explain.

● Do you think of yourself as mostly positive or negative? Explain.

Assign the following scripture passages to the small groups: Genesis 1:26-27, 31; Leviticus 19:18; 1 Samuel 16:7; Psalm 139:13-16; Proverbs 31:30; Jeremiah 31:3; Matthew 6:25-34; Mark 12:31; Luke 1:68; Luke 16:15; John 3:16; Romans 8:31, 38-39. Ask the small groups to look up their assignments and be prepared to share them with the total group.

After about 10 minutes, have a spokesperson for each group report on the scripture passage they were assigned. Then, within the small groups, discuss the survey results, the scripture messages and how they are related to our self-image.

We Are Free!—Bring the small groups back together by singing "We Are the Family of God" or some other song that celebrates our oneness even in the midst of our differences. With the group review some of the messages we have experienced during these two days. If you have scheduled a guest speaker at this time, be sure he or she covers the following material:

"All of us have moments when we feel ugly, dumb or unloved, especially while we are teenagers. Why? Because our values have been placed on us by others. We tend to look at what other people say, not what God says. We get confused about what has true and lasting value, because of what our society tells us.

"Others generally judge us in four ways: what we own (possessions); things we do (accomplishments); who we know (relationships); and the way we look (appearance). These things definitely influence us, but they are not the things that determine our self-value.

"Instead, the scripture passages we just read reveal three truths:

"*We are unique.* We are created by a living and personal God, and we have a personal contribution to make that is like no other's;

"*We have intelligence.* We are a rational people with potential to learn and change and be creative; and

"*God loves us.* Our Lord has paid the price for our freedom. We pay a token amount for the bread for our physical needs, but God paid the supreme price for us by sacrificing his only son for our spiritual needs.

"Therefore, we are free to celebrate! We are so special that God has taken care of our penalty of sin and death. We are loved by a God that has offered the best he has as a sacrifice for our mistakes. We are free!"

Ask one of the young people to close with a prayer that remem-

bers the difficulties of:
- the people in the past who stood up for their faith;
- Christians today who live in oppressive societies and must muster tremendous amounts of courage to stand up for their faith; and
- each of us as we stand up for our faith, whether in school, at home or in other circumstances.

After the prayer pass out pieces of paper to the participants. Ask them to write down individuals or groups or countries of people whom they recognize as needing courage in their lives. Ask them to pray for these individuals every day for the next month. Pass the offering tray and collect these papers. Offer these concerns and individuals to God as the group sings "Let There Be Peace on Earth" or another song that encourages us to support each other's courage.

Down With the Blahs

By Arlo Reichter

Each person, each family, each youth group experiences the "blahs" (a period when life becomes dull and uninteresting). Often the blahs come in the middle of winter—the school year seems as though it will never end. Christmas is past and the new year isn't really new. In the middle of these experiences, this retreat helps individuals as well as the entire group overcome the blahs.

In this retreat, the participants will:
- list personal sources of the blahs;
- identify blessings that overcome the blahs; and
- discover at least one new thing about their faith.

Before the Retreat—Consult *The Group Retreat Book* (Group Books) for help with planning a retreat.

Select a unique retreat location to help build excitement.

Collect Bibles, Bible dictionaries and Bible handbooks for the Bible Input time; items for the parade presentations such as newsprint, markers, crepe paper, tape, costumes; and, for each person, masking tape and one blue and one yellow sheet of construction paper for the Friends as Blessings time.

Make copies of the following for each person: Personal Covenant, Personal Interview Sheet, Blahs to Blessings Acrostics, Encouragers of My Faith and People I Can Encourage.

Recruit a song leader. Have that person look for songs that reflect blessings, as well as songs the group already knows and likes.

Ask two people to prepare brief devotions on Luke 12:22-25 and 1 Peter 5:7.

Arrange for refreshments for the breaks.

Enlist youth or adult leaders for each group of six to eight persons. Give each leader two sheets of newsprint, markers, tape, pencils and a copy of Bible Input Sheet.

Secure or arrange for special equipment for the Get Rid of the Blahs Fun Time.

For bad-weather alternatives during the Get Rid of the Blahs Fun

Time, use ideas from the *New Games Book* or *More New Games* (Doubleday). Other bad-weather alternatives might include table games such as Trivial Pursuit, card games such as Rook, plus Christian music records or tapes.

As you travel to the retreat site and as you tour the retreat area, have adults (or designated young people) listen for conversations that reflect the blahs, e.g., boredom, strained boy-girl relationships, family problems. Ask the listeners to be ready to tell what they heard (without betraying confidences) during the Friday night session. Also have the same people listen for conversations that reflect blessings, e.g., new friendships, new talents discovered, positive family experiences, excitement about the retreat, songs of joy.

Retreat Schedule

Friday
7:00 p.m. Unload and settle in rooms
7:30 p.m. Opening Fun Time
8:00 p.m. Orientation and Personal Covenants
8:30 p.m. Blah Sheets
9:00 p.m. Blessing Sheets
9:45 p.m. Refreshment break
10:15 p.m. Blahs and Blessings Worship
11:30 p.m. Rest well

Saturday
8:00 a.m. Breakfast and announcements
9:00 a.m. Bible Study
9:30 a.m. Personal Interviews
9:45 a.m. Preparing Blah Dramas
10:30 a.m. Refreshment break
11:00 a.m. Blah Dramas
Noon Lunch
1:00 p.m. Get Rid of the Blahs Fun Time

4:00 p.m. Sing-Along Fun Time
7:00 p.m. Bible Input
7:45 p.m. Bible Characters Parade
8:15 p.m. Refreshment break
9:15 p.m. Friends as Blessings
10:00 p.m. Blessings Worship
11:30 p.m. Rest well

Sunday
8:00 a.m. Breakfast and announcements
9:00 a.m. Worship Preparations: Blahs to Blessings Acrostics, Encouragers of My Faith and People I Can Encourage
10:30 a.m. Closing Worship
11:00 a.m. Pack and load
11:30 a.m. Lunch
Noon Depart for home

Retreat Ingredients

FRIDAY

Opening Fun Time—These crowdbreakers will help get things started.

● *Bumper Bods*—This game is from *The Best of Try This One* (Group Books). You'll need a large, clear area. No need for circles or lines for this one; just have each person bend over and hold his or her ankles firmly.

When the leader says "Go," each person attempts to bump everyone else over (to the floor). The object is to be the last person not bumped over. Players are out if bumped over or caught not holding their ankles.

● *Bent Out of Shape*—This game is from *Try This One . . . Too* (Group Books). Divide the group into three equal lines facing the caller. The caller says, "All those who _____," and continues, "grab the _____ of the person in front of (or behind) you."

Examples for the first blank: didn't take a bath today, own a stereo, watch MTV. Examples for the second blank: left knee, right shoulder, right elbow.

Example of a complete command: "All those who brushed their teeth within the last 24 hours grab the left foot of the person behind you." Continue giving commands until everyone is tied in knots.

Orientation and Personal Covenants—If the retreat location is new for your group, take time to meet the person in charge. Have that person welcome the group and tell about the facilities and behavior expectations.

Take the group on a brief walking tour of the site. Listen for blah and blessing statements. Examples of blah comments: the showers are in a separate building, there isn't any pool, the snow isn't deep enough for sledding. Examples of blessing comments: the fireplace is beautiful, the rooms look great, it's only a short distance to the dining hall.

As group members return to the meeting room, divide them into small groups of six to eight plus an adult or youth leader.

Give each small group leader copies of the Personal Covenant worksheet, one for each person in the group. Have each small group form a tight circle.

Discuss additional behavior expectations you have for the weekend and go over the schedule. Answer questions.

Then say: "The purpose of this weekend is to overcome the blahs in all our lives. You'll identify those things that are blahs and look for blessings to overcome the blahs. You need to work with the group to accomplish this goal.

"Your group leader will now give each of you a Personal Covenant for you to promise to do your part to make this a good weekend. Take time to read the covenant, ask questions about it and sign it. Then, one person at a time in the small group tapes his or her covenant onto the wall as the rest of the group shouts 'Hurray for (person's name).' The next person tapes his or her covenant onto the wall, is cheered by the group and so on until all group members' covenants are taped onto the wall."

Personal Covenant

I promise to do my best to make this weekend successful. I will look for blessings that overcome blahs. I will work with the group and will participate in the retreat activities. I will follow the group's guidelines for behavior and do my best to be a blessing to all group members both during the retreat and after we return home.

_____

Signature   Date

Blah Sheets—Give each small group a sheet of newsprint and markers. Have each group write on the sheet things that contribute to the blahs. This is the group's Blah Sheet. Allow 10 minutes for all groups to complete the sheets. Then have them tape the sheets onto the wall.

When all of the Blah Sheets are taped onto the wall, read things from the sheets that contribute to the blahs. After you read each group's sheet, have everyone say, "Oh, blah!" with great emotion.

Now ask the designated adults or young people to tell some of the comments they heard in travel conversations that reflected the blahs.

Blessing Sheets—Have your song leader lead the group in two or three songs to change the mood from blahs to blessings.

Then say: "Many things can do away with blahs—we call them blessings. Blessings might be friends, something good that happens to us, a smile or anything that makes us happy.

"The same people who told us about blahs they heard will now tell us about blessings they heard.''

After the listeners report on the blessings, have each small group list blessings on another sheet of newsprint. After 10 minutes, have each small group post its Blessing Sheet on the other side of the room from the Blah Sheets, have them use red markers and draw a large "X" through their Blah Sheets.

When all the sheets have been posted, read the items on the Blessing Sheets. Have the entire group shout "Hurray for blessings!" as you finish reading each sheet.

Blahs and Blessings Worship—Have the small groups form one large group and sit in front of the Blessing Sheets.

Sing positive and upbeat songs. Have someone give a devotion on Luke 12:22-25. Ask volunteers to share blahs that have now become blessings. After each person finishes, have the entire group shout the "Hurrah for blessings!" response used earlier.

Close with a prayer of thanksgiving for blessings and a good night's rest.

SATURDAY

Bible Study—Have group members sit in the same small groups in a tight circle. Read 2 Corinthians 5:17-18: "Therefore, if anyone is in Christ, he is a new creation; the old has gone, the new has come! All this is from God, who reconciled us to himself through Christ and gave us the ministry of reconciliation."

Say: "This retreat is an experience of being joined with a part of the body of Christ. In other words, this youth group is part of the church. In this setting we discover new things about our faith, our brothers and sisters in Christ and ourselves.

"I'll give you an incomplete sentence to answer. The leader of each small group will finish the sentence. Then the next person to the right does so, and so on around the circle. You may pass if you can't think of something to say. Please try to work with your group. I'll call time after two minutes for each sentence. Then I'll give you another one to complete."

Model this activity yourself by completing each sentence first.

The incomplete sentences:

● Other than getting up for breakfast, the biggest blah this morning so far is . . .

● The best thing about our church is . . .

● The best thing about our youth group is . . .

● One new thing I've learned at this retreat about my faith is . . .

● One thing I'm going to do on this retreat to be a better Christian friend is . . .

Have each small group decide on one thing it can do to be a blessing for the entire group. Examples: keeping the meeting area clean, being quiet after lights-out time.

Personal Interviews—Give each person a Personal Interview Sheet. Have everyone put his or her name on the top of the sheet. Say: "This exercise helps you meet people other than those in your small group. People are blessings who help overcome blahs. Follow the directions on the Personal Interview Sheet." (Note: Adjust the handout to fit the size of your group.)

Help kids who have difficulty filling in their boxes. When everyone finishes, read through the boxes and have volunteers name some of the people who fit the categories.

Have the group repeat after you: "Other people/are blessings/who help us/overcome the blahs!"

Preparing Blah Dramas—Have everyone sit in the same small group. Each small group is to create and share a skit with the entire

Personal Interview Sheet

Your name _____

Directions: Find a person who fits the qualifications listed in a box. Have that person sign the box. Each box must be signed by a different person.

Has a pet	Lives in an apartment	Has sung in a choir	Has lived on a farm	Is over 16
Is attending his or her first retreat	Is older than you are	Has done baby-sitting	Is active in a sport	Has a nice smile
Has sung a solo	Has dark hair	Has a 10-speed bike	Has lived in your community less than three years	Has blond hair
Has lived in your community all his or her life	Has older brothers or sisters	Loves to swim	Has younger brothers or sisters	Has painted a picture

group. Theme suggestions: a blah day in the life of a new student at our school; a blah day when I do everything the gang wants to do, but the gang does nothing I want to do; a blah day in the life of a nursing-home patient; a blah day in the life of an unpopular teacher at school; a blah day in the life of a youth leader.

Allow the groups 30 minutes to develop and rehearse the skits. Then break for refreshments.

Have each small group present its drama. This will be a time of laughter and startling realism. Cheer for each drama.

Get Rid of the Blahs Fun Time—Before the retreat, plan this fun time carefully. If your site has a special facility such as a pool or ski area, now is a good time to use it.

Here are other ideas: Build snow castles rather than sand castles, have a beach party in the snow, play softball in the snow, have a winter hay-ride.

Also, prepare bad-weather alternatives, just in case. Bring along table games such as Trivial Pursuit, card games such as Rook, or plan an afternoon using ideas in the *New Games Book* (Doubleday). Have good Christian music to listen to, and use your imagination to make this a time to overcome the blahs.

Sing-Along Fun Time—Have the song leader lead several upbeat songs.

To keep the spirit of the afternoon's fun alive, ask the group members to each name a blessing they experienced during the Get Rid of the Blahs Fun Time. When a person names a blessing, have the group respond with a cheer: "Hurrah for blessings!"

Bible Input—Have everyone sit in the same small group. Say: "We're going to help end the blahs by looking at the Bible in a fun way. We'll use old stories told in different ways.

"Your small group will be given a Bible person or Bible persons and supplies to plan a presentation for a parade. Make a float, dress up in costumes, design posters or plan a routine that presents your character(s) in a fun way. You have 30 minutes to get ready. Here is the information you'll need." (Hand out to each small group leader the Bible Input Sheet with one character role circled.) "Your group's character role is circled. The left column gives the references for the part I'll be reading from Hebrews 11.

"When I read your character role and then pause, you give your presentation. The right column gives a Bible reference for you to use to design your presentation. There are also Bible dictionaries and Bible handbooks to help you learn about your Bible person(s)."

Bible Characters Parade—For the parade, the narrator reads the verses indicated on the Bible Input Sheet, and pauses for each small group's presentation. Have the whole group give a cheer for each parade entry.

Friends as Blessings—Say: "Sometimes people around you are blessings who help you overcome the blahs. When a person does something nice for you or says something nice about you, it lifts your spirits.

"At this retreat, the members of your small group have become your special friends. Take time to think of one thing that each group member has done to help end the blahs."

Give each person one sheet of blue and one sheet of yellow construction paper and a pencil. Have the small groups sit in very tight circles.

Now say: "Take your sheet of blue construction paper and make a large capital 'B' by tearing the paper. The letter 'B' stands for the blahs. Use masking tape to stick the blue 'B' onto your back.

"Take your sheet of yellow construction paper and tear one star for each member of your small group except yourself. When you finish tearing stars, write each group member's name on a star. Then on each person's star, write one thing that this friend has done at this retreat to help overcome the blahs."

Give plenty of time but keep group members moving along.

Say: "In each small group, have one person at a time stand in the

---

Bible Input Sheet

During parade time, read the pasages in the left column. The passages in the right column are to help you prepare your part in the parade.

Narrator reads from Hebrews 11

References to help plan presentation (be sure to read footnotes)

Narrator reads from Hebrews 11	References
1-3—Faith defined	Narrator only
4—Abel	Genesis 4:1-7
5—Enoch	Genesis 5:21-24
6—Importance of faith	Narrator only
7—Noah	Genesis 6:11-22
8-10—Abraham	Genesis 12:1-8
11-16—Abraham's children	Narrator only
17-20—Abraham and Isaac	Genesis 22:1-10
21—Jacob	Genesis 32:22-29
22—Joseph	Genesis 37:5-24
23-29—Moses	Exodus 14:21-29

middle. All other group members, one at a time, tape the star for that person onto his or her 'B' and say, '(Name) helped end the blahs by . . . '

"When all group members finish and the person's 'B' is covered with stars, the entire group gives that person a group hug. Continue this process with each member of your group."

You might also have the small group members shout "Hurrah for blessings!" as they give the group hug to each person.

Blessings Worship—Have your song leader select songs about joy and blessings.

Have someone give a devotion based on 1 Peter 5:7 and have several people describe ways in which Jesus brings joy to their lives.

End with a circle prayer asking each person to thank God for one blessing they received this weekend.

SUNDAY

Blahs to Blessing Acrostic—As people arrive at the place for worship, have them sit in the same small groups. Hand out Blahs to Blessings Acrostics.

Say: "Complete the two acrostics—one using the word 'Blahs' and one using the word 'Blessings.' For the word 'Blahs,' list five words (the first beginning with 'B,' second with 'l,' third with 'a,' and so on) that cause the blahs in your life. For the word 'Blessings,' list words in the same manner that lift you out of the blahs. Bring your completed acrostics to the worship service."

Encouragers of My Faith—Hand out an Encouragers of My Faith sheet to each person and say: "List five people who are en-

---

Blahs to Blessings Acrostics

B _____   B _____
L _____   L _____
A _____   E _____
H _____   S _____
S _____   S _____
                               I _____
                               N _____
                               G _____
                               S _____

couragers of your faith. These may be people at the retreat or teachers, ministers, friends, parents or relatives who are not at the retreat. After each name, list ways this person encourages you. Save this list for the worship service also.''

Encouragers of My Faith

Name	How he or she encourages me
1.	
2.	
3.	
4.	
5.	

People I Can Encourage

Name	How I can encourage this person
1.	
2.	
3.	
4.	
5.	

People I Can Encourage—Hand out a People I Can Encourage sheet to each person and say: "List five people you can encourage in the faith. Also list ways you are or can be an encourager. Bring these to the worship service as well."

Closing Worship—Begin by singing songs that have been important at this retreat or during past experiences of the group. Read Philippians 4:8-9. Say: "As we worship, we give thanks for what God has given us at this retreat, but we also seek God's presence as we return home to put into practice what we've learned."

Ask group members to each share with one other person the acrostics they created. Now ask for several people to share their acrostics with the total group. Applaud all who share.

Have all the group members sit in one large circle. Ask each person to tell the name of one person who has been an encourager to his or her faith and a reason. After each person speaks, have the group say together: "We praise God for this encourager!"

Have each person look at the list of people he or she can encourage. Ask everyone to pray silently for each person on his or her list.

Have the group members stand, walk around, hug each other and say: "I'll encourage you! Please encourage me!"

Have your song leader lead a final song. Ask the group members to stand in a circle and hold hands. Give a brief closing prayer.

The Gift

By L. Jim Anthis

Life is a journey of gift-discovery and development. Invite young people to lay hold of the special gifts and talents God has given them and to begin using these gifts and talents. The Gift retreat is particularly effective during the Christmas season, but it can be used any time during the year.

This retreat will help the young people:
- become sensitive to the gifts and talents God has given them;
- seek ways to use these gifts and talents; and
- encourage each other's special qualities.

Before the Retreat—Make sure your retreat site has a meeting room with a soft carpet or comfortable chairs.

Gather marshmallows; wrapping paper; bright-colored ribbons and bows; a Christmas tree; newsprint; markers; tape; Bibles; refreshments; paper; and materials to make tree ornaments such as glue, scissors,

---

Retreat Schedule

Friday
7:00 p.m. Arrive and settle in
7:30 p.m. Gift Celebration
8:00 p.m. Your Surprising Gifts
9:00 p.m. Night hike—reflect on the beauty of all the gifts God gives us
10:00 p.m. Sing songs and roast marshmallows by the fireplace
11:00 p.m. Lights out

Saturday
7:30 a.m. Wake up

8:00 a.m. Breakfast Conversation
9:00 a.m. Defining Your Gifts
10:30 a.m. Break
11:00 a.m. The Gift Tree
Noon Lunch Conversation
1:00 p.m. Responding With Your Gifts
3:00 p.m. Worship Planning
4:00 p.m. Free time
5:00 p.m. Dinner Conversation
6:00 p.m. Closing Worship Celebration
7:00 p.m. Head for home

construction paper, magazines, glitter, pipe cleaners, cardboard and scraps of material. Each person will need a 3 x 5 card, pencil, candy bar, Gifts handout and Gift Award handout.

Make a surprise package for each person. Buy different types of candy bars (Mars, Snickers, etc.). Wrap one candy bar for each person; tie a bright-colored bow around it.

Set up a Christmas tree at the retreat site. Do this even if it is not Christmas! Place the surprise packages under the tree.

Write the conversation questions for each meal on newsprint. Post the questions during mealtime.

Retreat Ingredients

FRIDAY

Gift Celebration—Gather the kids around the Christmas tree. Say: "The purpose of this retreat is to help you discover your gifts. We're going to begin by opening some surprise packages."

Distribute one package to each person. Ask the participants each to open their package and then compare the gift to their thoughts about the retreat. For example, a person might receive a Snickers candy bar. He or she could say, "I hope to snicker and laugh and make new friends during this retreat." Let everyone have a chance to share, then eat the goodies!

Your Surprising Gifts—Gather the kids in a circle. Have them sit in a comfortable position, then say: "Once upon a time, Michelangelo pushed a huge slab of marble down a street. A curious neighbor sitting lazily on the porch of his house called out to him, 'Why do you labor so over an old piece of stone?'

"Michelangelo answered, 'Because there is an angel in that rock that wants to come out.'

"You and every young person in the world face the task of releasing the angels. You hold the raw materials of your lives. The exciting discovery of your gifts and abilities leads to your growth and to your becoming. The struggle to become who you are begins with that fascinating trip of gift discovery.

"As young people, you are full of surprises! Again and again throughout your lives you will be surprised as you discover your gifts. Close your eyes and think of these points."

Read the following four statements and pause for a few moments to let the kids reflect:

● God is my creator. I am created in his image. I, in turn, am the creator of gifts . . .

● I am here to discover and develop my gifts and abilities . . .

● I am responsible for my gifts . . .

● As long as my gifts are held back, I am not a whole person . . .

● A gift is not a gift until it is defined, developed and shared with all people . . .

● Imagine Christmas: You are standing by the tree, waiting to open your gifts . . . What do you hope to find?

Have the kids open their eyes, then distribute a 3×5 card and pencil to each one. Ask them two questions, and have them write their answers on their card.

● How would you define a gift?

● When you think of yourself, what is one gift you possess?

Gather in pairs and discuss the answers. When everyone is finished, gather the cards and wrap a bright-colored ribbon around them. Place the "package of gifts" under the tree.

SATURDAY

Breakfast Conversation—After saying a prayer of thanks for the food, draw the kids' attention to the newsprint with the discussion questions written on it. Ask them to discuss the questions with the others sitting at their table.

● What images come to your mind when you hear the term "youth"?

● What is one good aspect (or gift) about being young?

● If you could ask for one gift from an adult, what gift would you ask for? Why?

Defining Your Gifts—Gather in a large group and have the kids sit in a comfortable position. Invite the young people to let their imaginations go. Say: "Close your eyes and imagine a large movie screen . . . Project on the screen the most creative moment in your life . . . What did you do? Did you paint a picture? listen to a friend and help him or her solve a problem? come up with a solution to a family conflict? Remember the creative moment . . . Feel it . . . Taste it . . . Smell it . . . See it . . . Relive all of those images and feelings again, savoring that experience."

Bring the visualization exercise to a close by inviting the young people to open their eyes. Lead a discussion about the experiences by asking these questions:

● Describe your most creative experience.

● Why was it so unique that it flashed across your mental screen and lived again for you?

● What did you learn in re-experiencing it?

Give the young people each a Gifts handout and a pencil. On one side of their paper, have the kids draw or write all the gifts they see in others. Caution them this is not an exercise of artistic ability, but rather a discovery of gifts. On the other side of the paper, have them draw or write the gifts they see in themselves.

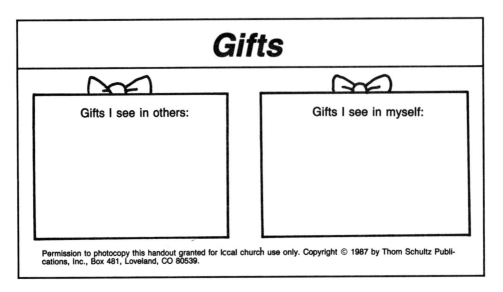

After 15 minutes, divide the group into small groups of three to four people. Give each small group a sheet of newsprint and a marker. On the sheet of newsprint have them write down all the gifts they see in themselves and others.

One at a time, ask each group to share its "gift list." Tape each list onto the wall and stick a bright-colored bow on it.

The Gift Tree—On a table, place glue, scissors, magazines, construction paper, glitter, pipe cleaners, cardboard and scraps of material. Invite the kids to each use the material on the table and make a "gift ornament" for the tree. Their ornament should reflect a shining, glittering gift they possess. For example, a person could make a circular ornament out of orange construction paper and glitter; it could represent his or her "sunshiny" personality.

After about 30 minutes, discuss the creations. One at a time, have the kids describe their gift, then hang the ornament on the tree.

Lunch Conversation—Note that within the Christian community the meal has always been a time of sharing God's gifts. Meals remind us of the gift of communion—the bread, wine, fellowship with others. Point to the list of questions you have taped to the wall. Have the kids discuss the questions at their tables.

● Who is a person you consider "great"? (Could be a grandparent, president, etc.)

● What is a gift that person gave you? others? the world?

● What action or quality made your person great?
● Describe a moment when you felt great.

Responding With Your Gifts—Gather the kids and ask them to sit in a comfortable position. Say: "When we are unsure of people's names, we tend to name them by their gifts; for example, the girl who beats everyone in pingpong, the guy who really can sing. Our gifts tell who we are."

Let the kids have a chance to think of a special gift they possess. Then go around the room and have everyone say his or her name and the gift. For example, "My name is David, and I'm a singer." The next person says his or her name and gift, then repeats David's name and gift. This continues until the last person says everyone's name and gift.

Then say: "Gifts are not really gifts until they are used and given to others. For example, singing in the shower may not be a great gift, but singing within the church choir is a great gift. At Christmas, we look for the right gift to give. The best gift is always the one that expresses who we are.

"Close your eyes and get comfortable. Using your senses, imagine it's the first Christmas with all of the excitement and enthusiasm of that time when Jesus was born. You are one of those coming to lay a gift at the foot of the manger. Stop and sense the atmosphere . . . Feel it . . . Smell it . . . Open your gift . . . the most special and unique gift you have to bring. Say to the Christ child, 'Jesus, I have brought you the most unique gift I have. It is . . .' Name your most special and unique gift . . ."

Have the kids open their eyes. Give them each a piece of paper and a pencil. Ask them to write down two or three gifts they want to develop.

Divide into small groups of four to five people. Have the members share the gifts they have listed. Encourage participants to listen and help each other work through their gifts. If they see a gift not on another's sheet, encourage them to name it and have the person write it down.

Gather all of the gift sheets and tie a ribbon around them. Place them under the tree.

Worship Planning—Have the participants stay in their small group and plan the closing worship. Assign each group a portion of the service. For example, one group could be in charge of a reading from the New Testament. The kids could choose the parable of the talents (Matthew 25:14-30). While one person reads it, the others could act it out. Another group could plan the sermon. They could lead a "group sermon" where everyone participates by filling in thoughts about the retreat. They could complete this sentence: "The one thing I won't forget about this retreat is . . ."

Part of the worship will be the giving of Gift Awards. Distribute a slip of paper and pencil to each of the group members. Have them write their name on the slip of paper. Gather the slips, mix them and redistribute them. Everybody should have a name other than his or her own. Next, give everyone a blank Gift Award. Have the kids fill out the award for the person whose name they drew. They should think of a special, unique gift that person possesses and write it in the appropriate blank. Save these awards for the worship service.

Gift Award

This award is given to _____

in honor of his/her gift of _____.

God has truly blessed you with this gift. Develop it and use it to your fullest potential.

_____

Signed

_____

Date

Dinner Conversation—Give thanks for the gifts of the kids and the gift of food. Then, call the kids' attention to the newsprint sign with discussion questions printed on it. Have them answer the questions at their table.

● Name one gift you have seen in others that really surprised you.

● What gift did you discover within yourself that surprised you the most?

● What is the most important gift you have to develop?

● What is the first thing you are going to do to develop it?

Closing Worship Celebration—Let the small groups each lead their portion of the service which they prepared. Close the service with the giving of Gift Awards. Say to the young people: "Opening gifts is one of the most exciting and fun things we do. God has given each of us so many great gifts—just waiting to be opened! We send you home with the hope that you will continually open up the gifts within your life, sharing them for the good of all people in the world."

—————————— 5 ——————————

Leadership–
Spiritual Gift

By David Olshine

L eadership is a unique gift. Some people have a natural ability to stand in front of a group and present themselves and their purpose with ease and dignity. Others lead best by organizing carefully, delegating authority and maintaining a constant vigil on how plans are proceeding. Some display their leadership skills by making people feel comfortable with what is going on. All of these forms of leadership have value in certain situations.

Most of us have some form of leadership ability. We may not lead in the same way as our best friend or our brothers and sisters. But just because our skills are different doesn't mean they are any less valuable. In the words of the Apostle Paul, "It was he who gave some to be apostles, some to be prophets, some to be evangelists, and some to be pastors and teachers, to prepare God's people for works of service, so that the body of Christ may be built up . . ." (Ephesians 4:11-12).

This retreat can help young people:
- be aware of the different kinds of spiritual gifts;
- identify their own spiritual gifts;
- realize how their spiritual gifts contribute to their leadership;
and
- understand that their gifts are needed in the body of Christ.

Before the Retreat—When you have a leadership retreat for young people, include them in the planning and decision-making for the event. Ask student leaders to meet with you and other adult sponsors to determine the role each will play during the retreat. Who will be in charge of the numerous responsibilities for preparing and running the retreat? Who will lead the community-building activities? Who will direct the worship? Who will make sure all the equipment arrives? Encourage your young people to become as involved as possi-

Nothing teaches leadership better than the act of leading.

Reserve a retreat center or campsite for a weekend. Prepare handouts for the studies on leadership and spiritual gifts. Look in the *Try This One* series or *Building Community in Youth Groups* (Group Books) for ideas on community-building and meaningful fun activities.

Read through the retreat and write all of the discussion questions on newsprint ahead of time.

For the Famous Leaders activity, prepare pieces of paper with the names of different leaders from the past and present. Divide your leaders into types with three to five leaders in each type. Include political leaders like the current President and Napoleon; religious leaders like Martin Luther and Gandhi; biblical leaders like Jesus and King David; scientists like Galileo and Jonas Salk; philosophers like Plato and Socrates; movie stars like Charlie Chaplin and Meryl Streep; musicians like Beethoven and Neil Diamond. Be sure to include enough different

Retreat Schedule

Friday

7:00 p.m. Registration and orientation

7:30 p.m. Group singing and community-building activities

8:00 p.m. Famous Leaders

8:30 p.m. What Makes a Leader?

9:00 p.m. Break

9:15 p.m. Peter: A Model for Leadership

10:15 p.m. Snacks and free time

11:30 p.m. Preparation for bed

Midnight Good night!

Saturday

7:30 a.m. Rise, shine and give God glory!

8:30 a.m. Breakfast

9:30 a.m. Group singing and community-building activities

10:00 a.m. Scavenger Hunt

10:45 a.m. Spiritual Gifts

Noon Lunch

1:00 p.m. Organized sports or games (volleyball, softball or tug of war)

2:00 p.m. Free time

4:00 p.m. Tabulation of Spiritual Gifts

5:00 p.m. Role play assignments

6:00 p.m. Dinner

7:00 p.m. Final preparation for role plays

7:30 p.m. Leadership Role Plays

8:30 p.m. The Disciples as Leaders

10:00 p.m. Snacks

10:45 p.m. Movie of your choice

Midnight Lights out

Sunday

7:30 a.m. Today is the day that the Lord has made!

8:30 a.m. Breakfast

9:00 a.m. Paul: A Leader in His Own Time

10:00 a.m. Personal Commitment

10:30 a.m. Peace Candle

11:00 a.m. Affirmation Event

Noon Communion

types of leaders that you can use this method to divide your group into smaller groups.

One option to the Spiritual Gifts handout used on Saturday morning is a personal inventory titled "Discovering Your Spiritual Gifts" written by Kenneth Kinghorn. By answering questions and tabulating the scores, your teenagers can determine the top three or four spiritual gifts toward which they lean. You will need one copy for each person. Order six weeks in advance from Kenneth Kinghorn, Asbury Theological Seminary, Wilmore, KY 40390.

Gather the following items for the Spiritual Gifts activity on Saturday morning: various colors of construction paper; magazines; tape; glue; pipe cleaners; markers; and, for each person, a one pound coffee can with lid or a half-gallon milk carton. You will also need enough 3×5 cards so that each person has a card for everyone else in the retreat.

In addition to these items, you will need paper; pencils; straight pins; a large roll of newsprint; a medium-size candle with a sturdy candleholder; equipment for the organized games on Saturday afternoon; and, for each person, a Bible and one stamped envelope.

For the movie on Saturday evening, you will need a movie projector or a television with a VCR. Try to choose a movie with a leadership theme or one that could stimulate some interesting conversation about leadership. For example, rent *Gandhi* or *Jesus of Nazareth* from your local video store.

All of the songs are from *Songs* (Songs and Creations, Inc.).

—————— Retreat Ingredients ——————

FRIDAY

Famous Leaders—Begin Friday evening's activities with singing and meaningful fun activities. Encourage everyone to bring a Bible, paper and a pencil to all sessions. To introduce the theme of leadership, play the following game.

Pin a piece of paper on each person's back. Don't let the participant see whose name is written on it. Explain to the group that the objective of this activity is for individuals to guess correctly the name on their back. Tell the group to mingle with each other and ask questions about who they are. Responses must be either yes, no or I don't know. Typical questions might be: "Am I living in the 20th century?" "Am I female?" "Am I an American?" "Am I a biblical character?" If a participant has difficulty discovering who he or she is, identify what *type* of leader he or she is like a politician, a musician, or a leader in religious history.

Once every person has identified the leader on his or her back, divide into small groups by the *types* of leaders. All the musicians will be in one group, the philosophers in another group and the biblical leaders in still another group. Remind participants to think about the different *types* of leaders they see represented.

What Makes a Leader?—Give each small group a What Makes a Leader? handout and have participants discuss the questions within their own group. After 20 or 30 minutes, ask the groups to come together as a total group and share at least one characteristic of leadership they noted during their discussions. Record these characteristics on the first of four large sheets of newsprint put up for everyone to see.

What Makes a Leader?

You have had a chance to look at the names of many different kinds of leaders during our game this evening. Think about the names you saw and discuss the following questions within your small groups:

1. What leader do you most admire and why?
2. Who do you think is the least effective leader?
3. What characteristics identify a strong leader?
4. What characteristics identify a weak leader?
5. What biblical character first comes to your mind when you think of leadership?
6. Do you feel you are a strong leader? Why?

Read aloud Matthew 10:1-4. Point out that Jesus worked with his disciples to build leaders. Ask the group to identify the leadership skills described in these verses that Jesus helped to develop within his disciples. Write these on the second sheet of newsprint.

On the third sheet of newsprint, ask the group to list Jesus' followers. Then take about 10 minutes to record what your young people know about each of these men. They may know a lot about Peter, James and John, but very little about disciples such as Thaddaeus, Philip and Bartholomew.

Peter: A Model for Leadership—Write the following scripture passages and numbers on separate pieces of paper and hand them out at the break. Ask individuals to read through the passages and be prepared to read them aloud to the total group. These will be read in order after the introduction.

1. Matthew 15:15
2. Matthew 16:15-16
3. Matthew 14:29
4. John 6:66-67
5. Matthew 16:18-19
6. Matthew 16:21-23
7. Matthew 26:31-35
8. John 21:15-17
9. 1 Peter 2:13-18
10. 1 Peter 2:21-23
11. 1 Peter 4:12-13
12. 1 Peter 5:5
13. 1 Peter 4:8

Introduce this study by reviewing some of the facts about Peter that are already listed on the newsprint at the front.

Ask if anyone knows why Simon's name was changed to Peter. Simon was a common name meaning "shifting" or "wishy-washy." Jesus changed this strong-willed man's name to Peter, which is Greek for "rock." Peter moved from being a "wishy-washy" fisherman to a strong and unwavering church leader.

Point out that Simon called Peter is the first disciple listed in Matthew 10:1-4. And after Jesus returned to heaven, Peter became the functional leader of the disciples.

Ask the kids to read their scripture passages in order. Then ask another young person in the group to summarize in a short phrase or word the leadership qualities evident in Peter's life. Write the participants' observations on the fourth sheet of newsprint. One young person might summarize Matthew 15:15 by saying, "Peter was curious and wanted to understand. He wasn't afraid to admit he didn't know something. Peter was *open* and *curious*." Point out that God used Peter as a leader even though he had weaknesses, like the rest of us!

Go through the list of scripture passages verse by verse and discuss Peter's life. When you get to the verses in 1 Peter, explain that Peter wrote this book later in his life. In it he mentions numerous keys to leadership. After each reading, ask the group, "What key words describe a leadership quality?" In 1 Peter 2:13-18, he suggests that we should submit to man's authority and show proper respect. In 1 Peter 2:21-23, the words, "be an example" and "do not retaliate" hold the message. In 1 Peter 4:12-13, we read that leaders should rejoice in their suffering because it teaches them to handle their personal struggles. In 1 Peter 5:5, we are told to be submissive to those who are older and show humility toward one another. In 1 Peter 4:8, we learn that a leader must love.

As the study on Peter draws to a close, summarize how Peter demonstrated his leadership characteristics. Be sure to point out that he made mistakes such as denying Jesus, but he was also the one who responded to Jesus, "You are the Christ." His life is an example of love, humility and submission, all accompanied by an inquisitive mind.

SATURDAY

Scavenger Hunt—Sometime before this activity begins, cut the Scavenger Hunt handouts in half. Give each group one of the top halves when the hunt begins, and save the bottom half for the group's discussion at the end of the hunt. After your singing and community-building activities, begin the hunt. Allow about 45 minutes for this activity, including the discussion at the end.

As participants return from the scavenger hunt, assign four individuals the following scripture passages to be read during the next session on Spiritual Gifts. Write these passages across the top of a

---

Scavenger Hunt

Your group will have 30 minutes to locate as many of these items as possible. The group that returns first with all or most of the items wins.

Acorn, or nut, still in shell
Drinking straw
Coke can
PBJ sandwich
A leaf from a plant
Plastic fork
Something fuzzy
Something treasured

Stick in the shape of a cross
Old sock with a hole in the toe
Smooth stone
Insect
King James Bible
Baby picture
Something hard

-- Cut here --

When you have returned from the scavenger hunt, discuss these questions as a small group:

1. Which individuals assumed leadership within your small group?
2. Who served as the director of the group?
3. Who was the most helpful?
4. Who was the most encouraging?
5. Who was the instructor or the person who explained how, when or what to do?
6. Did one person assume all of these roles, or did the leadership change?
7. Were there any individuals or forms of leadership that surprised you?

large sheet of newsprint and post it in the front of the room: Romans 12:1-8; 1 Corinthians 12:4-11, 28-30; Ephesians 4:7-12 and 1 Peter 4:9-11. (Remove the first sheet of newsprint from the night before. The other three will be used in later sessions.)

After the small group discussions, ask everyone to meet as a large group to discuss the leadership they saw during the scavenger hunt. Go through the discussion questions and review the characteristics of Peter's leadership that were listed the night before.

● Are there any significant similarities?

● Are there any significant differences?

● Did you make any new discoveries during this activity?

Spiritual Gifts—Ask individuals to read aloud the four scripture passages you assigned which deal with spiritual gifts. After each scripture, list the spiritual gifts mentioned and write them under that Bible verse on the newsprint. Remind participants that each person has spiritual gifts, and assure them that they do too.

Pass out one Spiritual Gifts handout to each person and explain how we can work together to help each person identify his or her own spiritual gifts. Tell the group: "You will participate in several activities with this handout, three of them this morning. First, everyone will decorate a can to reflect your own idea of your spiritual image. This activity is explained further in your handout. Next, you will use the list of spiritual gifts at the bottom of your handout to rank your own from 1 to 10. Write your rankings in the left-hand column at the bottom of this handout. Finally, refer to the same list of spiritual gifts and use a 3×5 card to identify the spiritual gifts in one another. List the three top gifts you see in each person and write them on a card. Then place this card in that person's spiritual-image can. The right-hand column of this Spiritual Gifts handout will be used later to tabulate the results of the 3×5 cards you are writing this morning."

Have all materials for this activity prepared ahead of time. Designate an area for the kids to place their spiritual-image cans when they have finished decorating them. Allow about one hour for this activity.

Tabulation of Spiritual Gifts—Following an afternoon of planned recreation and some free time, meet as a group to celebrate each other's spiritual gifts. After singing several songs like "We Are the Family of God" and "Everybody Has a Gift," ask participants to pick up their spiritual-image cans from the designated location. Have them remove their Spiritual Gifts handouts and 3×5 cards from the cans.

Then explain the tabulation procedure: "Using the right-hand side of your spiritual inventory, tabulate the results of your spiritual gift cards that others gave you. Each time someone mentions a spiritual gift, you get one point for that gift; order doesn't matter.

"After you have tabulated all the points from your 3×5 cards, add

Spiritual Gifts

1. Select one of the coffee cans. Cover the sides of the can with construction paper. Use a color that you feel creates the spiritual image you project to others.

Look at the list of spiritual gifts on the bottom of this handout. Try to portray the most dominant spiritual gift you believe you possess. For example, if you feel your best spiritual gift is the ability to write, cut a picture of a pencil from a magazine and glue it on your can.

Use any of the materials provided to decorate your can. Be sure your name is on the outside of the can in a way people can recognize it.

2. Look at the list of spiritual gifts again. This time rank your own spiritual gifts on a list from 1 to 10 (with 1 being the highest and 10 being the lowest). Use the left-hand column under Personal Ranking for your personal evaluation. For example, if your best spiritual gift is your ability to teach, put a 1 next to teaching.

3. After you have ranked your own spiritual gifts, pick up one 3×5 card for *each* participant at the retreat. Sign his or her name at the top of the card and list his or her top three spiritual gifts on that card. Choose from the gifts listed on this handout. You may sign the card if you wish, but it is not necessary. As you finish a person's spiritual gift card, place it in his or her spiritual-image can.

Spiritual Gifts

Personal Ranking (Use 1 to 10)		Others' Ranking (Tally cards here)
_____	Organized	_____
_____	Enthusiastic (about faith, life)	_____
_____	Giving (things)	_____
_____	Artistic (music, art, etc.)	_____
_____	Compassionate (cares)	_____
_____	Serving (helps)	_____
_____	Prayerful	_____
_____	Teacher	_____
_____	Writer	_____
_____	Speaker	_____

the points to determine which spiritual gifts others see as most dominant in you. Circle your top three or four spiritual gifts.''

While everyone is tabulating their spiritual gifts, locate the sheet of newsprint with the following questions on it and post it at the front of the room. When everyone is finished, ask the group to divide into their small groups. Have each person check both columns (the personal ranking and the ranking of others) to see how they compare. Ask the small groups to discuss these questions:

- Did others see you as you see yourself? Explain.
- Did others recognize the gifts you acknowledged? Explain.
- Did others see something in you of which you were not aware? If so, what was it and do you agree?

Caution the groups to listen to each other carefully. Remind them to clarify any misunderstandings and affirm new revelations for each other. As groups complete their discussions, ask them to put their cards and Spiritual Gifts handouts back in their cans, put the lids back on and display them again at the designated location. You will use the handouts one more time on Sunday morning.

Leadership Role Plays—On the Leadership Role Plays handout, circle a different situation on each sheet. While the small groups are still in session, pass out one handout to each group. Allow approximately one hour for the groups to develop the leadership role play circled on their handout. Remind them they will have about 30 minutes after dinner for their final preparations.

Leadership Role Plays

Role play the circled situation below. Leadership is needed. Create a specific situation and prepare to act it out for the rest of the group. You may portray your leadership as poor or effective. For example, role play poor leadership with a sports team by pretending several group members are energetic football players and another group member is a timid coach who whispers what the team should do.

Sports team	Cafeteria scene
Student council	Classroom
Dating relationship	Church planning meeting
Family fight	Peer pressure about drugs
Cheerleaders	School faculty
Business meeting	

After each group has presented its role play, discuss the style of leadership used. How effective was the leadership? What could have improved its effectiveness? On a large sheet of newsprint, list the style of leadership presented for each role play.

After all presentations are complete, try to determine which style of leadership was presented most often. Ask the group to discuss whether this type of leadership is a preferred style or one that comes easily because of experience.

Suggest they compare their own spiritual gifts with the styles of leadership presented by the role plays.

The Disciples as Leaders—Circle one of the disciples on each group's handout. Review or reread Matthew 10:1-4. Talk about the spiritual gifts God provided (see second sheet of newsprint). Review the newsprint where you listed information about the different disciples (third sheet). Divide the group by numbering off into 11 small groups to study the different disciples. (We have already studied Peter.) Give each group The Disciples as Leaders handout. Have them study the disciple circled on their paper.

Bring the small groups back together again to share their findings on the disciples and to list the leadership qualities they discovered. Write these leadership qualities on a sheet of newsprint for all to see. Talk about the fact that Bible characters do not always provide the best example of leadership, nor do they paint a pleasant picture of what leadership is.

After discussing the disciples' leadership, focus on your young people and their need to make a commitment to being a better leader for Christ. Ask them to be thinking about the leadership qualities they have seen in themselves and others. Close this session by asking the group to pray about how God wants them to use their spiritual gifts.

Remind participants to bring their Bibles, paper and pencils to the session tomorrow morning. Sing "Spirit of the Living God" to close this session.

SUNDAY

Paul: A Leader in His Own Time—Before this session, post the discussion questions on a sheet of newsprint for all to see. Read 1 Thessalonians 2:1-20. Ask the group to discuss these questions:

● What leadership characteristics can you identify in Paul?

● According to Paul, what should a leader do? what shouldn't a leader do?

● How is Paul's closing the sign of a good leader?

Personal Commitment—Make sure all participants have retrieved their spiritual inventories from their spiritual-image cans.

The Disciples as Leaders

Check to see which disciple is circled for your group study. Read the verses of scripture that apply to that disciple and discuss the following questions. Be prepared to share your findings with the rest of the total group. (If you finish early, you may choose one of the other disciples and study about them too.)

What do you notice about _____ (disciple's name)?
What leadership characteristics does he have?
In what specific ways does he use his abilities?

1. Andrew—John 1:40-42; 6:8-9; 12:20-22
2. James, son of Zebedee—Luke 9:51-56; Matthew 20:20-24; Acts 12:1-4
3. John—John 13:23; 20:2; 21:7; 19-24; 21:15-17
4. Philip—John 1:43-46; 6:5-7; 12:20-22
5. Bartholomew (or Nathaniel - names mean "son of Tolmi" and "Gift of God")—John 1:45-51
6. Matthew—Matthew 9:9-13; Mark 2:14-17
7. Thomas—John 11:14-16; 14:5; 20:24-29
8. James, son of Alpheas ("the less," probably in reference to his small size and young age)—Mark 15:40
9. Thaddeas—Matthew 10:3; John 14:21-24
10. Simon Zealot (the Canaanite)—Luke 6:15
11. Judas Iscariot—John 12:4-6; 13:10-11, 18-19; John 13:27-29; Matthew 26:16; John 18:24; Matthew 27:3-5

They will each need a piece of paper, a pencil and a stamped envelope. Have them make a Personal Commitment Chart by writing their name at the bottom of a piece of paper. Then they list their top three or four spiritual gifts across the top of the page, leaving space below for writing. (Make a sample of this on a sheet of newsprint as you explain it to your group.)

Ask your teenagers to move away from the central meeting area and spend some time alone looking at how they can use their spiritual gifts, both in their daily life and their experiences at church. Encourage them to listen to God and be prepared to share their thoughts with the group when they return. (Tell them they will have about 20 minutes for this activity, and they should return when they hear the music begin.)

One teenager with a gift for organization might see a need for a program to prepare upper-elementary children for participation in the youth group. Another young person with a gift for teaching might offer to lead a Bible study for the youth group once a quarter. A senior high student with caring skills could start a personal growth group with some junior high students. Some kids with a gift for compassion might want to get involved with a workcamp. Encourage the group to come up with as many ideas as possible on how they would like to use their spiritual gifts.

Ask adults and other youth leaders to wander about the area to help individuals who may be struggling with this activity. Instruct them not to give answers, but to ask questions to facilitate the

Personal Commitment Chart

Organized   Writer   Giving

Chris

teenagers' thinking process:

- What spiritual gift of leadership do you feel best about?
- How are you using that gift now?
- Where would you like to try to use it in the future?

Questions like these force adolescents to struggle with their own thoughts, not our ideas.

After individuals have had a chance to decide how they want to use their spiritual gifts, ask them to list their ideas on their paper, fold them and place them in envelopes on which they write their names and addresses. Suggest that they prepare their ideas as an offering in response to the One who *gave* them their spiritual gifts.

As the group returns to the central meeting area, collect their envelopes in a large basket as an offering to God. (Later you might want to make copies of these papers for the youth leaders so they will know how to help their young people use their gifts. One month after the retreat, return these lists to their owners to remind them of their ideas and plans on how they can use their spiritual gifts.)

Peace Candle—After the opportunity to examine their own gifts of leadership and how they will use them, try to help your young people commit themselves to being a better leader for Christ. Start playing some soft but meaningful music to let the kids know they should return to the central meeting place. Darken the area as much as possible. As participants enter, quietly indicate where they should place their envelopes and seat everyone on the floor in a circle.

Use only one candle, the Peace Candle, and place it in front of you. When everyone is seated, explain the significance of the Peace Candle. Say something like this:

"Perhaps God has talked to you this weekend. I hope so. Tonight each of us has a chance to share our faith with one another as this candle is passed to the right around the circle.

"The person with the candle is the only one allowed to speak. You may choose to pray out loud, share something God has taught you, thank a friend for something he or she has done or said or anything else that is on your heart." (As the leader, you can also direct the group to share specifically about something such as one new way they have decided to be a better leader for Christ.)

Encourage everyone to share briefly so all who wish to speak can. Let them know that if they don't want to say anything, they can merely pass the candle to the next person on the right. Expect individuals to open their hearts. Most will be serious. Some will cry, while others will rejoice and laugh.

After the candle has passed around the entire circle, close by giving words of encouragement. Stand up, sing a song, and then hug. It is beautiful how people express love, deep hurts or feelings during this time. The group will be glued together in a new dynamic way. Koinonia has happened!

Affirmation Event—As a final activity, ask everyone to team up in pairs. Each team should get a marker and two long sheets of newsprint. Have one individual trace around the other on his or her newsprint and reverse positions. Ask everyone to write his or her name on the top of the paper and then tape it onto the wall where others can write on it.

Read Hebrews 10:23-25. Take 20 minutes for the young people and adults to go around to the different pieces of paper and write positive statements of affirmation about the individual whose name is at the top of the paper. Everyone should try to write on as many papers as possible, but *not* their own. There will be wonderful, as well as funny statements such as "You are there when I need you" and "Great humor. Keep it up." No statements are to be signed by the writer.

The result of this event is that each person feels loved by the group. As the kids each take their paper home and look it over, they will be encouraged by the positive things others see in them.

Complete your retreat by reading Acts 2:42-47. Then sing some familiar songs and celebrate communion, using your lunch as the elements.

6

Self-Image Bloopers

By Mitch Olson

At some moments in our lives, we all suffer from feelings of low self-worth. We all need to cheer up and realize that we are valuable; that God loves us; and that we can learn to laugh at some of the mistakes we've made, make the best of the mistakes, and grow.

This one-day retreat focuses on self-image and the realization that each of us is useful in God's world. Throughout the day, kids will interact with each other and share quality experiences that will help them know they are valuable.

In this retreat, the kids will:
- examine the "bloopers" of their lives;
- learn to laugh at these bloopers;
- understand that others have similar problems; and
- encourage and affirm one another.

Before the Retreat—Since this retreat lasts only one day, you may want to have it in the church or at a member's home.

Order a film or video on "bloopers." It could be a film or video of funny mistakes made during football games, or funny errors made while filming movies or television programs. Check with a local video store for sports bloopers, or check with your local library for their listing on blooper films. Most libraries can order these films at little or no cost.

Gather construction paper; magazines; glue; newsprint; markers; Bibles; a film projector or videocassette player; a prize such as a candy bar or piece of fruit; refreshments; and, for each person, three 3×5 cards (two white, one green or other color), a pencil, a straight pin, one brown grocery sack and scissors. You also will need enough 3×5 cards so the kids can write an affirmation statement to each participant.

For the opening activity, prepare a "hidden message" for each person. Do this by writing, on separate 3×5 cards, statements such as "Ignore me," "I'm conceited" or "I have lots of money."

Retreat Schedule

Saturday
9:00 a.m. Arrive and register
9:15 a.m. Hidden Messages
10:15 a.m. Refreshment break
10:30 a.m. Me Sacks
Noon Lunch

1:00 p.m. Bible Bloopers
2:15 p.m. Break
2:30 p.m. Bloopers Today
3:45 p.m. You're-Okay Cards
5:00 p.m. Out for pizza

_____ Retreat Ingredients _____

SATURDAY

Hidden Messages—As the young people enter the room, pin a hidden-message card onto their backs. Don't let them see the statement that is written on their card. Instruct the members to treat everybody just like the signs on their backs say. Have the kids try to guess what their hidden message is. Once successful, they can remove their card. Award a prize to the last person who guesses his or her message.

Make the room a continuum. Say: "All those who thought Hidden Messages was a pleasant experience, stand on the left side of the room; all those who thought it was frustrating, stand on the right. If your feelings were between these two extremes, spread out accordingly on the continuum." Discuss why kids feel as they do. Why did some like the game? Why did some feel frustrated?

Next say: "Do we treat people certain ways because of how they look on the "outside"? Those who think we *always* treat people this way, stand on the right side of the room; all those who think we *never* treat people that way, stand on the left. If your feelings are between the two extremes, spread out accordingly on the continuum." Discuss kids' opinions. How can we stop treating others as they appear? How can we treat people as if they are unique and special?

Me Sacks—Tell the kids that they are going to make Me Sacks to represent their "real selves"—inside and outside. Give everybody a brown grocery sack, a pair of scissors, and some glue and magazines. Instruct the young people to search the magazines for pictures to symbolize how others view them (for example, sunshine and smiling faces). Ask them to glue these pictures on the outside of the sack. Then have the kids search the magazines for pictures to symbolize their "true selves"—how they are on the "inside" (for example, cloudy sky and teary eyes as well as sunshine and smiles). Ask them to glue these pictures on the inside of the sack. Once the kids are finished with this, have them cut the letters of their name out of construction paper and glue the letters onto the front of the sack.

Gather in small groups and discuss the Me Sacks. Let each person share his or her sack and symbols. Ask:

● Were you surprised at others' "outsides"? Explain.

● Were you surprised at others' "insides"? Explain.

● What is one thing you learned from this activity?

Line the sacks along one wall. They will be used later in the day for the You're-Okay Cards activity.

Bible Bloopers—Tell the participants: "We all have made mistakes in our lives. Some of these mistakes are hard to forget, and we keep kicking ourselves for them. As Christians we need to remember that we are human *and* we are forgiven. We need to learn from our mistakes and then forget them.

"Just as we make mistakes in our lives, Bible people made mistakes in their lives. In spite of their mistakes, God used them in powerful ways. Just as God used the Bible people and their mistakes for good, he can use us and our mistakes for good."

Divide into small groups and give each one a Bible, a sheet of newsprint and a marker. Let each group choose a person in the Bible who made a mistake (or blooper), yet God used that person for good. Examples are: Peter's denial (Matthew 26:69-75); James' and John's requests for special treatment (Matthew 20:20-24); David's adultery (2 Samuel 11:1—12:25). Have each group answer these questions and write the answers on their sheet of newsprint:

● Who is the Bible person?

● What was the blooper?

● How did God use this person for good?

● What does this mean for us today?

After every group is finished, share findings in a large group.

Bloopers Today—Show the film or video on bloopers. Discuss these questions and write the answers on newsprint:

● Which characters can you identify with? Do you know someone who might have experienced similar bloopers?

● What do the bloopers in life teach us?

● How can we learn from our bloopers, laugh a bit at ourselves and make the best of every situation?

● What are ways you can encourage others when they feel down about their mistakes?

Hand out two 3 × 5 cards (one white and one green) and a pencil to each person. On the white card have each person write two mistakes or bloopers he or she feels really rotten about. Then on the green card have each person write two things he or she feels really good about. Ask the kids not to sign their names to the cards. Collect all blooper cards and mix them so you won't give away anyone's mistakes. Place the blooper cards in one pile. Then collect all green cards and mix them so you won't give away anyone's answers. Place these in a pile.

Read the bloopers and list them on the newsprint. Note all duplicates. Point out that a lot of our bloopers are the same. If we think we are the only ones in the world with our specific problem, we are usually wrong. Ask the kids how they could affirm and encourage a person who's experienced these bloopers. An example of a blooper might be, "I feel bad because I let myself gain so much weight." An encouraging response might be, "We should affirm that person for who he or she is. We could compliment his or her attitudes, helpfulness and friendliness."

Go through the same process with the positive remarks. List and discuss them. This is a great encourager. Talk about how everyone in this group is gifted, and how everyone can overcome other people's bloopers with affirmation. Say: "We can overcome our own bloopers by shifting our focus. We should think of all our blessings and gifts, rather than all of our mistakes."

You're-Okay Cards—Give everybody enough 3 × 5 cards so they can write an affirmation for each person in the group. Ask them to focus on "inside" qualities rather than "outside" appearances. When the participants write their affirmations, have them place the cards in the respective Me Sacks. Don't let them read their affirming comments until they get home.

Gather in a circle and read 1 Samuel 16:7: "The Lord does not look at the things man looks at. Man looks at the outward appearance, but the Lord looks at the heart." Have everyone say one positive thing about the person on his or her right, focusing on the "heart" rather than appearance. Have everyone shout, "You're okay!" at the end of each affirmation.

Let everybody take home their Me Sacks. Go out for pizza to wrap up a fun day!

─── Section Two ───

Relationships

7

Back to School

By Alan Maki

In June, high school students seldom think about going back to school. But in early August, visions of returning to school begin dancing in everybody's head. With those visions come fears and concerns. Schedule this retreat before school starts to give kids a chance to get together and talk about the things they'll face when school starts.

What concerns do high schoolers have about the start of a new school year? Here are actual responses:

- "I'm worried about how people will treat me this year";
- "I'm concerned about passing all my classes";
- "I'm scared of the drinking and drug scene";
- "I need some new clothes"; and
- "There aren't any Christians in my school."

There are many more worries: adjusting to new schedules; getting desired teachers and classes; dealing with unpopular teachers; cheating pressures; making friends; being accepted socially; dating and sexual pressures; choosing extracurricular activities; and competing in sports, grades, cliques.

Back to School is designed to help young people:

- identify common back-to-school concerns and needs;
- realize it's not unusual to have back-to-school worries;
- explore solutions for common school problems; and
- discover ways to support one another in school.

Before the Retreat—Locate a room with enough open space to hold large "classroom" group activities. The location should be able to accommodate free-time options such as swimming, soccer, volleyball, softball and hiking.

Ask each participant to bring one school-related item that will be auctioned off at the retreat. (See Back-to-School Auction.) Also ask each member to bring two dollars for the auction.

Prepare enough Prayer Covenant, Discussion Questions and How Do I Act? handouts for each person.

Read the descriptions for Back-to-School Sports and Headband Sharing, and prepare the necessary materials.

Recruit a song leader who will lead the group in singing kindergarten and Christian songs. The song leader also leads singing in the Sunday worship. Remember to bring songbooks for all. Also bring maracas, tambourines, sandpaper blocks, finger cymbals, washboards and other simple instruments for the rhythm band.

Find volunteers to plan and lead the four devotions.

Form a recreation team for free periods. Have them bring all necessary equipment.

Arrange transportation and drivers.

Gather Bibles; the three handouts; plenty of 3 × 5 cards; several ballpoint pens; a black permanent marker; rhythm band instruments;

Retreat Schedule

Friday (Orientation)
7:30 p.m. Arrive and settle in
8:00 p.m. Singing
8:30 p.m. Ready-for-School Sports
8:45 p.m. Introduce retreat theme
9:00 p.m. Headband Sharing
10:00 p.m. Snack break
10:30 p.m. Buzz, Bonk, Boink
11:00 p.m. Devotions
1:30 p.m. Lights out

Saturday (Classes)
7:00 a.m. Up and at 'em (Get kids used to early rising again!)
7:45 a.m. Devotions
8:00 a.m. Breakfast
9:00 a.m. Homeroom: Rhythm Band and Friends Forever Autograph Party
9:45 a.m. First hour class: Dear School Board
10:30 a.m. Second hour class: School Skits
11:15 a.m. Third hour class: Peer Pressure
Noon Lunch
1:00 p.m. Recess: volleyball, swimming, softball

3:30 p.m. Fourth hour class: Back-to-School Auction
4:30 p.m. Fifth hour class: How to Treat Others
5:20 p.m. Sixth hour class: A "detention" at any of the recreation areas
6:00 p.m. Dinner
7:00 p.m. Extracurricular activity: Rhythm Band and singing
7:30 p.m. Film and discussion
9:30 p.m. Bonfire, hayride, snack time
11:20 p.m. Devotions
11:45 p.m. Lights out

Sunday (Graduation)
7:00 a.m. Up and at 'em
7:45 a.m. Devotions
8:00 a.m. Breakfast
9:00 a.m. Planning the worship service
10:30 a.m. Worship
11:15 a.m. Prayer Covenants
11:30 a.m. Pack and load up
Noon Leave for home

songbooks; 8 1/2×11 paper for auction fliers; extra auction items and extra cash; newsprint; a crazy prize (for example, a bag of bubble gum, silly notebook, colorful pen); two bowls or hats; tape player; Christian music tapes; recreation equipment; a film or video about school pressures; movie projector or video playback equipment; and, for each person, a white headband (or a 2×32-inch strip of white sheeting), a pencil and an envelope.

Retreat Ingredients

FRIDAY

Ready-for-School Sports—Divide young people into teams of four or five. Ahead of time write on 3×5 index cards the names of several sports—one sport to a card. For example, card #1—baseball; card #2—football. Have one team at a time come forward and select a card. The team then acts out—in slow motion—the sport named on the card—without touching each other. For example, if there are four team members and the sport is wrestling, two team members at a time would "wrestle." If there are four team members and the sport is baseball, one two-person team would "play" the other two-person team.

Headband Sharing—Before this activity, use a black permanent marker to print one of the following school concerns on each headband or in the middle of each strip, using one-inch letters: cheating, detention, failing, stress, boredom, passing, homework, teachers, cafeteria, partying, dating, friends, acceptance, loneliness, competition, sports, cliques, spirituality.

The rules: Give each person a headband, a pencil and a 3×5 card. After the kids put on their headbands, give them 15 minutes to talk one-on-one with other kids about the topic on their respective headbands. Have the kids each jot down on the cards the suggestions they receive for handling their problem. Change discussion partners every two minutes. At the end of 15 minutes, have everyone sit in a large circle. Go around the circle and have group members each summarize the suggestions they received about their headband topic. Suggest to the kids that they swap and wear their headbands throughout the retreat. Also, encourage kids to take them home as a retreat souvenir.

Buzz, Bonk, Boink—Arrange kids in circles of between eight and 13 people each. Each small group begins counting counterclockwise up to 35, substituting the word "buzz" for the number three and every multiple of three. If anyone goofs, the whole group must start over. Once they reach 35, they win that round. The second time, all groups must use "buzz" for three and every multiple of three, plus "bonk" for five and every multiple of five. The third time use "boink" for seven and multiples of seven. The first team to count to 35 correctly using all three (buzz, bonk and boink) is the winner if they can count up to 35 again with the other groups listening and watching. If they fail, the groups get back together again until one group wins.

Devotions—Gather the young people together for devotions and quiet time. Briefly discuss the kids' concerns about going back to school. (The list at the beginning of this retreat is a good start.) Have someone read Romans 12. Give each person a copy of the How Do I Act? checklist. Give them each 10 minutes to rate themselves by completing the checklist. Then ask kids to think about how their strengths and weaknesses relate to their concerns about going back to school. Close with a prayer that God will help them each think about ways to improve their self-image by being more like Christ.

How Do I Act?

Check the box that best represents your response to each statement.

	Always	Most of the time	Some of the time	Occasionally	Seldom
● I present myself as a living and holy sacrifice to God.					
● I refuse to conform to peer pressure, and do what is good and acceptable to God.					
● I accept others as part of the body of Christ, even if they're different from me.					
● I recognize each of us has unique gifts to share.					
● I support others in Christian love, sharing in their happiness and grief.					
● I reach out to those who have less than I do.					
● I am kind to people who've hurt me.					

SATURDAY

Morning Devotions—Have kids sit back-to-back on chairs or benches in the breakfast area. Have someone read 1 Corinthians 12:12-27. Discuss how we're all part of God's family who need one another, and how having different strengths and weaknesses is a positive thing. Close with a prayer that God will help group members recognize not only are they important to him, but others are too. Pray that God will help each person be kind to others and accept people for who they are.

Rhythm Band—Choose a few kids at a time to participate in a rhythm band. Use instruments such as maracas, sandpaper blocks, washboards, tambourines, combs. Have everyone sing kindergarten songs such as "Old MacDonald" and "Farmer in the Dell," while the band plays. The band may also want to play during group singing at other times throughout the retreat.

Friends Forever Autograph Party—Have five kids each remove one of their shoes and socks. Give them each a ballpoint pen and three minutes to get as many signatures as they can on the bottom of their feet. The winner gets a prize; everyone gains friends.

Dear School Board—Pass out two 3×5 cards and a pencil to each person. Say: "On one of your cards, write a short problem letter to the school board about one of the concerns named on your headbands last night. Ask the school board for advice similar to a 'Dear Abby' letter. You have five minutes to turn in your cards."

After the problem letters are collected, say: "On your remaining card, write the solution to your own problem letter. Turn in this card when you're done."

Put all problem letters in a bowl or hat and mix up the cards. Put the solutions in another bowl. Pick out a problem card and read it. Then randomly select a solution card and read it as the answer to the problem. The results are hilarious.

School Skits—Ask the group members to now think seriously about the problems they identified during the Dear School Board activity. Have group members prioritize the problems. Then divide members into small groups of five. Have each small group select one of the problems and prepare a short skit about a solution to the situation. Allow 20 minutes for preparation time, then have each group act out its problem and the solution.

Peer Pressure—If your group is larger than eight, have kids form a large circle, and count off to form small groups of five or six. Give a copy of the Discussion Questions to each group. Say: "Most kids give in to peer pressure because they have a poor self-image. Teenagers with low self-esteem usually go along with the crowd because they want to feel accepted. If the crowd does something negative, kids who need acceptance go along with it because they don't have the confidence to stand up for what they believe. Discuss the questions on the handout. Look up the scripture references as you go through the list. After you're through, we'll look at one last scripture together.''

Discussion Questions

1. What is positive peer pressure? negative peer pressure?
2. What kinds of things do other teenagers pressure you to do? Why are you tempted by peer pressure?
3. Name one or two things you'll be pressured to do this school year that you know now you don't want to do.
4. Read 1 Peter 3:17 and Proverbs 13:20. How can giving in to negative peer pressure cause you to suffer for doing evil, or to be destroyed?
5. Read 1 Peter 4:1-2, 19. Finish this sentence: Because I belong to Christ, I can't _____

_____

_____

After 20 minutes, have someone read Colossians 4:12. Say: "This greeting says that Epaphras was always praying for his friends that they may stand perfect and complete in God's will. Let's take time right now to pray for one another to stand strong in Christ." Have the group members form a large circle and join hands. Ask them to repeat the following prayer: "Lord, help us remember to pray for one another. Help us to stand up for what we know is right. Let us not be ashamed of our relationship with you. May we always be willing to tell others about our faith and trust in you. In Jesus' name, amen.''

Back-to-School Auction—Before the retreat, ask each person to bring one or two items for the Back-to-School Auction and two dollars for bidding money. (Some kids may forget, so bring extra items and extra cash.) Suggest the following school items: a school pennant, poster, yearbook, jersey, tote bag, pompons, athletic socks, notebook, paper, pencils, pens, rulers. Other great auction items: two free school lunches, a one-hour tutoring lesson from a teacher, a guy/girl who will carry your books between classes for a day. Be creative.

Have the group select an auctioneer. Generally there's a "natural" in the group and the kids will know who it is. Set a minimum for each item (20 cents). The auctioneer should joke around during the auction and keep it lively, attempting to get as much money as possible for each item.

Print auction bills beforehand listing every item. Hand these out before the auction begins so kids will know ahead of time what's available and can plan their bidding. Allow each member to take only two dollars to the auction so everyone has equal buying power. Play Christian music or school songs in the background.

How to Treat Others—Say to your group: "Many of you wonder how you're going to be treated by others during the new school year. But all the wondering in the world won't give you any real answers. So let's discuss what you *can* control."

Have kids form groups of four and choose a spokesperson for their group. Tell them they'll have two minutes to discuss each of the several questions and then report back to you. Use the Leader's Questions, one at a time. Write kids' responses on newsprint in one- or two-word phrases. When all the questions have been answered, ask kids to pray silently for two minutes; then close by asking God to help them develop the Christian qualities they desire.

Leader's Questions

1. How do you plan to treat others at school?
2. Will the way you treat others affect the way they treat you? Explain.
3. What do you look for in a friend? Talk about those qualities.
4. Which of these qualities do you possess? Which do you lack?
5. How can you get some of the qualities you don't have?
6. Read Galatians 5:22-23. Discuss these characteristics of a spiritual life. How are these qualities pleasing to others?
7. Read John 13:34; 15:12. What do these verses mean? What does it mean to love others as Christ has loved you?
8. Make a mental list of classmates you haven't treated well in the past. Think about ways you can treat these people with love.

Film and Discussion—Choose a film or video that relates directly to school life and school problems. A film dealing with peer pressure would be good. Preview the film and prepare questions and activities to use after the group sees the movie.

Two sources of Christian films are EcuFilm, 810 12th Avenue South, Nashville, TN 37203 and Gospel Films, Inc., Box 455, Muskegon, MI 49443. Or, contact Learning Corporation of America, 1350 Avenue of the Americas, New York, NY 10019 for a list of secular movies and videos about teenage concerns.

Devotions—Gather kids together in a large group. Have someone read 1 Peter 3:8-17. Discuss how we're to act toward one another; how we need to watch our speech as well as our actions; and how we should always be ready and willing to share with others about our hope in Christ. After two minutes of silent prayer, close by asking God to help the kids not be intimidated or troubled if someone at school teases them about not cheating, not getting mad at someone, or not trying to get even when someone does something bad to them.

SUNDAY

Devotions—Have kids again sit back-to-back in the breakfast area. Have someone read John 4:7-24. Discuss how we should follow Christ's example and befriend people we don't normally hang around with; how Christ knows all about us; and how God wants us to worship him in spirit and in truth. Have kids turn to someone and share one or two fears they have about talking to someone they don't know very well. After two or three minutes, close with a prayer that God will help each person reach out to others as a way of worshiping him.

Planning the Worship Service—Divide kids into five groups. Each group is responsible for designing one part of the worship service. Include:

● *The setting*—Have this group pick the location for the service and get it ready, including decoration, seating, songbooks.

● *Music*—Have this group, under the direction of your song leader, select songs and develop unique ways of singing them.

● *Prayer and praise*—Have this group write prayers and decide ways to deliver them. Have them plan ways of offering praise to the Lord throughout the service.

● *Scripture*—Have this group prepare creative presentations of two or more of the Bible readings used during this retreat.

● *The sending forth*—Have this group find ways to illustrate how the retreat's theme will be taken back home by each of the members.

Prayer Covenants—Have each young person fill out a Prayer Covenant at the end of the worship service. Give participants each an envelope and ask them to write their name and address on it. Have them place their covenant sheets in their envelopes and return them to you. On the first day of school, mail the covenants back to them.

By the time you leave for home, kids will be more mentally prepared for the problems they'll face at school. They'll know other kids' fears and others' solutions. They'll realize they're not alone. They'll discover ways to support one another.

They may even look *forward* to school starting.

Prayer Covenant

Name:_____

Peer pressure confronts me every school year. The start of this school year will be different from past years, as I promise to pray each day for God's strength and guidance in handling the pressures. I'll pray that God will help me to do the right things. I'll also pray specifically for: _____

_____

_____

I promise to keep this prayer covenant for the next _____ days.

Signed: _____

8

Love One Another

By Ben Sharpton

All kinds of people have communicated their thoughts on the topic of love. The definitions of love often seem as varied as the communicators themselves. Love One Another will help kids narrow down the varieties of definitions.

Use this retreat to help participants understand the meaning of biblical love as it relates to:

- relationships within a family;
- feelings between friends; and
- thoughts about God.

Before the Retreat—Gather a large metal pot; candle; matches; tempera paints; scraps of material; glue; scissors; newsprint; markers; tape; 3×5 cards; pencils; several apples; dish towels; cassette recorders; cassette tapes and microphones; and, for each person, a penny, raw egg, and copies of all handouts.

Make enough copies of Love Notes and I Care Coupons so each person can write one for every retreat participant.

Prepare Body Parts cards by writing on 3×5 cards the name of one body part. These will be used to form small groups. Each group should have two ears, two eyes, two arms, two feet, one mouth. (Make smaller groups by deleting some body parts.)

On separate 3×5 cards, write one of the case studies found in the Saturday morning session.

On separate 3×5 cards, write one of the following scriptures. You will need one card for each person: Galatians 6:1-2; Romans 14:1; Romans 14:13; 1 Timothy 5:19-20; Luke 17:3-4; Romans 15:1-3; James 5:19-20.

If you want to show a movie during free time, rent a video and equipment. Be sure to bring popcorn to munch on during the feature.

A couple of weeks prior to the retreat, contact the parents of your group members. Ask them to give you a brief note or letter addressed to their son or daughter expressing their love for him or her. These notes should be confidential and secret; you want to surprise the kids.

Retreat Schedule

Friday
4:00 p.m. Arrive at camp and settle in
5:30 p.m. Supper
7:00 p.m. What Is Love?
9:00 p.m. Group Noise Contest
11:00 p.m. Break
11:30 p.m. Lights out

Saturday
8:00 a.m. Breakfast
9:00 a.m. Love for Family, Part 1
10:30 a.m. Free time
Noon Lunch

1:00 p.m. Planned recreation (softball, volleyball, etc.)
3:00 p.m. Love for Family, Part 2
5:30 p.m. Supper
7:30 p.m. Love for Friends
9:30 p.m. Snacks (show an entertainment movie and pro-
vide popcorn)
11:30 p.m. Lights out

Sunday
8:00 a.m. Breakfast
9:00 a.m. Love for God
10:30 a.m. Pack and clean
Noon Lunch, then leave

Retreat Ingredients

FRIDAY

What Is Love?—This meeting will set the mood and focus for the remainder of the weekend. During this time you will encourage your young people to clarify their understanding of the meaning of love.

As people arrive, give them each a Body Parts card. Tell them to hang onto the card until you give further instructions.

Play the Hug Game. Explain that you are going to call out different characteristics, and everyone is supposed to hug one or more people who possess each characteristic. Add any to the following list:

Someone wearing red
Someone wearing glasses
Someone who plays in the band
Someone who is new to the group
A volunteer adult leader
Someone who has dimples
Someone who has received one or more speeding tickets

Ask the group members to take out their Body Parts cards. When you say "Go," they are to find enough people who possess different body parts to form a complete body. Each group must have two eyes, two ears, two arms, two feet and one mouth. Challenge each group to form a straight line starting with the tallest to the shortest. Next, have them line up according to birthdates. Now, have them line up according to shoe size. Recognize the first team to accomplish each feat.

Have the participants each place their hands on the waist of the person in front of them, so that each team forms a chain. Give the last person in each line a dish towel. Have them tuck it in their belt so that most of the towel is exposed. Explain that the goal of this game is for the person at the front of the line to try to snatch as many towels as he or she can (without losing his or her own team's towel). Teams cannot let go of one another. Play two or three rounds, changing the lineups so that different individuals get to play in the front or back.

After the games, have the group members each compare the body part listed on their card to their role during the games. For example, a person with the "arms" card could say, "I supported others during the games. I helped them up when they fell."

Have the teams each sit on the floor forming a circle. Explain the I Care Coupons and Love Notes. I Care Coupons are available for anyone to use during the retreat. Kids can fill out a coupon, sign their

---

I Care Coupon

To: _____

From: _____

To demonstrate that I care, I am willing to:

_____ take a walk with you _____ (when)

_____ give a smile

_____ share a meal _____(when)

_____ give a hug

_____ talk _____(where) _____(when)

_____ give a backrub _____(when)

_____ other _____

Note: Completing and signing this coupon indicates your willingness to complete the appropriate task(s).

Signed: _____

name to it, and give it to a friend. Love Notes are methods of affirming others anonymously. Kids can write a brief, positive affirmation or compliment to a person without signing their name. Love Notes can be delivered by a third party, or left in a conspicuous place (on the person's bed, in his or her shoe, etc.). Encourage young people to write at least one I Care Coupon and one Love Note for each participant.

Love Notes

Give the participants each a 3×5 card and a pencil. Ask them to complete this phrase on their card: "Love is . . . " Collect these love definitions and read them. Avoid evaluating them. Give each group a sheet of newsprint and a marker; assign each group one of the following tasks. If you have more than five groups, repeat the tasks.

1. Come up with at least 10 synonyms (meaning is the same) for the word "love."

2. List at least 10 antonyms (meaning is the opposite) for the word "love."

3. How would you define "love" to a 5-year-old child?

4. How would you define "love" to a 65-year-old person?

5. List at least 10 feelings that are associated with love.

Discuss each group's task and post the newsprint around the room. Then give each group a Bible and a Love Is handout. Ask each group to work through all of the questions.

Bring everyone back together. Explain that the Saturday morning session will deal with love for family members. To help everyone ex-

Love Is

Love is something you do:
1. Give examples of ways that we love others.
2. If we don't love others, are we Christians? Explain.
3. Read 1 John 3:11-18. As a group, sum up the meaning of these verses in one sentence.

Love is something that happens to us:
1. Give examples of ways that love affects us.
2. Can love ever be selfish? Why or why not?
3. Read 1 Corinthians 13:4-7. List five characteristics of love.

Love is a person:
1. What do we mean when we say that "God is love"?
2. Read 1 John 4:7-16. As a group, sum up the meaning of these verses in one sentence.

What is love? (Choose one of these descriptions and explain your answer.)
1. A person who comes to us and lives with (in) us.
2. A feeling that we experience.
3. A task we must do.

perience care for a family member, give each person (adults and youth) a raw egg to "parent" through the night. Their task is to first decorate their egg, then take care of it through the night, protect it from harm, and bring it to the morning session (in whatever shape it is in) to share their experience of parenting.

Pass out the eggs. Distribute markers, paints, cloth scraps, glue, scissors and other items. Allow time for participants to decorate their egg.

Close in a love prayer. As everyone prays silently, invite volunteers to share one word or a brief phrase that describes something (or someone) they love. After several people have prayed, close with the Lord's Prayer.

Group Noise Contest—After a fairly intense two-hour session, it's time to relax with a wild and creative game.

Divide into different groups of three to 10 people. Each group gets a cassette tape recorder, tape and microphone. Say: "Your group has 15 minutes to record the following sounds: a cattle drive; the start of the Indianapolis 500; a dog pound with a cat intruder; the shootout at the OK Corral. Each sound must last 10 to 15 seconds. All group members must contribute.''

Send the groups to different rooms. After 15 minutes the groups come back together. One at a time the groups play their first sound. Once all groups have played the first sound, each plays the second, and so on. Close by seeing which group can be the most quiet for one minute.

SATURDAY

Love for Family, Part 1—This session will help your young people identify problem areas they face with other members of their family, and will guide them to discover positive ways to show and improve their love for those relatives.

Ask each person to report on his or her ''egg parenting'' experiment. What happened to each egg? Were any people neglectful? How did it feel to be totally responsible for the well-being of something else? How do they think their folks feel about the responsibility of parenting?

Break into the same small groups you formed during the first session and play a game to wake up the kids on this early morning. Pass out pencils and sheets of scrap paper and have the participants each write down 10 things about themselves that the other members of their group may not know. They should not sign their name. After everyone has completed their list, have the leader in each group collect the sheets and read off the items from each list, one at a time. Members of the group should then attempt to guess who wrote that list.

Give an apple to each of the small groups. Have them pass the apple around the circle and ask each group member to say how the apple is similar to a family. For example, someone might point out that both bruise easily. Another might mention that a stem attaches it to a larger family (tree).

Write each of these case studies on a separate 3 x 5 card. Give each group one of the case studies. One person in each group should read the case study out loud, and ask others in the group to suggest possible solutions to the problem.

Case 1—Tom is a junior in high school. His mother and father have been talking about his school grades, which have dropped slightly during the last semester. Tom announces that school is boring and that he has decided to drop out to go to work full time at a local fast-food restaurant.

Case 2—Sarah told her parents that she was going to the church lock-in. They said goodbye at 7:00 p.m. At about 9:30 p.m. Sarah's mother noticed that Sarah had forgotten her socks, a necessity for late-night roller-skating. She drove to the church with a pair of fresh socks to find a fellowship hall full of kids and youth counselors, but no Sarah. She returned home and discussed the matter with her husband. They decided to call Sarah's boyfriend (Bill). His parents said that Bill was spending the night in his brother's apartment and gave them that number. Sarah's parents didn't bother calling the number, but drove to the apartment. They discovered Sarah and Bill eating pizza on the front steps. What punishment (if any) should be given?

Case 3—Mom and Dad are reading the newspaper in the living room. Karen comes in and announces that she is going out with Joe Schmitzer for the evening. Her parents are concerned because they have heard that Joe had been arrested previously for shoplifting.

Ask each small group to present its case to the large group by identifying each major character, identifying the specific problem or problems, and listing their suggestions. After each presentation, open the discussion to others in the large group.

Place a large pot in the middle of the room and pass out a penny to each group member. Explain that the pot is a "wishing well," and each person has a chance to share one wish he or she has about the family. One at a time, members can share their wish and toss the penny into the pot. Members should be given the freedom to avoid sharing their wish out loud.

Love for Family, Part 2—Prepare the Family Chart on newsprint. Distribute Bibles and ask volunteers to read the passages of scripture. Then ask kids to help fill in each column.

Family Chart			
Passage	**Children Must**	**Parents Must**	**Results**
Ephesians 6:1-4			
Colossians 3:18-21			

Next, ask the entire group the following questions:

● Are there times when total obedience to your parents is not wise? (For example, when one's life, health or faith is threatened.) If so, how does one know when to obey and when to refuse?

● Are the items listed in the Results column realistic? Why or why not?

● Is being obedient one way of showing love for family members? Explain.

Pass out the letters from home to each participant. Say that the rest of the afternoon is for reading and reflecting on the letters. Dismiss in silence, allowing each person to read his or her note in private.

Love for Friends—During this session you will examine ways we express love for friends.

Divide into the small groups created during the first session. Ask everyone to share something special that has happened during this retreat. Give individuals the opportunity to pass and listen closely to each item.

Give each group a sheet of newsprint and a marker. Have them brainstorm and create a list of qualities of true friends. After each group has written 10 or more characteristics, have them place a chair in the center of the group. One at a time, each member should sit in the chair while the rest of the group identifies those "true friend" characteristics they see in that person. Give everyone the opportunity to be affirmed in this way.

Read the following situations one at a time. Discuss each situation, to make sure that everyone understands the dynamics of that case, and then ask everyone to vote by raising hands as to how they would respond in those circumstances. (One vote per person for each situation.) Discuss responses after everyone has voted.

Situation	**Response**
1. Your friend didn't study for today's biology exam, and you overheard him say he had a "cheat sheet." You have never heard him admit to cheating before, and you figured he never did.	Do nothing Talk to him Talk to biology teacher Talk to his parents Talk to his friends
2. Your friend has always been active in your church and youth group. She is an outspoken leader and was one of the main reasons you became a Christian. Now she is dating Tom and doesn't seem to have time for God, the church or the church crowd.	Do nothing Talk to your friend Talk to Tom Talk to your youth counselor Talk to your other friends

3. Your friend is getting a bad reputation around school as being "easy." You honestly don't know who to believe because she seldom confides in you anymore. You have heard some pretty cruel rumors.

Do nothing
Talk to her
Write her an anonymous note
Talk to her parents

4. Your friend has been hanging around some members of the school "Christian" club. You have recently seen a big change in him. He seems to look down on you and is expressing beliefs totally foreign to your faith. He has even challenged you to a couple of arguments about his new beliefs.

Do nothing
Talk to him
Talk to your youth minister
Try the club out
Ignore the behavior
Talk to his friends
Talk to his parents

5. Your friend led the biggest raid of all on this retreat. Some items were damaged and some people got their feelings hurt, but the youth director slept through it all. Tonight they're talking about an even bigger raid (and the counselors just purchased a life-time supply of Sominex). Raids are against camp rules.

Do nothing
Talk to your friend
Talk to the youth counselor
Find a place to hide
Talk to the group
Call home
Buy squirt guns

6. Your friend seems to love being disruptive during youth group discussions. He and his friends are leaders and tend to control the mood of the class. Many people in the group don't share because they are afraid of being put down by your friend.

Do nothing
Talk to him
Talk to your friends
Talk to the youth director
Tell him to shut up
Talk to his friends

Bring everyone back into one large group. Pass out copies of the scripture cards and a Bible to each person. Each card should contain one of these verses: Galatians 6:1-2; Romans 14:1; Romans 14:13; 1 Timothy 5:19-20; Luke 17:3-4; Romans 15:1-3; James 5:19-20. Give everyone time to read the cards, and then to exchange them with one other person. Would any of the kids' responses to the situations have changed if they had read these verses earlier? What do the verses say we should do in these sticky situations with our friends?

Distribute copies of the I Am Your Friend handout. Ask the kids each to find one partner; someone they trust. Ask them to share one difficult situation they are now facing, to pray about that situation with their partner and then have both people sign the sheet. Bring the entire group back together and close in prayer, asking God to make us responsible and accountable for each other's actions.

I Am Your Friend

"Brothers, if someone is caught in a sin, you who are spiritual should restore him gently. But watch yourself, or you also may be tempted. Carry each other's burdens, and in this way you will fulfill the law of Christ" (Galatians 6:1-2).

I want to be available to you as a friend, confidant and support. I agree to pray for you and to help you through tough times. Please feel free to call on me at any time.

Signed: _____

Signed: _____

SUNDAY

Love for God—During this session, young people will be encouraged to evaluate the ways they express their love for God, and challenged to seek more opportunities to share that love.

Brainstorm together and list on newsprint practical suggestions for establishing and maintaining a good relationship with people. Some ideas your group might list could be "spend time together," "always place your friend first" and "share similar interests." After you have accumulated a good list, have the group vote to identify the "top 10" suggestions, then number the top 10.

Divide into small groups and instruct them each to stand close together in a clear section of the room. Explain that you will read several statements that describe qualities of faith. After a statement, each person should reach out and place his or her hand on the shoulder of someone in the group who has exhibited that quality during this retreat. Thus, the entire group could be touching and touched at the same time. Use these qualities and add others:

You are loving	You are compassionate
You are giving	You are supportive
You are wise	You are friendly

You are full of hope   You are very patient
You are righteous   You are full of peace
You are gentle   You are kind

Pass out 3×5 cards and pencils. Have the kids each write the numbers 1 through 10 on the left-hand side of their card. Direct their attention back to the newsprint listing the top 10 ideas for quality relationships. Ask the kids each to grade themselves according to how well they carry out each suggestion in their friendship with God. (A = Wonderful, fantastic. B = Pretty good. C = Average, could improve. D = Definite need for improvement. F = Help!) For instance, if a person successfully holds a daily quiet time with God, he or she should place an "A" by that idea. Finally, ask each of the young people to pick one area where they would like to improve their grade. Share all grades in the small group.

Place a lighted candle in the center of the room and invite everyone to sit in a circle around the candle. Ask two volunteers to read these verses: Psalm 25:14; John 15:9-17.

Pass the candle around the circle. As the candle comes to each person, give that person an opportunity to share anything he or she would like to share with the group.

Pass the candle around once again. Each person who holds the candle is the one who will receive affirmations from all the other group members. Have each member complete this sentence as a celebration of the candle-holding person: "You are a light in the world. I like your . . . " (smiles, enthusiasm, cheerfulness, etc.). Blow out the candles, turn on the lights, and have everybody hug at least five others before they head to the cabins to pack.

9

Playing on God's Team

By Rickey Short

Playing on God's Team focuses on Christian sportsmanship and gives the young people an opportunity to participate in a multitude of sporting events. Plan this retreat in the late spring before you begin to step up your recreational programs. Create extra excitement by inviting other churches and group members' friends to participate. This type of retreat could also be an effective outreach event for adding members to your youth group.

Use this retreat to:

● teach young people about sportsmanship, not only in sports, but in their daily lives;

● add a different dimension to your youth ministry programming;

● give kids a chance to participate in fun activities; and

● allow young people quality time with their friends.

Before the Retreat—Several weeks in advance, ask young people to prepare the devotions (or chalk talks). Read the retreat for more details on each one.

Contact a local Christian coach or a representative from Fellowship of Christian Athletes to be the guest speaker on Sunday morning. Have him or her speak about God as the source for team spirit.

Select games and activities for some of the time slots listed in this retreat design. Use resources such as the *New Games Book* (Doubleday), *Fun -N- Games* (Zondervan), the *Try This One* series and *Building Community in Youth Groups* (Group Books). Collect all equipment needed for the games.

Gather Bibles; paper; crayons; pencils; copies of the handouts; and a prize for each person such as tennis balls, golf balls or sweat bands. You also will need several heavy, bulky overcoats and several clunky pairs of boots.

Ask kids to bring a hillbilly outfit for the Picking and Grinning hootenanny. They can bring straw hats, jeans, bandannas, etc.

It's important that you stress that this retreat is not only for athletes. All people are welcome, because the focus is winning on God's team!

Retreat Schedule

Friday
6:00 p.m. Arrive at the retreat location
6:30 p.m. Organized group activity such as flag football, softball, volleyball and tag
8:30 p.m. Refreshments
9:00 p.m. Picking and Grinning
10:00 p.m. The Vision of a Champion (Youth Group Chalk Talk)
11:00 p.m. Free time
Midnight Go to bed

Saturday
7:00 a.m. Breakfast
8:00 a.m. The Spiritual Fruit of the Christian (Youth Group Chalk Talk)
9:30 a.m. Individual track and field sports such as 50-yard dash, 100-yard dash, relays, mile run, etc.
10:30 a.m. Snacking break plus visit the old waterhole
10:45 a.m. Non-competitive team games such as Hug Tag and Hide and Go Seek

Noon Lunch
1:00 p.m. The Value of Winning
2:00 p.m. Skilled team sports such as softball, basketball and volleyball
4:00 p.m. Anything goes team sports such as sack races and water fights
6:00 p.m. Supper
7:30 p.m. Group Share Time
9:30 p.m. Break
10:00 p.m. Preparing to Win (Youth Group Chalk Talk)
11:00 p.m. Night hike to look for "night creatures" and make bird sounds
Midnight Go to bed

Sunday
8:00 a.m. Breakfast, then personal devotions on The Necessity of Self-Limitation
10:00 a.m. Guest Speaker
11:30 a.m. Awards Ceremony
Noon Lunch
1:00 p.m. Pack and leave

Retreat Ingredients

FRIDAY

Picking and Grinning—Start out the retreat with an old-fashioned hootenanny. Sing some hillbilly twangy songs such as "I've

Been Working on the Railroad'' or ''She'll Be Coming 'Round the Mountain.'' Pick songs that are ideal for a lot of hand clapping and foot stomping. Have everyone dress up like hillbillies and improvise some fun instruments such as clacking spoons together, banging on a pan or blowing into an empty bottle. Between songs, see who can tell the corniest jokes.

The Vision of a Champion (Youth Group Chalk Talk)—Prior to the retreat, share the following story and questions with a young person. Ask him or her to elaborate on it and be prepared to present a 10- to 15-minute devotion.

''There is nothing unique about having a dream or vision of what we want to accomplish. Everyone dreams of being a champion. A story is told of an eagle who had been raised in a barnyard with chickens. One day he observed an eagle in the sky, and from that day on he began to dream of being an eagle and soaring up in the sky. But he never did. He was convinced that he was a chicken and that he must peck around and flop about with the rest of the chickens.''

● Have you ever dreamed of being an eagle and then reminded yourself that you are only a chicken? If so, when?

● Can you dare to believe that you could be an eagle? Why is this difficult?

● What does it take to make a vision become a reality?

After the young person has presented the devotion, distribute pencils, Bibles and the Champions for God handout. Allow 15 minutes for kids to complete the handouts, then discuss answers in small groups.

After the small groups have discussed the handouts, follow up by asking everybody these questions:

● What do the words ''champion'' and ''championship'' mean to you?

● What is the dream that would have to come true for you to be a champion?

● Can a person be a true champion if he or she psychologically or physically hurts others on purpose in order to win? Explain.

● Do you think a person becomes ''better'' because he or she has won? Why or why not? What do you mean by ''better''?

● Is there a personal sort of championship that can be won without showing a win in the record book? Explain.

● Is winning or losing most likely to change a person? Why?

SATURDAY

The Spiritual Fruit of the Christian (Youth Group Chalk Talk)—Prior to the retreat, ask one of the group members to prepare some devotional thoughts on this topic. Have this person read John

Champions for God

In this Bible study we will take a look at two men who faced great spiritual challenges which they had to overcome in order to become champions for God. Read the passages, then answer the questions:

1. What was Nehemiah's vision and dream? (Nehemiah 2:1-6)

2. What kind of opposition did he face? (Nehemiah 4:1, 7-8, 11)

3. What did he do about it? (Nehemiah 4:16-23)

4. Did he achieve his dream? (Nehemiah 6:15)

5. In your opinion was Nehemiah a champion? Explain:

6. When Jeremiah was called to be a preacher, what was he told to do? (Jeremiah 1:4-8)

7. Do you think it would take a lot of courage to do what God asked Jeremiah to do? Explain:

8. How did God promise to help Jeremiah be a champion in the faith?

9. What are the things you think it takes to make a spiritual champion?

10. How does God show you how you can be a champion for him?

11. How does God help you accomplish your goals?

15:1-8, then ask these questions to the large group:
● How does the life cycle of a fruit tree compare to the life of a Christian?
● What problems do fruit trees have which keep them from bearing fruit?
● What problems do Christians have which keep them from bearing fruit? (Don't forget poor sportsmanship!)
● How can we increase our potential for bearing fruit?

After the chalk talk, distribute paper and crayons. Tell the participants they are to draw a sports figure, and list ways that athlete could bear fruit (use terms that go along with that sport). For example, someone can draw a picture of a baseball player. He or she can list ways of bearing fruit such as "Never cry 'foul,' always forgive," "If you strike out and feel you've sinned, ask for God's forgiveness and accept it" or "Live life as if each day is a home run." Share the drawings in a large group. Post them on the wall.

The Value of Winning—Introduce this session by saying: "We're going to see how Jesus and David handled competition and opposition." Distribute pencils, Bibles and A Look at Jesus and David handouts. Have kids complete then discuss the handouts in small groups of threes.

Group Share Time—Gather the kids in a circle. Have them take turns sitting in the center. Ask group members to share one observation about the person in the middle. Have them begin their observation this way: "A positive thing I have observed about you on this retreat regarding your Christian walk and your competitive edge is . . . " Let everyone have a chance to sit in the middle for these affirmations. Then go around the circle and ask kids to share one way they want to be different in their sportsmanship because they are a Christian. Say that sportsmanship refers to sports as well as everyday life.

Preparing to Win (Youth Group Chalk Talk)—Prior to the retreat, ask a young person to prepare a 10- to 15-minute devotional on this subject. The devotional could include some thoughts about winning in sports as well as winning in spiritual matters. Here are some thoughts you could share with the teenager to get him or her started:

"In his letter to the Corinthian church, Paul had something to say about winning. Paul felt like he was free to do about anything he wanted even as a Christian, but there were some things he chose not to do. He knew they would not help him run the race and win the prize he was after. Paul encourages us to lay aside every weight that hinders us in the race (1 Corinthians 9:24-27). For instance, it would be foolish to try and run a foot race in a heavy overcoat. You could choose to do it but it would really hinder your efforts."

After the chalk talk, run a relay race. Divide into teams and give the first person in each line a heavy overcoat and two huge boots. At the word "Go," have them put on these items of clothing, run to the other end of the room, do 10 jumping jacks, run back to the line and tag the next person, who repeats the process. First team done wins. Then run the relay again only don't use the overcoats and boots. Afterward, gather the teams in a circle and discuss how much easier it was to run without extra weight and bulk. Compare the relay to Paul's teaching.

A Look at Jesus and David

1. When Jesus was a small boy playing games do you think he pushed and shoved to get the ball? Explain. Do you think Jesus ever lost a game? Explain.

2. Jesus has been called a fierce competitor by those who have studied his actions and behaviors. Can you think of a situation in which Jesus showed he was not afraid of strong opposition? (For example, Jesus chasing the money changers out of the temple, or Jesus before Pilate.) What did Jesus do in this situation?

3. In order to bring us to eternal life, do you think Jesus had an overall game plan in mind? Explain.

4. How does John 3:16-17 sum up this game plan?

5. Was Jesus able to stick with his game plan? Explain.

6. Do you think this was difficult for Jesus? Why or why not?

7. Winning requires a number of qualities. How did Jesus show each of these:

Commitment	Dedication
Sacrifice	Character
Self-discipline	

8. How did Jesus act on the cross when he had apparently lost?

9. How do we know that Jesus really won?

10. Read 1 Samuel 17 and take a look at David. Why did it seem apparent that David could not defeat Goliath? List as many reasons as you can.

11. List the qualities, traits and skills that David had going for him as he entered the battle.

12. How was David able to defeat Goliath?

13. Why did David say he was able to win the victory?

14. What do you think is the central lesson in this story?

15. How do we win spiritual battles?

16. Do we need a game plan to win spiritual battles? Write out your game plan:

a.

b.

c.

d.

e.

17. List the spiritual armor of Ephesians 6:10-18.

18. Which one of the above pieces of armor do you most need to add? How will it help you?

SUNDAY

The Necessity of Self-Limitation—After breakfast, give everybody a Bible, pencil and Self-Limitations handout. Give the kids one hour to complete the questions as part of their personal devotions.

At the end of the devotion time, gather the kids and give them each a Personal Limitations Commitment Sheet. Ask them to read the sheet, sign it, and get two others to be "witnesses" and sign it also to make it "legal."

Guest Speaker and Awards Ceremony—Invite the Christian coach or representative of Fellowship of Christian Athletes to speak on God as the source for team spirit. Emphasize that team spirit doesn't

---

Self-Limitations

1. Read Daniel 1:3-20. What kind of limits did Daniel set for himself? Why? What were the results?

2. Read Daniel 3:4-29. What kind of limits did Shadrach, Meshach and Abednego set for themselves? Why? What was the result?

3. Read Genesis 39:2-23; 41:41-43. What kind of limit did Joseph set? Why? What was the final result?

4. Read Matthew 14:6-12. What kind of limit did Herod set? Why? What was the result?

5. Why are the following types of self-limits important today?

    a. Food and drink (Is there still royal food and wine to avoid?)

    b. What we worship (Do we worship false gods?)

    c. Moral behavior (Should we avoid certain acts even if we are pressured to do them?)

    d. Promises and commitments (Do we still have to follow through with what we say we will do?)

    e. Entertainment (Will the wrong kind of entertainment influence our judgment and decisions?)

6. How can failing to limit ourselves in these areas cause us trouble in our spiritual life?

7. What are some personal limits you have chosen in these areas?

Food and drink:

Worship:

Moral behavior:

Promises and commitments:

Entertainment:

Other:

8. Christians face many temptations in life's everyday challenges. How can a Christian avoid temptation and stay within the limits he or she has set?

Personal Limitations Commitment Sheet

1. I will not become involved in any activity or endeavor which would discredit my school, the name of Jesus or my reputation as a Christian.

2. I will not physically or verbally insult anyone.

3. I will not involve myself in any potentially dangerous habits such as taking drugs. I will care for my body as I would care for the temple of the Lord.

4. I will eat a balanced diet that is proper and sufficient nourishment for my lifestyle.

5. I will set a personal curfew which will give me enough rest to perform at my best.

6. I will limit myself by striving for excellence in those things I choose to do. I will set a reasonable limit on what I attempt to do so that I might be at my best.

7. I will not use curse words to communicate.

8. I will read or watch entertainment that can inspire and lift me. I will try to avoid entertainment based on violent and sexual themes.

9. I will never insult a person in authority, whether he or she is a teacher, parent, coach or referee. I will be supportive of his or her decisions.

10. I will never become so busy that I outrun God. I will spend 15 to 30 minutes each day in personal devotion, prayer and meditation.

Signed _____ Date _____

Witness _____ Date _____

Witness _____ Date _____

only apply to sports, it applies to our everyday lives—how we get along with others, how we uplift and encourage others, etc.

Allow time for discussion, then close with an Awards Ceremony. Give prizes for "Most Valuable Discussion Leader," "Most Positive," "Most Endurance," etc. Make sure you award a prize for everyone and thank them for being such good sports at this retreat!

10

The Power Game

By Kristine Tomasik

Power. This is a crucial issue in relationships between parents and teenagers. Many adolescents think they are powerless with their parents. They assume the only way to gain any control is to strike out and take what they want. Or they may choose to be passive-aggressive and quietly resist their parents at every step. Parents can feel just as powerless as their teenagers do. This is especially true if the teenagers are aggressive toward their parents.

The teenage years are particularly tense because the relationship's balance of power is shifting.

Use this retreat to:

● help parents learn how to relax their power gradually;

● help teenagers recognize personal responsibility for their own choices;

● teach both parents and teenagers how to use, rather than abuse their power.

This retreat is designed to defuse the power struggle between teenagers and their parents by teaching them the skills to negotiate their needs and wishes. By engaging in friendly collaboration, parents and teenagers can demonstrate respect for each other, as well as for themselves. Neither party loses, yet neither party feels abused.

Before the Retreat—This retreat is outlined for an overnight for both parents and their teenagers. Since the retreat teaches negotiation skills, stress collaboration between parents and teenagers in all activities. Mix parents and adolescents on all cooking and cleanup teams. Provide sports and fun activities that require cooperation. Avoid assigning a teenager to the same small team with his or her own parents. The idea is simply to let parents and kids see each other as real human beings.

Ideally, each teenager will have one or both parents in attendance at the retreat. If a teenager's parents cannot attend, enlist the help of an adult sponsor for that young person. Be sure the adult is willing to spend some time with the teenager's parents after the retreat to share some of the insights and experiences he or she had with their child.

In addition to the food, utensils, and other general supplies you normally need for a retreat, specific items are necessary for the planned activities that follow: Sign-Up Mixer sheets; bandannas or blindfolds; a long rope, strong enough for a tug of war; a roll of newsprint; masking tape; pencils; green, purple, red, and black markers; Power Line sheets; supplies for Relationship Collages (magazines, newspapers, glue, scissors, etc.) and supplies to create ice cream sundaes. Ice cream and toppings are basic, plus any items that would make a creative sundae critter—sugar wafers for legs, candy mints for eyes or shredded coconut for fur. Include anything edible—chocolate bits, mini-marshmallows, licorice sticks, etc. Be creative!

Retreat Schedule

Friday
7:00 p.m. Arrive and settle in
7:30 p.m. Welcome
7:50 p.m. Tug of War
8:15 p.m. Power Search
9:00 p.m. Break
9:15 p.m. Abuse or Wise Use?
10:00 p.m. Snacks, quiet board games, etc.
Midnight Lights out

Saturday
8:00 a.m. Breakfast
9:00 a.m. A Shifting Balance of Power

10:00 a.m. Break
10:15 a.m. Personal Power Lines
11:15 a.m. Games or free time
Noon Lunch
1:00 p.m. Games with teams divided into parents and teenagers
2:30 p.m. Relationship Collages
4:00 p.m. Pack and get ready to leave
5:00 p.m. Supper (minus dessert)
6:00 p.m. Negotiation, Not Compromise
8:00 p.m. Negotiating Can Be Fun!
8:30 p.m. Return home

Retreat Ingredients

FRIDAY

Welcome—When everyone has arrived at your retreat site, begin with some rousing crowdbreakers. Try Sign-Up Mixer from *The Best of Try This One* (Group Books). Pass out the Sign-Up Mixer sheets to both parents and teenagers. Instruct them to follow the directions at the top of the page. Allow 10 minutes for this activity.

Tug of War—Split everyone into two groups with all of the parents in one group and all of the teenagers in the other. Encourage

Sign-Up Mixer

Find someone to sign their name for each item on the list below. You can ask a person only one question. If the answer is no, you must go to someone else before returning to this person with another question. If the answer is yes, have the person sign your list next to the item. After 10 minutes, the person with the most names will be declared the winner.

_____ I use mouthwash regularly.

_____ I lie about my age.

_____ I have a hole in my sock right now.

_____ I have no cavities in my teeth.

_____ I watch Sesame Street.

_____ I read Peanuts.

_____ I was born 1,000 miles from here.

_____ I love Bach.

_____ I like to play chess.

_____ I like to read Hemingway.

_____ I believe in women's lib.

_____ I cry at movies.

_____ I eat raw oysters.

_____ I mash the toothpaste tube in the middle.

_____ I dance the Charleston.

_____ I refuse to walk under a ladder.

everyone's participation! If some are hesitant, they can be at the end of the line.

Tie a bandanna in the center of your long rope. Draw two lines five feet to either side of the bandanna. Line up the two teams behind the lines on each side. Explain that when one side pulls the bandanna past the line on their side, they have won. Caution your participants not to let go of the rope at the end of the contest. Now tug away! The winner will be the team with the best two out of three pulls.

When the tugging is complete and the winning team has been decided, have both groups sit down and wipe off the sweat. Once the panting has stopped, ask the group to share briefly how the parent and teenage relationship is sometimes like a tug of war.

Then point out in your own words how power can be a big issue in the relationship between parents and teenagers. Say: "Even though you might not recognize it, both parties in the parent and teenage relationship have power. This weekend we're here to learn how to use that power for good. We're here to learn how to negotiate, instead of turning this relationship into a tug of war."

Power Search—Divide parents and teenagers into separate brainstorming groups. Be sure the two groups are in separate rooms and cannot hear or see the others' responses. Give each group large sheets of newsprint. Give the parents purple markers and the teenagers green markers.

Parents should brainstorm the following topics, recording their ideas on newsprint:

● What are the ways *teenagers* have power in the parent/teenager relationship?

● What are the ways *parents* have power in the parent/teenager relationship?

The teenagers should brainstorm the same two topics, recording their ideas with the green markers and beginning with the ways parents have power.

Allow at least 30 minutes for brainstorming. Then, bring the groups back together. Collect the large sheets from both groups and post them side by side, by similar topics. You'll be able to tell which is which by the color coding.

As a group, discuss the comparisons and contrasts between the parents' and the teenagers' ideas. How did the parents think their children have power? How did the teenagers think their parents have power? Use a red marker and draw arrows between similar ideas. Ask both groups to think about what surprises there were in the other group's thinking. Mark the surprises for each group with a red star.

After most individuals have had a chance to share their observations and thoughts, ask the groups what they learned by doing this comparison. Record these comments with a red marker on a new sheet of paper.

Summarize these thoughts in your own words. You might say something like, "As you can see, each party in the parent and teenager relationship does have power! No one is really powerless. But how happy the relationship is depends upon whether we abuse or wisely use that power."

Abuse or Wise Use?—Set up a fishbowl discussion. One group will be in the center, facing inward to discuss a question. They are "in the fishbowl." All of the others form a circle around them to listen in and not comment.

Encourage those in the fishbowl to speak as anonymously as possible so as not to point the finger at their own parent or teenager. Encourage those on the outside of the fishbowl to really listen and learn from the ideas and opinions of those inside the fishbowl.

Let the parents (or a representative group of six to eight parents) be in the fishbowl first. They should discuss the following two issues:

● Teenagers abuse their power when they . . .
● Teenagers use power wisely when they . . .

After the parents' discussion, let the teenagers be in the fishbowl, discussing two similar issues:

● Parents abuse their power when they . . .
● Parents use their power wisely when they . . .

When the teenagers have completed their fishbowl discussion, bring the groups together to discuss what they have learned from listening to each other.

Ask the teenagers, "What do your parents want? Is that reasonable?"

Ask the parents, "What do your teenagers want? Is that reasonable?"

Distribute paper and pencils to the participants. Based on what was learned in the preceding discussion, have each person write down a personal resolution, indicating specific ways he or she will begin to change. Ask them to complete this sentence:

I will use my power wisely by:

1. _____
2. _____
3. _____ etc.

When individuals have completed writing their resolutions, they should put them away until tomorrow's evening session.

SATURDAY

A Shifting Balance of Power—Pretend to set up another tug of war between parents and teenagers. But this time stop the activity in the middle of the tug. Ask the total group what would happen if one side would simply drop the rope. Once the participants bring out the possibilities of falling, injury, lack of control, etc., ask both groups to put down the rope carefully and sit down where they are. Then discuss the following questions:

● Why is it important for parents to "let go" gradually?
● Why is it important for parents to "let go" at all?

Point out the following in your own words: "The balance of power in the parent and teenage relationship is shifting. Parental control appropriate for a child at age 6 doesn't work when the child is

16! But that shift of power is difficult for everyone."

Divide once more into all-parent and all-teenager brainstorming groups of about three to five people each. Provide the groups with large sheets of newsprint plus the purple markers for the parents and the green markers for the teenagers. Each group is responsible for developing a suggested power continuum on the following questions:

● How should the power shift from when a young person is 7 to 11 to 16, in the following areas: dress, curfew, music, friends, studies, and church.

● What issues and how much should the parents decide?

● What issues and how much should the teenagers decide?

● What factors might determine how the decision-making power shifts?

After 30 minutes pull the groups together, post their continuums side by side, and let them briefly share their ideas.

Personal Power Lines—After the break distribute the Personal Power Line sheets to all participants. Individuals should privately complete their sheets by placing an "X" anywhere along the power lines, at the place that most closely expresses their feelings.

After 15 minutes meet in small groups divided into parents and teenagers to let participants air their feelings about their power lines. Are there parents who are having a difficult time letting go of their control? How can they be helped to let their young person grow up? Are there teenagers who are feeling totally powerless? How can they be helped to recognize the powers they do have? Make sure a staff person is present within each group to facilitate discussions and make constructive suggestions.

Then ask participants to look at their power lines again. Have them locate three areas on their power lines where they feel most powerless. Ask them to write specific changes they would like to see. For instance, a teenager might write, "I want to come in at midnight on weekends instead of 10 p.m. like my weekday curfew." A parent might write, "I want my teenager to call me if he or she is going to be late." Encourage participants not to think about whether the other party is going to grant their request, but simply to get in touch with their own deepest wishes. Once individuals have identified what they want, suggest they also write down some simple reasons for their request—not arguments, but reasons.

Close this session by putting the following idea into your own words: "Negotiation is the key to working out our power conflicts. In our next session, we will learn how to negotiate successfully so everyone wins."

Relationship Collages—After the games and activities following lunch, provide materials for each individual to create a collage that

Teenager's/Parent's Personal Power Line

Check one of the following blanks to indicate whether you are a teenager or parent:

_____ teenager

_____ parent

Mark the continuum for each of the following areas:

● In my relationship with my parents/teenager, overall I feel:

Powerful (I have a say and am listened to)	So-so (Things could be better)	Powerless (I feel weak, helpless, squashed)
L_____|_____J		

● I feel powerful/powerless in these specific areas:

	Powerful, (I have a say and am listened to)	So-so (Things could be better)	Powerless (I feel weak, helpless, squashed)
Music	L_____|_____J		
Privacy	L_____|_____J		
Curfew	L_____|_____J		
Friends	L_____|_____J		
Church	L_____|_____J		
Use of telephone	L_____|_____J		
Style of dress	L_____|_____J		
Cleanliness	L_____|_____J		
Language	L_____|_____J		
Expression of feelings	L_____|_____J		
School work	L_____|_____J		
Sharing confidences	L_____|_____J		
Other	L_____|_____J		

represents the positive aspects of the parent/teenager relationship within his or her own home. Encourage everyone to use as many colors, textures, and ideas as possible to touch all of those special areas of relationships. Divide into small groups containing both parents and teenagers and have individuals share their collages and what they mean.

Negotiation, Not Compromise—When parents and teenagers don't know how to resolve their power conflicts, their conflicts may regress into a tug of war. In this kind of situation, one party wins and one party loses, unless there's an endless stalemate. A tug of war is a lousy way to resolve a power conflict.

But trying to resolve conflict by avoiding it is just as bad as a tug of war. Some people try to handle their conflict by running away. Avoiding the problem is like letting go of the rope; it lets the other party down with a crash and doesn't really solve anything. In fact, it may even make the other party more angry!

Negotiation is the best way to resolve a power conflict. In negotiation, each party gets some of what they want, and each party gives in a little, but all of the "give-and-take" is based on listening and understanding the needs of the other. Therefore, when a negotiated decision is finally met, there is a renewed awareness of the issue for both parties.

Negotiation is different from compromise. In compromise, one party gives in to the other just to keep the peace. Compromise is not the preferred way to solve problems, because one party still wins and the other loses. But in negotiation, both parties win.

Explain how negotiation works. (You may want to write these guidelines on a sheet of newsprint for everyone to see.)

● Each party states clearly what he or she wants and why. Be sure to hear each other out without interrupting!

● Each party states what he or she can and can't accept about the other person's proposal.

● Together, they work to come up with a third proposal that both can live with. Each party must give a little in order to gain. But in order for true negotiation to take place, both parties must be able to live with the final solution. If something continues to bother one party about the solution, adjust the solution till everyone can live with it.

Role play a simple negotiation before the total group. One staff member should take the part of the parent, while another takes the part of the teenager. Try to make sure there are some glaring errors in your role play.

Ask the group to critique your role play according to the three guidelines you presented earlier.

1. Did both parties state what they wanted?
2. Did they state why they wanted this?
3. Did each party listen without interrupting?
4. Did each party state what he or she could accept about the

other's proposal?

5. Did each party state what he or she could not accept about the other's proposal?

6. Did they work for a third proposal with which both could live?

7. Did they succeed?

8. Examine the feelings of both parties individually. Did you feel you gave up an essential? Did you feel good about the results of your negotiation?

Practice Negotiation #1 (Teenager, parent, observer)—Divide the total group into threes with a teenager, an adult who isn't a parent to that particular teenager and an observer. The observer may be an adult or a teenager. As a team they should select a sample negotiation, using one of the situations from the teenager's Power Line sheet. The teenager should explain to the others what stance he thinks his parents will take. The parent should assume that stance for the sake of the negotiation. But both individuals should try to come up with a reasonable third alternative

The teenager and the parent should briefly negotiate the chosen situation, with the observer silently looking on. After a third alternative is reached, the observer should guide the teenager and the adult through the negotiation guidelines and point out both the positive and negative examples of how the negotiation went. Then the teenager and the adult should have a chance to respond to each other and the observer in how they felt about the process. After the small groups have been through this practice session, meet as a total group to discuss the question, "What did you learn about negotiating?"

Practice Negotiation #2 (Teenager with his or her own parent)—Ask the teenagers to group with their actual parents. Then have one family group with another family. (There should be no more than two families represented in each group, unless one of the teenagers has a youth sponsor as a stand-in for his or her parent.)

Have the first family group negotiate an actual situation from their teenager's Power Line sheet, while the second family observes. The second family should look for positive and negative examples of the negotiation process. After the discussion they may make observations and mediating suggestions if they like. Remember, the objective of negotiation is to arrive at an acceptable conclusion for the family discussing the situation, not the observing family.

Then switch positions. The second family should negotiate an issue from their teenager's Power Line sheet and the first family will observe. Walk around the room as the negotiations proceed. Your role is to facilitate the negotiation process so each family can bring their negotiation to an acceptable conclusion. Be sure you point out that sometimes an acceptable conclusion is, "We agree to work on this issue further on (date, time)." This decision to delay negotiations is a realistic way to avoid degenerating into fights and destroying the negotiation process.

Negotiating Can Be Fun!—Close your retreat with a purely delightful negotiation. Divide the total group into teams of parents and teenagers, making sure family members are not together. Each team should have access to all the makings for an ice cream sundae. Tell the teams they are to negotiate to come up with the most creative sundae critter!

Turn them loose, judge quickly, and dig in and enjoy!

11

Risking to Reach Out

By Bob Valleau

Cliques and interpersonal barriers destroy a youth group. They hinder young people from reaching out to others. Young people need to learn how to reach out and commit themselves to one another.

Use this retreat to help your young people:
- discuss what it means to reach out to someone;
- reflect on what hinders us from reaching out;
- talk about commitment and how risky it is; and
- try to improve their "reaching out" skills.

Before the Retreat—Gather 3×5 cards, pencils, markers, notebook paper, red construction paper, a coat, scissors, newsprint, copies

---

Retreat Schedule

Friday
7:00 p.m. Arrive at retreat site and settle in
7:30 p.m. Get-Acquainted Time
8:00 p.m. Reaching Out to One Another
10:00 p.m. Refreshments
10:30 p.m. Quiet Time
11:00 p.m. Lights out

Saturday
8:00 a.m. Breakfast
9:00 a.m. Hindrances to Reaching Out
11:30 a.m. Break
Noon Lunch
1:30 p.m. What Is Commitment?
3:00 p.m. Break

5:30 p.m. Dinner
7:00 p.m. Commitment to One Another
9:00 p.m. Break
10:00 p.m. Singing
10:30 p.m. Quiet Time
11:00 p.m. Lights out

Sunday
6:00 a.m. Sunrise devotions (Gather outside and watch the sunrise. Quietly meditate on all that was learned at the retreat)
7:00 a.m. Breakfast
8:00 a.m. Clean up, pack and departure

of the handouts and Bibles. You also will need a CD or cassette player and DC Talk's CD (or cassette) titled *Free at Last* (available from Forefront or your local Christian bookstore).

Read the retreat and copy discussion questions on newsprint.

—————— Retreat Ingredients ——————

FRIDAY

Get-Acquainted Time—Here's a quick get-acquainted activity that both introduces the kids to each other and introduces the retreat topic.

Divide kids into groups of eight (or some other even-numbered divisions). Next, set chairs back-to-back in a circle with the outer chairs closely facing an inner chair as shown in the pod below:

Set up as many pods as needed. Have one person each sit in a middle chair facing an outer chair. Then have one person each sit in an outer chair and face a person in the middle.

Tell the outer-chair people they will ask the inner-chair people three questions about themselves. Instruct the inner-chair people to only respond to the questions. Say that a prerequisite for asking and answering questions is to introduce themselves to each other. Here are the questions (post these on newsprint so all can see):

● What cartoon character best describes you and why?

● What was the greatest gift you've given someone and how did he or she respond?

● What was the most important thing you've done for someone and how did it make you feel?

Set a three-minute time limit for the questions and brief responses. When the time is up say, "Rotate." Have the outer-chair people rotate one chair to their left and have the inner-chair people stay put. Then say, "Go." The outer-chair people start asking their new inner-chair people the same three questions. Keep going until everyone is facing his or her original partner. Then say, "Switch." The outer-chair people switch seats with the inner-chair people and the process is repeated. This now gives the new inner-chair people a chance to respond to the questions.

At the end of the activity, tell the young people that they've just shared three personal things about themselves and learned three important things from several others. Tell them to begin thinking of what reaching out to one another means to them as they gather for the next session.

Reaching Out to One Another—Say: "The Bible tells us that reaching out to one another is necessary for Christian growth and community. If we as group members do not reach out to one another, then we place limits on ourselves. Spiritually we stagnate, wither and die. We need each other." Illustrate this by reading Matthew 25:31-46. Break into small groups. Give each small group a Bible, piece of paper and pencil. Have them make a modern-day story from the parable. For example, "When Jesus and his angels come again, he'll gather all people in front of a glorious throne. He will put those who have reached out on his right, and those who haven't on his left. And he'll say to those at his right, 'Enter with me to my Father's place. For when a new person came to your school, you welcomed her; when your church needed help with food drives, you freely gave your time and money; when your neighbor was old and lonely, you visited him . . .' " Share the modern-day versions as a large group.

Hand the members in each small group a One Another Chart and a pencil. Allow 30 minutes for this exercise. Instruct the young people to look up as many scriptures listed on the chart as time permits. In the middle column of the chart, have them jot down key "one another" words (the first two are examples). Then, in the third column, have them write specific ways they can live out these verses.

When time is up, ask them to share key words they found, as well as some of their third-column responses. Discuss as many verses as time allows.

As you close the session in prayer, ask God to help everyone reach out to one another during the retreat. Then break for refreshments.

Quiet Time—Hand each person a pencil and three 3×5 cards. Have the kids pick three verses from the One Another Chart they feel they can put into action during the retreat. Tell them to write out one verse per index card. Then have them write their third-column response to each verse on the back of each respective card. Instruct them to carry these cards and refer to them throughout the retreat.

SATURDAY

Hindrances to Reaching Out—Explain to the kids that everyone, at some time, has difficulty reaching out to someone. Fear, mistrust or shyness has hindered many just to talk to one another. It's

One Another Chart

Verse	Key "One Another" Words	I can realistically do this in my life by:
John 13:34-35	"Love one another"	Going out of my way to say something kind to someone
Romans 12:5	"Members of one another" (Dependent on each other)	Asking someone to pray for me; reaching out to someone for advice
Romans 12:10 (two of them) Romans 12:16 Romans 14:13 Romans 15:7 Romans 15:14 Romans 16:16 1 Corinthians 11:33 1 Corinthians 12:25 Galatians 5:13 Galatians 6:2 Ephesians 4:32 (two of them) Ephesians 5:21 Colossians 3:13 1 Thessalonians 5:11 (two of them) 1 Thessalonians 5:11 Hebrews 10:24 James 4:11 James 5:9 James 5:16 (two of them) 1 Peter 4:9 1 Peter 4:10 1 Peter 5:5 1 John 1:7		

important to recognize our hindrances so that we may work on them.

Play the DC Talk song "Say the Words," then discuss these questions:

1. Why is it important that we tell others that we love them?

2. Why do people push their feelings inside them?

3. The song says that we tend to hide our feelings. And no matter how good some relationships are, we still feel unsure about sharing our true feelings at times.

● How does that affect our relationships?

● When we get a splinter or sliver under our skin, we hunt for a tweezer to get it out. How can we rid ourselves of "splinters" of being unwilling to say, "I love you"?

4. The song indicates there is a universal problem of people not really wanting to talk or reach out to one another. It says we need to make a special effort to tear down the walls that have been built between ourselves and others. (Hang up a sheet of newsprint in front of the young people. Ask them to list things that can be considered walls between people. For example, unforgiveness, mistrust, criticism, judgment and hate.)

Leave enough room on the newsprint to list the opposite of each one. Then ask the kids what are some specific ways we can tear down these walls. Stress that we have to tear down walls stone by stone or brick by brick. We can't tunnel our way underneath, go around or over a wall. If we choose any other way of getting to the other side of the wall—we are ignoring the wall.

Bring out a coat, then tell the kids: "You're going to better understand this discussion of reaching out to others by doing an activity called Pass the Coat. The person who has the coat represents the person reaching out. I'll go first. As I place the coat on someone, I'll portray by my facial expressions or actions the feelings I have when I reach out. For example, I could hide behind the coat to signify fear. Or I could give it and then take it back, thinking that the other person didn't really want what I had to give. To represent shyness, I could close my eyes as I slowly drape the coat over someone's shoulder. The person receiving the coat must respond to how he or she feels toward me. The person I give the coat to will give it to another person, and so on, until everyone has had a turn reaching out as well as receiving. No one can say a word."

After the activity, allow the kids to explain their feelings. Ask them to describe the meaning of their facial expressions or actions (when they gave the coat away and when they received the coat from another person).

Pass out the Watch-Me-Change sheets and a pencil to each person.

Watch Me Change

List, in order or priority, the five main hindrances that keep you from reaching out to others:

+ = I handled this hindrance well today.

✔ = I didn't handle this hindrance well today.

1) _____ 2) _____ 3) _____ 4) _____ 5) _____

	+	✔	+	✔	+	✔	+	✔	+	✔
SUNDAY										
MONDAY										
TUESDAY										
WEDNESDAY										
THURSDAY										
FRIDAY										
SATURDAY										
Totals										

This week's evaluation:

I'm getting better at handling number(s) _____ (+'s)

I need to really watch number(s) _____ (✔'s)

I did "okay" with number(s) _____ (tie)

Tell the kids to spend some time thinking about this exercise before they begin writing anything down. This sheet will help them this next week after the retreat as they reflect back upon the topic. Tell them to list in order of priority five hindrances that keep them from reaching out to others. Then have them place a check mark or a plus in the block that applies for that day. The plus or check mark represents how they handled a particular hindrance they have listed. At the end of next week they are to add all pluses and check marks at the bottom of the sheet. The evaluation portion is designed to help them gauge how they are doing with each hindrance every week. Pass out as many sheets as each person requests for additional weeks. Play the

Brown Bannister song again as they fill out the sheet.

Conclude the session with prayer. Ask God to help each person tear down the walls in their lives and give them strength to reach out to others.

What Is Commitment?—Commitment means making a pledge or promise to do something for someone. It means a liability to another person. It also means to unselfishly think about others. We cannot truly be committed to one another if all we do is think about ourselves.

For this session, divide the kids into groups of three or more. Appoint one person in each group as recorder and give him or her a pencil and a piece of notebook paper. Give groups 30 minutes to list examples of what commitment means to them (examples can be biblical, personal or symbolic). Near the end of the allotted time, say that each group must come up with only one sentence and one example describing commitment. Gather back together and discuss each group's response.

Read John 12:25: "The man who loves his life will lose it, while the man who hates his life in this world will keep it for eternal life." Ask these questions:

● What is meant by if we "love our life we will lose it"?
● How does a person love his or her life?
● How can we lose our life?
● What's the difference between needs and wants?
● Is anything wrong with satisfying our own wants and desires?

Reread the verse with these alterations: "The man who is committed to satisfying his own life loses it, while the man who commits his life to serving others will keep it forever."

Have the kids observe what the verse means now and explain their answers.

Commitment to One Another—Commitment to one another is a spiritual experience. Commitment to another person cannot be created by a formula or structure from without, but springs from inside a heart filled with the love of Christ. Christ's dynamic love exploding in our hearts produces commitment to one another.

Explain to the group that reaching out and being committed to one another is also risky. Risks occur when we expose ourselves to injury, damage or loss. But just because relationships are risky doesn't mean we should stop reaching out.

To help the kids understand risks, draw a line down the middle of a sheet of newsprint. Label the left column "Losses," and the right column "Gains." Then ask these questions:

● What are some risks involved in reaching out or committing ourselves to others? (For example, "Fear of being misunderstood," or

"Doubting the other person's friendship." Put their ideas in the left column under "Losses." List as many responses as the paper will allow.)

● What do you think would be the opposite of some of these things we have listed? (For example, the opposite of "Fear of being misunderstood" could be "Faith in the other person's judgment or discretion." The opposite of "Doubting the other person's friendship" could be "Trust that what I say or do is acceptable.")

Discuss the ways Jesus risked in his relationships. For example, Jesus risked being misunderstood many times by being controversial (Luke 16:1-15). Jesus risked rejection by being truthful (John 3:1-21). Remind the kids that even though Jesus was scoffed at and mistreated, he still reached out to others. He was still committed to loving and serving other people.

At the end of the discussion, say: "I did this listing of Losses and Gains hoping you could see that everything listed under Losses actually has to do with selfishness. When we reach out and commit ourselves to another person we lose a lot of these selfish traits (point to the left column). We focus in on the other person instead of ourselves. As we do this, we have much to gain from the relationship (point to the right column). In other words, we lose our selfishness and gain a friend when we risk reaching out.

"Of course, verbally saying we are committed to one another isn't quite as convincing as demonstrating our love."

Ask everyone to stand and join hands. Have them think of one way they can demonstrate their love to another person this upcoming week. Pray for God's strength and help as the kids risk these actions.

Quiet Time—Give each person a sheet of red construction paper, marker and scissors. Have everyone quietly cut a heart shape from the construction paper. After they've cut out the heart, have them write a sentence or two on the heart expressing their thanks to God for Christ's commitment to them. Then have them pledge to God one act of love they will do this next week as a demonstration of their commitment to one another. Offer them these examples:

● Pray for my youth leader.

● Pray daily for my best friend.

● Make it a point to look for unhappy people at school or church and go out of my way to cheer them up.

● Call someone on the telephone to let him or her know I care.

● Give someone an inexpensive gift such as a card or small poster.

● Take someone out for a Coke.

Tell them to keep the hearts as reminders of the pledge they've made.

12

Welcome to the Family

By Dick Hardel

When a family gets bigger—too big for a hug, too many to hear a single cry of hurt and pain, too busy to play together, too old to laugh together, too important to recognize common needs—it will soon fracture and fall in pieces. Welcome to the Family is a retreat designed for youth in a congregation to:

- become familiar with one another;
- discover a meaning for family; and
- spend a weekend "familying."

Before the Retreat—Adequate planning and preparation are essential for a positive retreat experience. First, acquaint yourself with the suggested schedule. Then read each of the retreat ingredients.

Find a retreat setting with enough open space to hold special large-group activities. Most of the activities need a large "family" room. The setting should also provide some fun activity options such as hiking or swimming.

Ask each participant to bring a favorite family game, a favorite family snack to share and home movies (optional).

Select family devotion planning groups from the list of participants. Assign them to plan devotions for Friday and Saturday evenings.

Designate at least one person to be the family photographer. It's good to use an instant-print camera. Place these instant pictures on the Name Wall (to be described later). Fill the youth ministry bulletin board at church with pictures from the retreat when you get back.

Prepare enough handouts, one for each participant. Include Personal Covenant; Family Covenant; Me, a Familiar; Continuums; and Blessed Be the Pie That Binds.

Gather Bibles, newsprint, markers, crayons, transparent tape, masking tape, 8½ × 11 paper, construction paper, scissors, balloons (7 inches or larger in diameter), old magazines and glue. A film about families is optional.

One week before the retreat, have participants complete and discuss their Personal Covenant and Family Covenant sheets.

Immediately before departing for the retreat, complete the Wor-

---

Retreat Schedule

Friday (Familiarizing)
- 6:00 p.m. Worship Just Before Leaving
- 7:30 p.m. Arrive and get settled
- 8:00 p.m. Name Wall
- 8:30 p.m. Me, a Familiar
- 8:50 p.m. Belt and Buckle Design
- 9:45 p.m. Upset the Family Table
- 10:00 p.m. Family Games
- 10:20 p.m. Write a family meal song
- 10:45 p.m. Eat family snacks
- 11:00 p.m. Do pre-planned family devotions
- 11:20 p.m. Read Ephesians 1 before going to sleep
- 11:30 p.m. Rest well

Saturday ("Familying")
- 7:00 a.m. Get up and get ready
- 7:50 a.m. Read Ephesians 2 before breakfast
- 8:00 a.m. Eat breakfast and complete the Meal Event
- 9:00 a.m. Experience a small family hike
- 9:20 a.m. Play a favorite family game
- 9:30 a.m. Blessed Be the Pie That Binds
- 10:20 a.m. Break
- 11:00 a.m. Family "Together" Stunt
- Noon Eat lunch and have a Meal Event
- 1:30 p.m. Read Ephesians 3 and take a small family hike

- 2:00 p.m. Family Outing
- 4:00 p.m. Family Sculptures
- 4:20 p.m. Rate Your Family
- 5:00 p.m. Break
- 6:00 p.m. Eat supper and have a Meal Event
- 7:30 p.m. Read Ephesians 4 and take a small family hike
- 7:50 p.m. Balloon Collages
- 8:15 p.m. Invent family TV game shows (or play more favorite family games, or watch old home movies or a film on families)
- 9:30 p.m. Celebrate an evening outing with favorite family vacation stories
- 11:00 p.m. Sing songs and do pre-planned family devotions
- 11:45 p.m. Read Ephesians 5 before sleeping
- Midnight Rest well

Sunday (Celebrating Family)
- 7:00 a.m. Get up and get ready
- 7:50 a.m. Read Ephesians 6
- 8:00 a.m. Eat breakfast and have a Meal Event
- 9:00 a.m. Have a family worship service (Design your own or go as a family to a nearby congregation's worship service)
- 11:00 a.m. There Is One Body

ship Just Before Leaving activity. Enjoy a special time together growing closer as the family of God. Unless otherwise indicated, consider "family" the whole group at the retreat.

_____ Retreat Ingredients _____

PRE-RETREAT

Covenants—In any family traveling and living together, it's essential for each member to be clear about the purpose of the weekend together and the commitment to one another. Have each person complete the Personal Covenant sheet individually. Then divide into small

---

Personal Covenant

Name _____

Goals

   The following are my personal goals for this retreat. They represent things I wish to learn, experience and be responsible for. They are things for which I will commit time and energy during the retreat.

   1. _____
   2. _____
   3. _____
   4. _____

Family Gifts

   Things I can do well are:

   Three things I have to offer this retreat family are:

Family Expectations

   What I'd like to see happen to this family on the retreat is:

   Things the retreat family can help me with are:

   How I'll treat others on this retreat is:

   How I want to be treated by others on this retreat is:

   What I need to be responsible for in order for the family covenant to be accomplished is:

---

groups; ask each person to read through his or her covenant. Work through the Family Covenant with the complete group.

FRIDAY

Worship Just Before Leaving—Read the following parable:

"Once there was a small family who wanted to be together. They went on a journey to see 'together.' It was a new beginning. They always asked, 'What does this mean?' They looked at trees and plants and asked, 'What does this mean?' They looked at maps and signs and asked, 'What does this mean?' They listened to birds and even to their stomachs growl and asked, 'What does this mean?' They listened to God speak, they looked at each other, they hugged and asked, 'What does this mean?' Suddenly they all knew, for they were 'together.'

Family Covenant

Family Life

1. We commit ourselves to deal with one another as follows:

2. We plan to help one another as follows:

3. Leadership in our retreat family will be handled as follows:

4. We will deal with persons who have or assume leadership as follows:

5. We are handling the following behavior issues as follows:
   sleep:
   drugs/alcohol:
   opposite sex relationships/couples:
   disagreements:
   when someone breaks the covenant:
   eating habits:

6. We will make decisions as follows:

7. Who is responsible for maintaining this covenant?

8. We encourage individuals in our retreat family to exercise the following freedoms (for example: form new friendships, take time alone, express ideas which may be different from others):

Together is a beginning.''

Assign young people as readers for the following parts:

Reader 1: We begin our journey together in Christ.

Reader 2: Help us, Lord, to grow together.

Reader 3: Give us vision to look closely together.

Reader 4: Strengthen us so we'll listen together with our faith.

Reader 5: Move our lips to celebrate you and each other.

Reader 6: Open our lives so we can see your love in the plain and ordinary.

Reader 7: Perform the miracle of your love in us.

Reader 8: Beginning today—together!

Name Wall—Put up several large pieces of newsprint on a wall or window. Have each participant use markers or crayons to decorate his or her name on the newsprint in a way that describes his or her uniqueness. The Name Wall provides a visualization of the retreat family.

For an interesting variation, have participants write letters to each other on the Name Wall.

Me, a Familiar—The word ''familiar'' means ''closely acquainted, intimate, of or relating to a family.'' Me, a Familiar is a beginning for participants to move closer together. Ask each participant to fill out the Me, a Familiar sheet. Then in small groups of two to six have the participants discuss the sheets with one another.

Me, A Familiar

My nickname _____

My full name_____
          (first)   (middle)   (family)

My middle name was chosen for me by _____

because_____

Coin-wise, today, I feel like a _____

Usually, I feel like a _____

The symbol below which best describes me is: (Circle it.)

☐   △   ϩ   ○

If I wrote a book today, its title would be:

Belt and Buckle Design—In the western part of the United States, many people wear belts with their names carved or stamped on the leather. Many also have large belt buckles designed to say something unique about them. Using strips of construction paper, have participants design their own belts. Have them creatively design their family names on the outside of the belts. Then each person should design a belt buckle which shows his or her greatest accomplishment. Tape the belt and buckle together.

Belts and buckles not only show family names, or hold up jeans, but also hold in feelings others don't see. On the inside of the belts have each participant write personal feelings other people don't see. The participants should wear their belts and in small groups of six to eight share some of the hidden feelings. After sharing, take all the belts and buckles, link them together, and hang them around the meeting room.

Upset the Family Table—This is the same game as Fruitbasket Upset. Have participants put chairs together to form a large circle. There should be one less chair than the number of participants. The participants are seated in chairs with one person standing in the center of the circle. Give each participant (including the one in the center of the circle) the name of something that can be found on the family table. Depending on the size of the retreat family, use only a few items so that every three or four people have the same item. For example: plate, fork, cup, glass. The person in the center calls out one of the items and all those people with that item exchange chairs. Players cannot go back to their original chair. During the exchange the person in the center tries to sit in any one of the vacant chairs. Thus a new person should be in the center. The new person in the center may also say, "Upset the family table." That's when all players must find new seats at least two chairs from where they last were sitting.

Family Games—Have each participant bring and lead his or her favorite family game during the retreat. The games can be used anywhere during the schedule. Play together as a family. Learn new favorites. Other games can be found in the books *Playfair* (Impact Publishers), *New Games* and *More New Games* (both Doubleday), and the *Try This One* series (Group Books).

Family Meal Song—During the Friday night session have participants design songs which will be used for prayers before and after meals. Break group members into smaller groups and give them a familiar melody such as "Edelweiss" or "I've Been Working on the Railroad." Write words on newsprint and practice singing the verses. Use the songs at each meal event.

SATURDAY

Meal Events—Make every meal a celebration event. Celebrate birthdays or each person's baptism birthday during the Meal Events. Let the "celebrated" person go first in line for food. Sing "Happy Baptism Birthday" or "Happy Family to You." You could even draw names before the retreat and during the retreat make special gifts for people. The gifts would be presented at the meal in which they are being celebrated.

Meditations and Family Hikes—The book of Ephesians is a letter to another special family called the "Saints at Ephesus." In the

---

Blessed Be the Pie That Binds

1. Autograph a slice of everyone's pie.
2. When I hear the word "bound," I usually think of . . . (Choose one word and share it with the group.)
   - stuck with
   - determined
   - connected
   - shared
   - prune juice
   - committed
   - strapped
   - glued
   - tied

AUTOGRAPH PIE

3. Think of a special friend. What type of binding is there in that relationship? (Share answers with the group.)
   - ring
   - pin
   - official document
   - membership card
   - picture
   - clothing
   - gift
   - special event
   - other _____
4. Choose one person from the group to whisper the following parable just loudly enough for all to hear:
   "Once there was a church who wanted to understand community. They had no theologian to theol-o-gize. No pastor to pastor-o-ize. No youth leader to leader-o-ize.
   "All they had was each other, some leftover dough and a bowl of cherries. They surrounded the table and looked at the cherries from every angle and squinted at each other. Each put a fingerprint in the dough.
   "One person shouted 'A cherry pie!' Others licked their lips. Some sniffed and smiled. Then one began to sing 'Blessed be the pie that binds!' They laughed and laughed. Who would have thought that a pie could be a tie?"
5. Describe a dessert you've had with a special friend.
6. Read Colossians 3:12-17 aloud together three times. Each time be in a different "binding" position. (For example, all lying on your backs in a circle linking arms and/or legs, each lying down with your heads on one another's stomachs, etc.)
7. Complete this sentence and share:
   - The most important binding to me is . . .

schedule, occasionally a small family hike follows the personal meditation. After all have read the assigned portion of scripture, have them
go for a hike in groups of three. During this 20-minute hike they are
to talk about being a saint in a family. Discussion could include what
they liked best about the verses, what they didn't understand, what
Ephesians says about "family" at this retreat, at home, with friends.

Blessed Be the Pie That Binds—Use this Bible study for small
groups of six to 10 people. Make sure everyone has the opportunity to
talk. This Bible study is designed so the participants see the importance of visible signs of loving relationships and so they celebrate their
relationships in Christ.

8. Complete one of the following sentences and share:
   - Sometimes being bound to someone can be a problem when . . .
   - Once I had a closely bound relationship broken when . . .
   - To heal a broken bond between people, one must . . .
9. Write a limerick about Colossians 3:12-17 and share it with the group. (A
   limerick is a type of five-line poetry in which the first, second and fifth
   lines rhyme, and the third and fourth lines rhyme.)
   Example: You are the branches and I am the vine
                   I have chosen you and you are mine
                   I have given you the ability
                   To love with kindness and humility
                   And to bind all together you have my sign

   Complete the last line:
                   The peace that Christ gave is to be our guide
                   As you and I in love abide
                   With Christ's message truly in our hearts
                   This community will never be apart

   _____

   Now write your own:
   _____
   _____
   _____
   _____
   _____

10. Complete one of the following sentences and share:
    - Some brokenness in my life that needs binding is . . .
    - I'm afraid to be bound so closely in Christ because . . .
    - What I need most from you to feel bound is . . .
11. Close by planning a visual sign of your binding love in Christ to be done
    at mealtime—perhaps over a piece of pie.

A Family "Together" Stunt—Do one or more stunts such as building a pyramid, or seeing how many people can get on a stump, log or tire. Do stunts that require everyone's participation in some way. Take pictures.

Family Outing—The family outing depends on the retreat setting. Do all kinds of things together. If there's a beach, bury one another in the sand or build huge sand castles together. If you're in the city visit a museum, an amusement park or a planetarium. Don't forget to take pictures!

Family Sculptures—Divide members into groups no greater than six. Have one person be the sculptor and the others the clay. The sculptor should shape the clay to show how families feel inside. For example, the group could be tangled to show confusion or tightly bound to show closeness. Talk about the feelings shown.

Rate Your Family—Pass out copies of Continuums. (See next page.) Have the participants rate themselves and their parents by placing a "D" for Dad, "M" for Mom, and "S" for Self on each continuum. Share ratings in small groups of two to six.

Balloon Collages—Have the participants make "family" collages on balloons instead of posterboard. Ask participants to inflate a 7-inch balloon or larger and tie a knot on the end. Have them cut out and paste pictures and words from magazine articles on their balloon. They should cover the whole balloon so that it can no longer be seen. When everyone is finished, hang the balloon collages from the ceiling.

SUNDAY

There Is One Body—This is the closure event. Each participant needs a piece of newsprint large enough to trace a life-size body outline. After everyone does the drawing, ask the participants to write their own name on their drawing. Have participants use scissors and construction paper to cut out a part of the body (eye, lips, blood vessel, certain muscle, certain bone, nose, etc.) for each participant including themselves. Also have them put the construction paper parts so that they can remember which part belongs to whom.

Have the participants sit forming a large circle. Give each person an opportunity to sit in the middle with his or her life-size drawing on the floor next to him or her. One at a time the others tape onto the life-size drawing the part of the body that they chose for the person in the center. Each person responds with the reason that part of the body was chosen. For example, "Bobby, I chose the clavicle for you because you always give me a strong shoulder to cry on."

When everyone has taped the parts on the drawing, the person in the center puts his or her own part on the drawing and tells why that

Continuums

Awfully Autocratic	1	Impossibly Permissive
Largely Legalistic Faith-wise	2	Nothing Faith-wise
Immovably Rigid	3	Pitifully Pliable
Tightly Together	4	Insensitively Separate
Constantly Clammed-up	5	Invariably Babbling

(Try a couple of your own.)

6
7

part was chosen.

When all have finished, read Ephesians 4:6-16 aloud. This closure activity takes a lot of time depending on the size of the retreat family, but it provides great affirmation. Keep the life-size drawings with the parts taped on and hang them in the youth room or in the church halls after the retreat.

Section Three

Issues

Life Stages

By Laurence Packard

Your life flashes before your eyes—past, present and future. You look at life with a new perspective. You ask the question, "Does it really make a difference to live as a Christian?" You know that it certainly does. Such is the impact of a retreat concerning the stages of life.

Use this retreat to help your young people:

● experience a weekend adventure;

Retreat Schedule

Friday
7:00 p.m. Arrive at camp
7:30 p.m. Who Am I?
8:00 p.m. Baby Photo Fun
8:30 p.m. "Birth" Narration
9:00 p.m. Partner Time
10:00 p.m. Personal Discoveries
11:00 p.m. Refreshments and free
time
Midnight Lights out

Saturday
8:00 a.m. Breakfast
8:30 a.m. Morning Warm-Up
9:00 a.m. "Adolescence"
Narration
9:30 a.m. Music and Film
10:30 a.m. Personal Discoveries
11:30 a.m. Lunch
1:00 p.m. Afternoon Warm-Up
1:30 p.m. "Adulthood" Narration
2:00 p.m. Group Discussion

2:30 p.m. Personal Discoveries
3:30 p.m. Music
4:00 p.m. Free time
5:00 p.m. Dinner
6:00 p.m. "Elderly" Narration
6:30 p.m. Walking a Mile
7:00 p.m. Making a Mural
8:00 p.m. Break
9:00 p.m. Personal Discoveries
10:00 p.m. Music
10:30 p.m. Free time and
refreshments
11:30 p.m. Lights out

Sunday
8:00 a.m. Breakfast
8:30 a.m. Film
9:00 a.m. "Eyewitness" Narration
9:30 a.m. Partner Time
10:00 a.m. Worship
11:00 a.m. Retreat Mementos
11:30 a.m. Pack and head for
home

- learn to include God in every part of their lives;
- explore the five life stages, from birth to death; and
- see how, for a Christian, each life stage has special meaning.

Before the Retreat—Recruit four group members to be narrators and to tape interviews. Ask them to read the following retreat and record the necessary narrations and questions. Ask one adult, ideally a sponsor for the retreat, to improvise and narrate the "eyewitness account" to be used on Sunday morning. (Suggested narrations and interview questions appear in the sections where they will be used.)

Select music representative of the different stages of life. This outline refers to songs from Tedd McNabb's album *Walker of the Way*, available at most Christian bookstores.

Give each group member a "blank book" to use as a journal during the retreat. Find these in book or card stores. The clothbound books make especially nice retreat mementos.

Gather Bibles, films (as noted), projector, screen, newsprint, markers, arts and crafts materials for making a giant mural, paper for the mural, guitars and songbooks, cassette tape recorders, baby photo of each person, earplugs, nose plugs, gloves, plastic bags, elastic bandages, eye patches or foggy plastic, and tape. You'll also need several copies of the Discussion Questions handouts.

_____ Retreat Ingredients _____

FRIDAY

Who Am I?—The theme for Friday is birth; the objective is to compare physical birth with spiritual birth.

Have everyone sit in a circle. Give a mirror to the first person, who looks in the mirror and says "Who am I?" and then states an adjective that starts with the first letter of his or her name, and the name. (For example, "I'm crazy Chris!") He or she then hands the mirror to the next person, who says, "You are _____; but who am I?" The person holding the mirror then says an adjective and his or her name, and passes the mirror to the next person, who repeats all names to that point and continues. The last person names everyone.

Baby Photo Fun—Gather everybody's baby pictures and tape them onto the wall. Assign a number to each photo, then let everyone try to guess who's who. Have people vote on who looks most like his or her baby picture.

"Birth" Narration—Play the prerecorded tape. The tape begins with a narrator/interviewer saying, "My name is Birth; I am a miracle of God," followed by a recording of an infant crying (10 seconds).

"I become a child," continues the narrator/interviewer and then the sounds of children laughing, talking and playing follow (15 seconds).

The narrator/interviewer then reads Psalm 8:2-5 above the sounds of the children.

Partner Time—Ask group members to choose partners and go outside for a short walk. Have each pair find a place to sit and read Psalm 8. Keeping in mind the scripture passage, each person completes the sentence "I am . . ." 10 different ways. (For example, "I am only a little lower than the angels.") The partners record each other's answers in the owner's blank book.

Personal Discoveries—Gather inside and begin by having two group members act out the encounter between Jesus and Nicodemus, as recorded in John 3:1-15; or invite one articulate group member to portray Nicodemus and tell a friend about the encounter he just had with Jesus; or ask a person to read the scripture passage.

Divide group members into small groups of three or four members (they'll keep the same small groups all weekend). Encourage them to record in their blank books discoveries such as new ideas, thoughts and feelings. Give each small group a Discussion Questions #1 handout.

Discussion Questions #1

- What are some similarities between physical and spiritual births? (For example, new beginnings.)
- Newborn babies can't exist apart from their parents, can't eat solid food, can't be left alone for long, etc. How do these qualities compare with qualities of spiritual "newborns"?
- How do you know when a physical birth has occurred? How do you know when a spiritual birth has occurred?
- If Nicodemus came to you today and asked what it means to be born again, how would you answer him?

SATURDAY

Morning Warm-Up—The theme for the morning is adolescence;

the objective is to see God's work in our lives as we go through changes.

Begin with a group exercise. Assemble the kids in the small groups. Tell each group to "get as close together as you can." Then run a string around the widest part of each group and cut it where it meets. Measure strings to determine the shortest.

"Adolescence" Narration—Play the prerecorded tape. The narrator/interviewer says, "My name is Adolescence; I am a time of change." Then the tape continues with various teenagers answering these questions:

● What changes are you experiencing in your life right now?

● How is your relationship with your parents changing? How do you feel about these changes?

● How do you feel about being a teenager?

● Do you think these are the "best years of your life"? Why or why not?

● What do you like best about being a teenager? least?

● What will you remember about your adolescence when you're 75?

Music and Film—Play "Tears" from McNabb's album. Say that it's okay to cry, or feel like crying, when facing so many changes.

View *Changes*, part one of the "Begin With Goodbye" series by EcuFilm, 810 12th Ave. S., Nashville, TN 37203. Discuss favorite and least-liked parts. Have group members get into their small groups again and talk about which scenes they could most relate to and why.

Personal Discoveries—Gather everyone and select some group members to act out the change in Abraham's life as recorded in Genesis 12:1-6, or have one person read the scripture passage.

Divide into small groups, once again, encourage the young people to record thoughts and feelings in their blank books. Give each group a Discussion Questions #2 handout.

Afternoon Warm-Up—The theme for the afternoon is adulthood; the objective is to see how God helps us grow through making choices.

Gather everyone for a group exercise. Give each group member a 12-inch piece of string and tell everyone to tie the ends of the string onto other members' strings. Give them three minutes. Note the many different-size groups created by doing this exercise. Discuss that, just as group members chose whom to "tie onto," we must choose in life which groups to join, which friends to have, etc.

"Adulthood" Narration—Play the prerecorded tape. The narrator/interviewer begins this section of the tape with, "My name is Adulthood; I am a time of making choices." Then the tape continues with some adults answering these questions:

Discussion Questions #2

● How was God involved in this major change in Abraham's life?

● What is a recent change in your life? How is God involved? (If you can't think of ways God is involved, ask other small group members to suggest ways.)

● What are some different reactions we have toward change?

● When might we want something to change? When might we resist change?

● Can we ever know whether changes will be good or bad? Why or why not?

● Whether a change is good or bad, what difference can it make to believe that God is involved in your life?

● What are ways you can know that God is with you always, no matter what changes? (See Matthew 28:20).

● Describe a change in your life and how you chose to handle it.

● What are some difficult decisions you've faced? (For example, how to set your teenager's curfew, when and how to discipline your children.)

● How did you choose your friends? Do you always feel certain you make the best choices? Why or why not?

Group Discussion—Have each person tell one important choice he or she made recently. Also ask the kids to describe the decision-making process they went through to make those choices. As the group discusses these ideas, have someone list on newsprint the possible steps for decision-making.

Personal Discoveries—Begin by having a group member recount the story of the feeding of the 5,000 found in John 6:1-14, as though he or she had been one of the 5,000; or have two group members portray Jerusalem residents, excitedly discussing the unbelievable story they just heard; or simply tell this story to your group members while they pass around a loaf of bread and eat bits of it.

Again, divide group members into their small groups and encourage the kids to record thoughts and feelings in their blank books. Give each small group a Discussion Questions #3 handout.

Music—Play the song "Daily Bread" from McNabb's album. Sing some of the group's favorite songs before breaking for free time.

"Elderly" Narration—The theme for Saturday evening is the

Discussion Questions #3

● Which do you think most satisfied the hunger of the 5,000—the food or Jesus' presence?

● Read John 6:27, 35. How is Jesus the bread of life for you? How does he help you to make decisions?

● How does Jesus enable you to be strong in your faith and better prepared to make choices? (For example, through studying the Bible, being with other Christians, praying.)

● Complete this prayer in your blank book: "Jesus, please help me to let you feed me more. Help me be prepared to make the right decision in my life right now about . . ."

elderly years; the objective is to see how God provides fulfillment through community and giving.

Play the prerecorded tape. The narrator/interviewer begins the tape saying, "My name is Old Age; I am a time for enjoying others and giving of myself." Then the tape continues with some elderly people answering these questions:

● Do you consider yourself an elderly person? Explain.

● In what ways are you fulfilled in life more now than ever before?

● What do you feel are your special gifts and abilities?

● How do you give of yourself to others?

Walking a Mile—Invite members to "walk a mile" in the elderly's shoes. Tell them that they will briefly experience simulated handicaps that many elderly people live with daily.

Distribute among group members: earplugs to impair hearing; nose plugs to stifle smell; gloves and plastic bags to make hand movement awkward and slow, as though arthritic; elastic bandages to hinder arm and leg movements; eye patches or foggy plastic to limit and blur vision.

Instruct everyone to remain in their handicapped state until the mural-making activity (next) is finished.

Explain that the birth change, growth and fulfillment processes discussed so far are not isolated to particular times in life. While it's true that certain life stages are characterized more by one or another, all of these processes can occur any time during our lives.

Ask group members to sit comfortably, close their eyes, and silently reflect on these elements in their lives. Ask aloud: "What times of new beginnings or renewal have you experienced? times of change? times of growth? times of fulfillment?"

Making a Mural—Tell group members to open their eyes. Challenge them to create a giant "life voyage" mural using the arts and crafts materials. Encourage everyone to think of memories about new beginnings, renewal, change, growth and fulfillment, and represent those times on the mural. For example, some might create symbols for birth (a crib), baptism (water or a dove), changes (a drivers license or a moving van), etc. Also tell group members to include illustrations of their dreams for the future on the mural (for example, college, a family, etc.).

At the end of this activity, let the kids "take off" their handicaps and discuss the difficulties they encountered.

Personal Discoveries—Again, have group members divide into their small groups and take their blank books for notes.

Give each group an Instructions handout.

Instructions

● One person reads aloud 1 Corinthians 12:4-12. Discuss spiritual gifts you think you and others in your group may have.

● All the members write on the top of a page in their blank books: "Gifts I've given to . . ." Then, one at a time, pass the blank books around the small group. As a member gets another person's book, he or she thanks that person for giving, for example, a listening ear, and then writes in the book his or her own name and the gift received from the book's owner. For example, Carrie might write "Carrie, a listening ear" in Laura's book.

● Pray together, thanking God for the gift of each small group member, and asking that each member will realize his or her special contributions to the whole group.

Music—Play McNabb's "Let It Shine" as prayers end. Roast marshmallows around a fire, sing songs and enjoy being together.

SUNDAY

Film—The theme for Sunday is death and resurrection; the objective is to see how life with Christ goes full circle from birth to death, a new form of birth.

Show *That's Life* by Floyd Shaffer, available from Mass Media Ministries, 2116 N. Charles St. Baltimore, MD 21218.

Discuss immediate impressions about the film. Ask group members to name as many examples of signs of rebirth after "death" that they know. List these on newsprint.

"Eyewitness" Narration—Play the tape, which has the prerecorded "eyewitness account" of one of Jesus' followers who met the risen Christ on the road to Emmaus (Luke 24:13-24).

Be sure to choose an articulate, expressive adult to summarize these events on tape. Have the person include in the narration his or her feeling as the events transpired.

Partner Time—Have Friday evening's partners get together for another brief walk. Give pairs the Discussion Questions #4 handout to answer and record in their blank books.

Discussion Questions #4

- Read the Emmaus road story in Luke 24:13-24.
- Why didn't Jesus' followers recognize him at first? When are you likely not to recognize Jesus in your life?
- What does Jesus' Resurrection mean to you?
- How can you know you belong to Jesus?
- List five ways Jesus makes a difference in your life.
- Pray for your partner's relationship with Jesus to be strong throughout all of life, even death.

Worship—Play McNabb's title song, "Walker of the Way," to call group members into a worshipful attitude.

Give a brief talk on how our voyage through life is complete only when we find meaning through Jesus. Physical birth is not enough; spiritual birth and growth are necessary.

Invite small groups to contribute to the worship service in any ways they would like.

Close with singing and a prayer.

Retreat Mementos—Suggest that all group members autograph blank books (yearbook-style) and add a special message or note about the weekend.

14

Popularity Pursuit

By Elaine Clanton Harpine

The popularity game. Young people play it by joining clubs and hanging around with the "right" crowd. Usually they lose, and end up lonely. But it's not enough to say, "Don't worry about being popular."

Help your group members go beyond the shallowness of what popularity is supposed to be, and learn deeper qualities of communication and friendship.

Use this retreat to:

● help young people evaluate the cost of being popular;

● demonstrate that "true popularity" comes from being a kind, loving and trustworthy friend—not from going along with the crowd;

● teach communication skills; and

● help group members feel better about not always being accepted or liked by everyone.

Before the Retreat—Form a retreat planning committee of kids and adults. The committee decides the retreat date, site, publicity, transportation and meals. The committee will also be in charge of distributing and collecting permission and health forms, and collecting money.

Gather the following supplies: newsprint, posterboard, masking tape, markers, magazines, scissors, glue, 3×5 cards, different-colored construction paper, popcorn, snacks; for every four group members, a paper sack and the scavenger hunt list; and for each group member, paper, a pencil, a shoe box and a Bible.

Prepare the I Think and My Reflection handouts, according to the examples given. Photocopy enough handouts so each group member has one.

For the Love Puzzle, draw a crossword puzzle design on newsprint. Write the letters "L-O-V-E" in large letters in four of the squares near the center of the puzzle.

Draw the Bible Treasure Hunt Puzzle on newsprint following the format given, including the Bible verses.

For the Finding Love activity, write the word "ACCEPTANCE" on a large piece of posterboard, and write "Acts 10:34-35" in one corner. Then cut the posterboard into as many jigsaw puzzle pieces as you have group members.

Draw The Popularity Game board on large pieces of posterboard—one for every five group members.

For Unscramble the Words, write on newsprint scrambled versions of these words: righteousness, spirit, blessed, merciful, meek, peacemakers, persecuted, poor, children and hunger.

Write on newsprint the questions for Sunday's morning Bible study.

Gather as many creative worship resources—books with worship ideas, poetry, songs and drama—as you can find.

Retreat Schedule

Friday
7:00 p.m. Arrive and unpack
7:15 p.m. Love Puzzle
7:45 p.m. We're Alike, but We're Different
8:30 p.m. Free time
8:45 p.m. I Think
9:15 p.m. Inside-Outside
10:00 p.m. Snack and group singing
10:30 p.m. A Bible Treasure Hunt
11:15 p.m. Lights out

Saturday
7:30 a.m. Finding Love
7:45 a.m. Breakfast
9:00 a.m. My Reflection
10:00 a.m. Break
10:15 a.m. In Search of Popularity
Noon Lunch
1:00 p.m. Planning Sunday's Worship Service

2:00 p.m. Group recreation time: Plan a game such as volleyball, or in bad weather, paint a mural on a long roll of newsprint
5:00 p.m. Dinner
6:00 p.m. The Popularity Game
7:30 p.m. Snack and Bible charades
8:30 p.m. Finish planning Sunday's worship service
10:00 p.m. Sharing Our Love
11:15 p.m. Lights out

Sunday
7:30 a.m. Unscramble the Words
7:45 a.m. Breakfast
9:00 a.m. Morning Bible Study
10:00 a.m. Worship service
11:00 a.m. Clean up and pack
11:30 a.m. Love Circle

Retreat Ingredients

FRIDAY

Love Puzzle—Tape the Love Puzzle onto the wall; place markers nearby.

Explain that the group will be making a crossword puzzle using members' names. Have each person find a letter—either in the word "love" or in someone else's name—that his or her name can cross with. Put someone in charge of blackening the squares before and after each name.

Emphasize that everyone is a part of the group, and that the common bond is love. Display the puzzle throughout the retreat.

Briefly review the schedule and discuss rules for the weekend. (Have the young people help establish the rules, then they're more likely to cooperate cheerfully.) Have everyone join hands, right arm over left, to form a Love Circle. Make a group commitment to work together. Close in prayer.

We're Alike, but We're Different—Give each person a sheet of paper. Have the kids draw a large square on their paper, and then divide the large square into 16 equal squares, four across and four down. Have each person write in each square a word that describes his or her personality; for example, kind, impatient, friendly or shy.

When everyone has finished, have group members mingle and discover who shares similar personality characteristics to their own. Have them write in the appropriate square on their handouts the name of the person who shares that particular characteristic. (A person's name can appear in more than one square.) Group members try to find a name to write in all 16 squares.

Emphasize that we're all similar in some ways and different in others, and that one purpose of this retreat is to get to know one another better.

I Think—Give each person an I Think handout. Explain that the activity will explore the meaning of true popularity. Have everyone turn to John 12:1-29.

I Think

Complete the following sentences.
1. People who drink beer are _____
_____.
2. My friends are_____
_____.
3. Illegal drugs make you _____
_____.
4. Fashion styles are _____
_____.
5. My parents think _____
_____.
6. The most important thing in life is_____
_____.
7. Dating is _____
_____.
8. I want to be_____
_____.
9. I hope my friends think I'm_____
_____.
10. It's more important to _____
_____.

First, read John 12:1-8. Discuss these questions:

● How did Jesus respond when Mary anointed him with oil? (Note to leaders: Anointing is a sign of honor.)

● Why is it important for us to let others do nice things for us? Then, read John 12:9-19. Discuss these questions:

● How do you think Jesus felt knowing that many of these people would turn against him less than a week later?

● How do you feel about friends who turn their back on you?

● How can you avoid being that kind of "fair-weather" friend?

Finally, read John 12:20-29. Ask:

● What did Jesus mean by what he said?

● Do you think this idea only applies to eternal life? Why or why not?

● How does a true friend give of himself or herself?

Have everyone complete the sentences on the handout. Then have the group divide into pairs and compare answers. Remind everyone that there are no right or wrong answers.

Inside-Outside—Give each group member a shoe box. Make available magazines, scissors and glue.

Ask each group member to make a collage on the outside of the box illustrating how others see him or her. The collage may include pictures or words from the magazines. Have the young people make their collages so the lid can be lifted off.

After everyone has finished, have each group member make another collage inside the box. This collage illustrates how each person sees himself or herself. Call the inside collage "the real you."

Allow volunteers to present their two collages. Discuss the differences. (Let the collages dry with the lids off, so they don't become glued on.)

A Bible Treasure Hunt—Give each participant a Bible. Display the newsprint with the Bible Treasure Hunt Puzzle on it.

Explain the rules: Everyone will get a chance to guess a letter. If the person guesses correctly, the letter will be placed in the appropriate square(s). If the guess is incorrect, then the person must look up one of the Bible verses listed on the newsprint and figure out a correct letter for his or her next turn. A key word in each Bible passage begins with the letter in the box number that corresponds with the clue number. (The answer is: "Be true to yourself and to God.")

After guessing a correct letter, a player can guess the complete phrase. After someone solves the puzzle, discuss how to be true to yourself and to God in the face of so many adverse pressures.

Close by singing and by forming a Love Circle. Make a commitment to continue learning and growing throughout the retreat. Offer a silent prayer of thanksgiving for each young person.

SATURDAY

Finding Love—As the group gathers for breakfast, give each person a piece of the ACCEPTANCE puzzle. Supply Bibles. Encourage

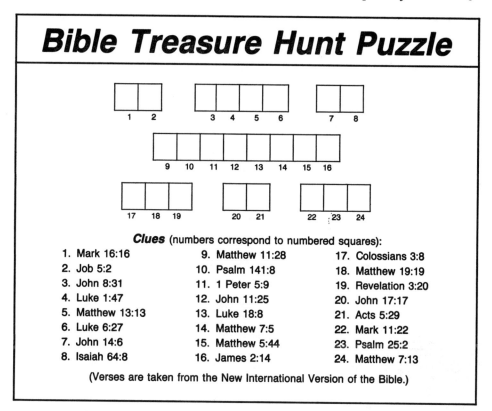

Bible Treasure Hunt Puzzle

Clues (numbers correspond to numbered squares):

1. Mark 16:16	9. Matthew 11:28	17. Colossians 3:8
2. Job 5:2	10. Psalm 141:8	18. Matthew 19:19
3. John 8:31	11. 1 Peter 5:9	19. Revelation 3:20
4. Luke 1:47	12. John 11:25	20. John 17:17
5. Matthew 13:13	13. Luke 18:8	21. Acts 5:29
6. Luke 6:27	14. Matthew 7:5	22. Mark 11:22
7. John 14:6	15. Matthew 5:44	23. Psalm 25:2
8. Isaiah 64:8	16. James 2:14	24. Matthew 7:13

(Verses are taken from the New International Version of the Bible.)

group members to solve the puzzle together. When the puzzle is completed, read the verses out loud. Ask group members to tell what "acceptance" means to them.

My Reflection—Give each person a copy of the My Reflection handout. Ask everyone to complete the three sentences on the mirror.

Form small groups of three to five members. Have each small group circle words on the mirror, or add in words, that describe a truly popular person. Each group member should contribute at least one word that he or she feels defines popularity.

Ask each group, from its word choices, to write a description of a "popular" person. Have each small group share its description with the entire group. To compile a description of "true popularity," write each group's suggestions on newsprint.

Refer to the sentences in the center of the mirror. Ask: "Do we ever pretend to be or do something just because we think it'll make us popular? Explain. What extremes will some people take to be popular?"

Close by having a "mirror prayer." Ask group members to get into pairs and face their partners, holding hands. Each person takes a turn praying—thanking God for the positive qualities he or she sees in

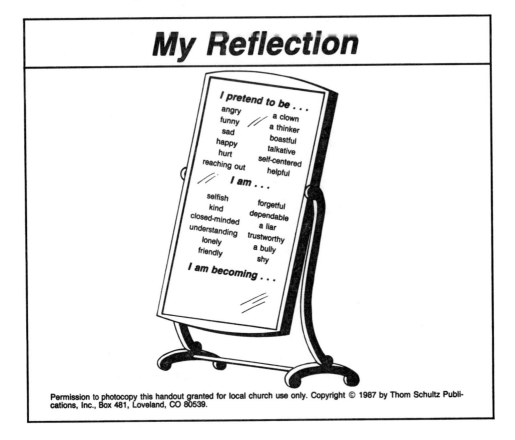

the other person, and praying that the partner can develop the characteristics of "true popularity."

In Search of Popularity—Form teams of four for an outdoor scavenger hunt. Give each team a list of items. Make sure everyone understands the deadline to return. Stress that all items must be natural, not man-made, but teams can make things from materials they find. Give each team a paper sack for collecting items, and send them out.

Teams should find things that represent the following:

1. something that makes you feel better than the other teams
2. a status symbol
3. something that will make others jealous
4. something fashionable
5. something that makes you feel important
6. something you like
7. something to brag about
8. something cold
9. something you don't have to care about
10. an example of peer pressure
11. someone's hurt feelings

12. love

13. something to share with everyone

14. friendship

15. an act of kindness

After everyone returns, have each group explain its items.

Planning Sunday's Worship Service—Form small groups of four to six. Have each small group suggest five ideas for the Sunday worship service. Suggestions can range from the kind of service to what to include—poems, skits, songs, prayers and Bible passages.

Bring everyone back together. From the suggestions, help the group outline the worship service. After the outline is decided, have the small groups select a part of the service to work on. Make sure all parts are taken.

Make worship resources available. Remind group members that they'll have another work session later.

The Popularity Game—Form groups of five. Give each group a game board and a bowl of popcorn.

Have everyone take a 3×5 card and cut a one-inch square to use as a game token. Give each person a marker to design the game token to reflect his or her personality.

Give each small group five 3×5 cards. Have groups write on one side of each card a different number between 1 and 5. Each person draws a card at his or her turn. The number on the card determines how many spaces the person moves. Shuffle the cards after each turn. If a player lands on a space already occupied, he or she must go backward until finding an empty space.

The player responds to the question or reads the Bible passage written on the space. After the player answers a question, the rest of the group discusses the answer and votes on whether the answer would help or hurt a friendship. For each positive vote, the player gets a piece of popcorn.

To land on "finish," a player needs to draw a card with the exact number of spaces needed. If the number is greater, the player must move back the extra number of spaces after reaching the finish line.

Write the following questions on newsprint. If small groups have enough time after finishing the game, they can discuss the questions.

● How did you feel when you had to go backward because someone else was sitting on a space? Is it fair if groups you want to join limit the number of participants—such as football or cheerleading? Why or why not?

● Was it frustrating to be so close to finishing the game and then have to go backward? Why or why not? Friendships can seem to go back and forth—best friends one minute, almost not talking the next. How do you deal with that? How can you tell if someone is really

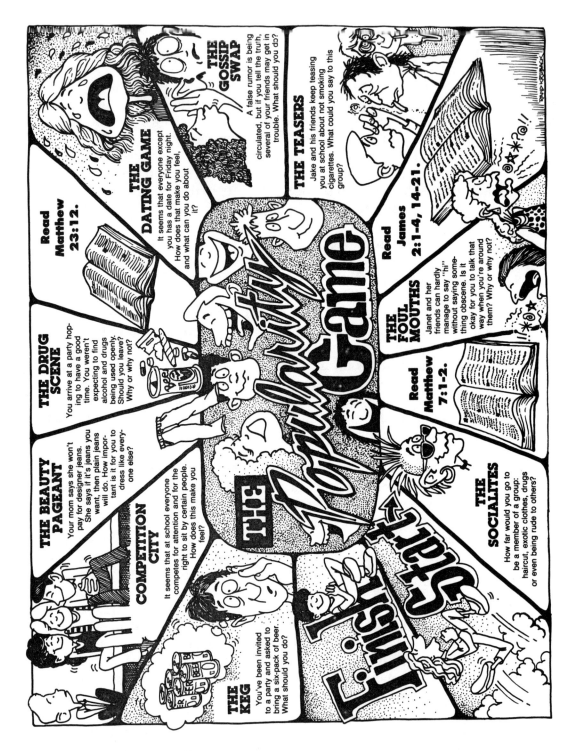

THE POPULARITY GAME

THE GOSSIP SWAP
A false rumor is being circulated, but if you tell the truth, several of your friends may get in trouble. What should you do?

THE TEASERS
Jake and his friends keep teasing you at school about not smoking cigarettes. What could you say to this group?

THE DATING GAME
It seems that everyone except you has a date for Friday night. How does that make you feel, and what can you do about it?

Read Matthew 23:12.

Read James 2:1-4, 14-21.

THE FOUL MOUTHS
Janet and her friends can hardly manage to say "hi" without saying something obscene. Is it okay for you to talk that way when you're around them? Why or why not?

THE DRUG SCENE
You arrive at a party hoping to have a good time. You weren't expecting to find alcohol and drugs being used openly. Should you leave? Why or why not?

Read Matthew 7:1-2.

THE BEAUTY PAGEANT
Your mom says she won't pay for designer jeans. She says if it's jeans you want, then plain jeans will do. How important is it for you to dress like everyone else?

COMPETITION CITY
It seems that at school everyone competes for attention and for the right to sit by certain people. How does this make you feel?

THE SOCIALITES
How far would you go to be a member of a group: haircut, exotic clothes, drugs or even being rude to others?

THE KEG
You've been invited to a party and asked to bring a six-pack of beer. What should you do?

FINISH Start

your friend?

● What's the price that must be paid for playing the popularity game at school or at youth group?

Sharing Our Love—Have craft supplies available on a table: scissors, markers and different-colored construction paper. Ask each person to make a badge that says, "I'm popular because . . ." and write on the badge one reason the person thinks he or she is popular. Challenge members to write responses such as "because I'm easy to talk with" or "because I'm a trustworthy friend," instead of "because I'm a cheerleader (or football player)."

Then have everyone find another group member whom they don't know well. Have them write on each other's badge one positive reason why the person they've selected is popular.

Have partners discuss the difference between seeming popular because you belong to many organizations at school and being popular because of the type of person you are.

Close with a Love Circle—praying, singing or reading a Bible passage.

SUNDAY

Unscramble the Words—As members gather before breakfast, divide the group into teams. Display on newsprint the words to unscramble. Give each team a Bible. Tell teams the key to unscrambling the words is Matthew 5:3-12.

Close by having someone read the Bible passage out loud as a blessing.

Morning Bible Study—Form four groups. Give each group a Bible. Assign each group one of these Bible characters and passages: Jonah (Jonah 1-2); Jesus (Mark 6:1-6); Zacchaeus (Luke 19:1-10); and Saul (Acts 9:1-31).

Display on newsprint these questions, and have the groups discuss them:

● Was the person in the passage popular? Why or why not?

● How did the person deal with popularity (or lack of it)?

Have the small groups share their answers with the entire group. Ask: "How did God's love influence each person's circumstances? How can it help you deal with unpopularity?"

Love Circle—Have everyone join hands, right over left, and form a circle. Go around the circle and invite each participant to thank God for the person on his or her right.

15

Shaping Christian Views of Sexuality

By Rickey Short

T he object of this retreat is to provide high school and junior high school young people with correct information and a biblical view of God's design for dating, courtship and sex inside marriage. This retreat does not dictate the level or the exact teachings that you should use; it gives you a model to organize your thoughts and theology into an effective presentation.

Use this retreat to:
- give kids a chance to think of their own sexuality;
- rely on God's Word as a teaching resource to help teenagers make good moral decisions; and
- help kids think of ways they can have a sensible, yet fun dating life.

Before the Retreat—Host a parents meeting one evening at least two weeks before the retreat. Their contributions and support will help you have a much more effective retreat.

Start with welcome and greetings, make any needed introductions and have prayer. Introduce the idea of a retreat with the teenagers to focus on sexual issues. Give the main reasons for the proposed retreat:
- All teenagers will have to make moral decisions in sexual areas.
- We need to provide them guidance.
- God has spoken clearly and strongly in these areas.

Continue by saying: "Teenagers will have to make a number of important life-shaping moral decisions between 11 and 19 years of age. As they mature, the decisions they make in sexual areas can defeat or enrich their spiritual life.

"Teenagers today are not satisfied with just a rule. Most moral rules which a church will emphasize are good and helpful to a young person, but at some point in time a teenager must establish a personal value system in his or her heart, without needing any outside pressure.''

Tell of contemporary sexual attitudes and behaviors among teenagers by stating local, state and national statistics. Find these results from your school district offices, library, or write to Search Institute, 122 W. Franklin Ave., Suite 525, Minneapolis, MN 55404-9990.

Discuss ways to best help teenagers in this situation. Say: "We can help and support each other as parents; we can listen to our teenagers at home, and freely answer their questions; and, as a youth group, we can provide support and information in making moral decisions.''

Briefly review the material to be covered at the retreat—pass out copies of all materials. Allow time for a discussion. Ask for parents' input to make the retreat more effective, and answer any questions they have.

Suggest the parents (as well as retreat leaders, youth sponsors and young people) read one or more of the following books: *Almost Twelve* by Kenneth Taylor (Tyndale); *Running the Red Lights* by Charles Mylander (Regal); *Talking Together About Love and Sexuality* by Mildred Tengbom (Bethany House); *Sex, Dating and Love* by Ray Short (Augsburg); *Creative Dating* by Doug Fields and Todd Temple (Thomas Nelson).

Invite a pastor or school counselor to come to the Sunday session and talk about "How to Have a Sensible, Yet Super Dating Life." Ask

---

Retreat Schedule

Friday
7:00 p.m. Arrive at retreat site and settle in
8:00 p.m. Getting Started
9:30 p.m. Roundtable Discussion Group
10:00 p.m. Games and free time
Midnight Lights out

Saturday
7:00 a.m. Breakfast
8:00 a.m. Group hike
9:00 a.m. What's the Bible Say About Sexuality?
11:00 a.m. Break
Noon Lunch
1:00 p.m. Tense Situations

3:00 p.m. Free time
5:30 p.m. Dinner
7:00 p.m. Heavy Issues
9:00 p.m. Volleycup
10:00 p.m. Campfire and snacks
11:30 p.m. Lights out

Sunday
8:00 a.m. Breakfast
8:30 a.m. Hour of meditation and silence
9:30 a.m. How to Have a Sensible, Yet Super Dating Life
10:30 a.m. Pack and clean up
11:30 a.m. Lunch, then leave for home

him or her to present guidelines for dating and how to avoid getting into tempting situations.

Gather newsprint, markers, 3×5 cards, scissors, paper cups, tape, Bibles, pencils and a soccer ball (or Nerf ball). Make a copy of the Pretest and What the Bible Says About Sexual Sin for each teenager. You also will need one towel for every two people.

Cut two circles about the size of a quarter out of a 3×5 card. Color one side of the circles green; color the other side red. Bring $10 in quarters for prizes. (Or you could award winners with other prizes such as candy or fruit.)

Retreat Ingredients

FRIDAY

Getting Started—Plan a rousing crowdbreaker like Towel Soccer from *The Return of Try This One* (Group Books). If the weather is nice and it's still light, play this game outside and use a regular soccer ball; if the weather is bad, find a large meeting room, move all chairs to the side so you have a spacious playing area, and use a Nerf ball instead of a soccer ball. Set up a soccer field with two goals. Divide the group into two even-numbered teams. Players then select someone from their team to be their partner, including goalies. Give a towel to every two people. They must hold the towel by the corners throughout the entire game. After the ball is thrown into play, partners must catch the ball in their towel and either pass it to another pair of kids on their team by flipping the ball up off the towel, or throwing it toward the goalies by flinging the ball from the towel.

Partners are allowed to take only three steps when they have the ball in their towel, then they must either pass it or try for a goal.

When the ball drops to the ground, the other team takes possession. Scoring is the same as regular soccer. The fun is partners trying to avoid getting tangled up with each other as they try to make a goal for their team.

After the game, tell the kids you are going to conduct an informal survey on opinions about sexuality. Stress that the survey results will be kept anonymous. Distribute a pencil and a Pretest to each person. Allow about 15 minutes for the kids to complete it.

Gather the Pretests and tell the kids you will tally the test and report the findings at the next session. The next part of this session deals with the subject of why God made rules for us to live by. This lesson is designed to make the teenagers discover some answers without the leader drawing a hard-and-fast conclusion.

Pretest

Age_____   Male/Female_____

Have you ever had serious conversations about sex, birth control, pregnancy, or Christian views about human sexuality with (write yes or no for each part of the question):

your parents _____   a doctor _____
a school teacher _____   a nurse _____
a school counselor _____   a male friend _____
a preacher_____   a female friend_____
                                   other _____

What is your main source of information about sex, birth control and pregnancy? Check one.

_____ friends   _____ parents
_____ books   _____ school
_____ movies   _____ other
_____ magazines

Have you ever attended a program related to human sexuality? _____
If yes, where? _____

Have you ever attended a program related to a Christian view of human sexuality?_____If yes, where? _____

What in your opinion are the three main teachings in the Bible concerning sex:
1.
2.
3.

Two ways to sin sexually are:
1.
2.

A person who sins sexually should:

Two things you can do to avoid sexual sins:
1.
2.

What is fornication and adultery? _____
What is "sexual immorality"? _____

Circle True or False for each of the following:

In the eyes of God the only purpose for sex is to have babies. True False
Sexual sins are the worst sins. True False
Sex makes a man and woman one in God's eyes and serves as the means to create one in the image of God. True False
If a couple has sex then they are married in the eyes of God. True False

Begin by taping a sheet of newsprint onto the wall where everyone can see it. Recruit one of the artistic teenagers to come forward and be your "official drawer." Tell the young people they have seven sheep in this wide open space. (Have your official drawer draw seven sheep.) Then say that there is also a terrible wolf running around loose. (Have your official drawer draw a wolf in one corner.) Say: "You have been appointed shepherd of these sheep in this wide open space. What will you do to keep them safe and help them live a wonderful life? We need to draw in everything these sheep need." (Have the official drawer draw a shepherd and whatever the kids list as things the sheep need.) The teenagers will suggest things like a fence to keep the wolf out, a barn, sun, grass, pond, animal hospital and trees.

When the picture is complete, give the official drawer a big round of applause. Then ask:

● Where is the real freedom for these sheep? Is it inside the fence or outside the fence? Why?

● How will these sheep get into trouble? (Answers could be: going outside the fence; sticking their neck out to eat grass on the other side of the fence, etc.) Why would these sheep risk getting into trouble after all we have given them?

● (This final question is to be asked without discussion or comment and before a concluding prayer.) Why do you suppose God has set some boundaries and rules in sexual areas for us to live by?

Close with a brief prayer.

Roundtable Discussion Group—Begin by going over the results of the Pretest. The results should inspire a lot of questions from the kids. Distribute a pencil and several 3 × 5 cards to each person. Have the kids each write questions they have about sexuality—one question per card. Gather the cards and ask everyone to sit in a circle for the Roundtable Discussion. One at a time, ask the questions. Encourage everyone to respond. You probably won't have enough time to discuss even half of these questions. Save the rest for the Saturday evening session on Heavy Issues.

SATURDAY

What's the Bible Say About Sexuality?—Begin this session with a game about trust. Call up a "couple"—one boy and one girl. Choose boys and girls at random. Give each person one of the colored circles you prepared earlier.

The object of this game is to make a dollar in any of the following manners. When the teenagers are asked to show their paper, they may show a green or a red side. If both teenagers show a green side, they each win 25 cents. If one shows green and one shows red, red wins 50 cents. If both show red, nobody wins anything. No talking allowed between the couple. Keep repeating the process until one teenager wins a dollar. Then let another couple try. Repeat the rules each time so that everybody is well aware of them.

Cut this game off while the teenagers are still screaming to go next and before you have run out of Coke money. This game creates a simple trust problem. "If I show green . . . can my partner be trusted to show green or will he or she take advantage of me?"

At the conclusion of the game ask the teenagers to sit down in a circle. Ask them to discuss their feelings about the game. What did they discover? Ask if being able to talk to each other would have changed the nature of the game. Continue the discussion with these questions:

● How would you describe a green/red relationship between a boy and girl? What would a red/red be like? What would a green/green be like? Which relationship is most like the relationship Jesus would want a Christian couple to have? Explain.

● What is the importance of open communication in a relationship?

● How would you feel if you were trying to be open in a relationship and the other person was lying to you or just using you?

● What is the importance of trust in dating, courtship and marriage? Why is it so important to be careful in whom you put your trust? How well and how long do you have to know a person before you really trust him or her?

● How can we all be "winners" in our dating relationships?

Say: "In all areas of life God has demonstrated his love for us. He desires the best for us. Sometimes God has to say no to things that appear to us to be good or desirable. When God says to avoid something it is because he has something better for us in mind. This is also true in the area of our expression of love to each other in a sexual manner.

"Here is a simple definition of sin: when we choose to do what God has said not to do. We can also sin against each other or even ourselves by what we do and think in the area of sexuality.

"The term 'sexual immorality,' is found in many newer translations of the Bible. It includes as part of its meaning the terms adultery, fornication, rape, incest, prostitution, homosexuality, lust, bestiality, pornography and group sex. Quite a list. You're going to get a chance to see what the Bible says about sexuality by completing a handout. Take about 30 minutes to answer the questions."

Distribute pencils, Bibles and handouts. After the kids have completed the handout, review their answers in a large group.

What the Bible Says About Sexual Sin

1. What does Romans 12:1-2 tell us to do with our bodies?

2. Read Acts 15:20-29. This letter was written by the early church to new Christians. What did it urge?

3. Read 1 Corinthians 6:9-10. Who will not inherit the kingdom of God?

4. Read Galatians 5:19-21. These verses tell us:

5. Read 1 Corinthians 6:13. The body:

6. Read 1 Corinthians 6:18-20. What do these verses tell us?

7. Read Colossians 3:5. It urges us to:

8. Copy 1 Thessalonians 4:3:

   Continue by reading 1 Thessalonians 4:4-8.
9. Read Matthew 5:27-29. In your own words, define lust.

10. Read Exodus 20:14. It says:

    What does this mean?

11. Read 1 Corinthians 10:13. What is the central promise in this verse?

12. Read 1 John 1:9. When we sin we should:

    God will:

Tense Situations—Divide your kids into small groups. Have them each choose a tension-packed situation when dealing with sexuality. For example, a girl finds out she is pregnant and doesn't know what to do. She goes in to see her school counselor for advice.

Have the small groups each present their tense situation in a skit format. Ask them each to prepare several discussion questions for the large group after they present their skit.

Heavy Issues—Form a panel of some of your mature teenagers as well as a few adults. Ask them to field questions from the floor or to respond to written questions. You can use the rest of the questions from the Roundtable Discussion time. Begin the session with a few questions you have prepared in advance:

What are the reasons for dating?

How old should a person be before he or she begins dating?

How do you say no when you don't want to go out with a person?

How do you pick a date? What do you look for?

What about going steady? What does it mean at this age?

What do you think of teenage marriage?

What would you say to a person who is slipping out to meet someone his parents do not want him to see?

Is sex before marriage ever right? I mean, what if you are really in love and planning on being married?

I know this girl who is afraid she will lose this guy if she doesn't have sex with him. What would you say to her and to him if you had the chance?

Is "going too far" an individual thing? Would it be different for different people? How would you know if you were going too far and you were going to end up doing something you would regret later? How would you stop? How could you avoid the situation in the future?

Volleycup—Loosen up after the intense discussion by playing Volleycup from *Try This One . . . Too* (Group Books). All you need are a few paper cups, a table and two teams. Divide into two teams of equal size. Have them sit at opposite sides of the table. One side starts out as the serving side (Side A). Side B is the receiving side. Side A serves one cup to the other side by simply hitting it with their hands. Side B attempts to hit it back in the same manner. The game continues until the cup is either hit off the table, missed or destroyed. Then Side B serves a new cup to Side A. Play as long as you like.

SUNDAY

How to Have a Sensible, Yet Super Dating Life—Gather and have the kids get comfortable. Introduce the topic and the guest speaker. Afterward, divide kids into small groups. Give each group a sheet of newsprint and a marker. Have them think of the Ten Commandments of Dating Life, then write them on their sheet of newsprint. Commandments could be: Thou shalt always be honest with your parents. Never lie about who you are dating. Or, thou shalt honor your partner and remember that he (or she) is a child of God. Or, thou shalt remember that no matter how badly you mess up, God forgives you if you ask him to.

After everyone is done, have the small groups present their lists. After each commandment is read, have everybody shout "Amen!"

16

Tough Times

By Ben Sharpton

Although life is difficult, we, as Christians, have access to a power that will give us strength and peace to withstand problems and face challenges. This retreat is designed to lead young people and adults into a deeper understanding of how God helps us through rough situations.

Use this retreat to help your young people deal with:
- times when they are lonely;
- feelings of guilt; and
- strong emotions of grief.

Before the Retreat—Publicize this event through church newsletters and special fliers. Be sure to personally invite those young people whom you feel are ready for deeper growth. Be selective in recruiting leadership; look for those who display maturity and sensitivity.

As you choose retreat sites, consider one close enough to a city that would allow you to drive in for the optional tour of a nursing home or hospital on the second day. If you plan to show a film, order that well in advance. Choose a film like *Ordinary People* or *Breakfast Club* (or a more current one) which shows people going through tough times. Also, make arrangements for popcorn and pop as snacks during the movie.

Pray for this retreat and ask your young people to pray about it as well.

Gather newsprint, markers, 3 × 5 cards, paper, pencils, masking tape, Bibles (the same version), an apple, flashlight, boiled egg, toothbrush, knife, any cassette tape, all handouts, and Guilt Game cards (read the retreat for directions). You'll need supplies for the Chain Relay such as paper, newspaper, scissors, marshmallows and balloons.

Read the retreat and write the discussion questions for the sessions on newsprint. Write on newsprint the Scripture Chart found in the session on loneliness.

Retreat Schedule

Friday
7:00 p.m. Chain Relay
7:30 p.m. From Loneliness to
Love
9:00 p.m. Show a movie, eat
popcorn
11:30 p.m. Lights out

Saturday
7:00 a.m. Wake up
8:00 a.m. Breakfast

9:00 a.m. The Verdict: Guilty
10:30 a.m. Free time
Noon Lunch
2:00 p.m. Planned recreation (softball, volleyball, etc.) or
tour an inner-city nurs-
ing home or hospital
5:30 p.m. Supper
7:30 p.m. Good Grief
9:30 p.m. Pack and leave

Retreat Ingredients

FRIDAY

Chain Relay—Open the session with any special announcements or schedule changes. Then play Chain Relay from *More . . . Try This One* (Group Books). There are two main differences between this and an ordinary relay. First, instead of team members performing individually, they are all joined at the hands (and secured with masking tape), and must do everything together. Second, instead of performing tasks in a given order, the different tasks are at stations around the room, and teams may try them in any order they wish (except for the final task).

Teams of three or more people join hands to form a line. Join hands by wrapping them with masking tape. This is to ensure that the group stays together.

There must be at least two more tasks than teams. Use tasks that require two hands. Some suggested tasks are: fold a paper airplane, cut out a shape from a piece of paper, roll up a newspaper and put a rubber band around it, untie and tie the shoe of the middle person, feed each member of the group a marshmallow, blow up and tie a balloon. The final task: The whole team must do a somersault together without breaking its grip.

There are only two rules to this game:

1. The final task must be done last.

2. If a grip is broken, the whole team must return to the leader to have the grip retaped before continuing.

From Loneliness to Love—Gather the kids in a circle and introduce the session by saying: "We all face tough times throughout our lives. During this retreat we'll focus on tough times caused by loneliness, guilt and grief. This session deals with causes, feelings and solutions to loneliness."

Give each person a pencil and a Who Are You? handout. Tell the participants to complete the handout and await further instructions.

Who Are You?

DIRECTIONS: Fill in the blanks with the appropriate number.

How many different houses have you lived in? _____

How many brothers/sisters do you have? _____

How many pets do you have? _____

How many times have you gone to the dentist these past 12 months? _____

Have you ever worn glasses/contacts? (no = 1; yes = 2) _____

Have you ever worn braces? (no = 1; yes = 2) _____

After everyone has added their total score, have them find one other person who has a score similar to theirs. This person will be their partner for the remainder of the retreat. Encourage them to make time to become better acquainted with this person by discussing the information from the handout, and by discussing the following information. Write these items on newsprint: Share your earliest recollection of church; share what your family is like; share a time when you were lonely.

Read the following information (Time, September 5, 1977, p. 45).

● The coronary rate among widows (age 25-34) is five times that of married women in the same age group.

● Divorced people are twice as likely as married people to develop lung cancer or suffer a stroke.

● Cirrhosis of the liver is seven times as likely in divorced, white males.

● Tuberculosis is 10 times more common in divorced, white males.

● Petting and stroking a dog profoundly affects the cardiovascular system of that animal.

Ask how the kids felt when these statistics were read. How many were surprised by the statistics?

Combine pairs in such a way as to form three small groups. Give each group a sheet of newsprint, a Bible and a marker, and assign one of the following tasks. Ask for their report after everyone has completed their job.

Group 1—Create your best definitions for "lonely" and "alone."

Group 2—List as many causes of loneliness as you can. Mark the five greatest causes.

Group 3—List as many methods of avoiding loneliness as you can. Be specific.

Post the following Scripture Chart on newsprint where all can see. Assign each pair one or two of the scripture passages on the chart. If you have more than seven pairs of people, combine them into small groups. Tell them to read their passage, decide who was lonely, what caused the loneliness, and how that person dealt with lonely feelings. Tell them to list their findings in the appropriate places on the newsprint chart. After everyone has finished this task, have them share their information with the group.

Scripture Chart			
Scripture	**Who feels lonely?**	**What is the cause?**	**What does he/she do?**
1 Kings 19:1-13			
Job 19:13-27			
Psalm 41:7-13			
Matthew 27:32-50			
Luke 15:11-24			
John 5:1-9			

After the chart has been completed, ask everyone to look over the findings and identify those situations in which people were lonely for the companionship of other people, and those situations in which they were lonely for a relationship with God. Does this difference help in understanding causes of loneliness? Explain. (For other passages when Jesus probably faced loneliness, see Mark 1:12-13; 6:1-3; Luke 22:39-46.)

Discuss some solutions to loneliness. Explain that you will read some different solutions. If the kids think the solution is unrealistic, have them cross their arms in front of them; if they think it makes sense, have them give a thumbs-up sign; if they don't know, have them shrug their shoulders. After you read each solution and the kids make their motions, discuss the various responses. Here are the solutions:

● Increase your self-esteem, or the value you place on your life. Perform a task that will help you experience success. Make friends with those who make you feel worthwhile. Be proud of your actions.

● Commitment is the key. It is not enough to have friends. One needs to have friends who are committed to him or her; who will be there when needed; who will accept him or her unconditionally; and who can be trusted. To know such trust, one must entrust himself or herself to others. Reach out to trustworthy friends and they will reach out to you.

● The problem of loneliness is basically a problem of spiritual emptiness. To overcome loneliness one should pray and ask God to fill the void in his or her life with a purpose and with the Spirit of God.

● If you want a friend, be friendly. Reach out to others and they'll reach out to you. Throw a party. Invite people to go out to dinner with you. Share yourself.

On one sheet of newsprint, ask the group members to help you list several capabilities that people possess that could help *them* deal with their own lonely feelings. Then on another sheet of newsprint, list capabilities that people possess that could help *others* through lonely times.

Ask everyone to examine the two lists. What are the similarities? differences? Gather in a circle. Ask the group members to affirm one another by mentioning one at a time a person's name and one capability he or she has exhibited that would be helpful in lonely times. Make sure that everyone is affirmed in this way.

Close in an open-eye prayer; ask each person to look around the room as he or she prays. Thank God for those present, and ask him to teach your group to support one another through lonely times, to be sensitive to each other and to help carry each other's burdens.

SATURDAY

The Verdict: Guilty—This session will help your young people better understand another toughie: guilty feelings. During this time together you will discover constructive ways to respond to guilt.

Have the participants stand in a circle facing toward the middle. Ask them to imagine that there are spokes or lines running from the center of the circle outward. Each person is to imagine he or she is standing on one of these lines. The center of the circle represents "guilt free." "Guilty feelings" increase as one moves away from the center.

Read the following statements, then ask members in your group to indicate how much guilt that activity would bring to them by moving in or out of the circle. Thus, if little guilt would be produced by "yelling at my parents," the kids would stand as close to the center as they can. If a lot of guilt would be produced, they would back away from the center of the circle.

After naming each activity, discuss their responses: yelling at my parents; making fun of a teacher; telling a lie to my best friend; telling a white lie to my best friend; telling a lie to an acquaintance; leaving chewing gum on my lunch tray; winning a state championship; shoplifting some gum; getting drunk; tearing off the "do not remove" label from a pillow; forgetting to carry out a promise; hurting someone in an automobile accident; cheating on an exam; getting caught cheating on an exam.

Ask for volunteers to share any insights into causes of guilty feelings. Jot down their suggestions on newsprint. Then play the Guilt Game. If your group is small, have partners compete against other partners. If your group is large, divide into small groups of eight or more. (Ask the kids to stay with their partners and be on a team together.) Prior to the game write each of the following items on separate 3×5 cards. Duplicate each item until you have three cards for each person.

Items for 3×5 Cards

Read 1 John 1:9 to your group. (5 points)

Read Matthew 5:23-24 to your group and explain what it says to you about guilt. (5 points)

Read Matthew 9:2-8 to your group and explain what it says to you about guilt. (5 points)

When you feel guilty, how do you relieve guilt? Tell your group. (5 points)

Read Ephesians 2:8-10 to your group and explain what it says to you about guilt. (5 points)

Tell a situation in which you were guilty over the last week or two. (5 points)

Tell the group what one thing would make you feel the most guilty. (10 points)

"Unrealistic guilt," feeling more guilty than is normal, is not only useless, but is destructive. Do you agree or disagree? Explain your answer. (10 points)

"Guilt is good." Do you agree or disagree? Explain your answer. (5 points)

Stand up and say, "Guilt can be helpful" five times as loudly as you can. (5 points)

Tell of a situation in your past that made you feel guilty. (5 points)

Tell of a situation in your past that may have made someone else feel guilty, but in which you didn't feel any guilt. (10 points)

If God offers forgiveness so readily, tell your group why it often seems so hard to grasp the joy of forgiveness and acceptance. (10 points)

Tell of a time in which you apologized to someone after feeling guilty, and explain how that made you feel. (10 points)

Tell the group your earliest (recalled) experience with guilt. (5 points)

Tell of something that is bothering you right now about which you feel guilty. (25 points)

Tell the group of a time that you were blamed for doing something you didn't do. (5 points)

Pass out three cards to each person; and, to each group, a Bible, piece of paper and pencil. Sitting in a circle, the kids each take a turn choosing a card from their "hand" and giving that card to their partner. The partner will either follow the instructions on the card or pass. (He or she doesn't have to read the instructions out loud.) If the partner follows the instructions, he or she gains that many points for the team. If he or she passes, the team neither gains nor loses points. Ask one person per group to keep track of the points the team is accumulating.

After all the cards have been used once, collect, shuffle and pass them out again. Play another round. After two or three rounds, ask for individuals to comment on what took place during this activity. Which team won the most points? Was it difficult to be open and honest about feelings of guilt? Go around the room and share "I Learned . . ." statements, giving each person a chance to share one thing he or she learned during this activity.

Tell everyone to read John 8:3-11. Ask those who were born in January through April to concern themselves with the woman in the story; those born in May through August should concentrate on Jesus; and those born in September through December should look at the Pharisees' perspective. Divide into three small groups and have them relate to their characters by answering these questions which you have posted on newsprint:

1. Create five sentences that your character(s) might say to themselves in verses 3-6. What words would you use to describe your character(s) feelings?

2. Create five sentences that your character(s) might say to themselves in verses 7-9. What words would you use to describe your character(s) feelings?

3. Create five sentences that your character(s) might say to themselves in verses 10-11. What words would you use to describe your character(s) feelings?

Share the sentences the various groups came up with. Then use the following questions to help your group learn more about guilt.

● What is good about being capable of feeling guilt?

● What is negative about being capable of feeling guilt?

● How can one tell if the guilt he or she is experiencing is positive or negative?

● What steps must one take to remove guilt? (Realize that a problem exists; confess sin to God or others; and accept the forgiveness offered from God.)

Make sure that everyone has the same version of the Bible and read together responsively Psalm 51:1-17. This passage is from David, after having committed adultery with Bathsheba. Look over the passage again and ask members to identify those verses in which David realizes his sin, those in which he confesses his sin and those in which he obviously accepts the forgiveness offered from God.

Ask your group members to hold hands together in a circle. Request that they stand next to their retreat partner. Ask each person to pray silently about his or her need for forgiveness, or about another member of the group's need for forgiveness. After a few moments of silent prayer, read aloud 1 John 1:9. Then, instruct each person to turn to and look at his or her partner, and say, "God forgives you.

We all forgive you. I forgive you." Encourage everyone to "go in peace" and dismiss the group.

Optional Session—Take your group to a nursing home, to an inner-city community or to a hospital. Let them explore the area with their partners, and ask them to find instances of loneliness, guilt and grief. Tell them their one goal for the time is to find a hurting person and comfort him or her. For example, if you go to a nursing home, partners could talk to lonely residents and cheer up their day. Gather back at the retreat site and discuss the experiences.

Good Grief—This session deals with one of the toughest theological issues that has ever been faced. Allow your group members to share openly their feelings about grief. Help them identify with others who suffer. Encourage them to contract together to support their partner when he or she experiences painful situations.

Ask your kids to find their partners and to combine with two other pairs to form small groups of six. Try to arrange to have at least one adult in each small group. Give one of the following items to each group: apple, flashlight, boiled egg, toothbrush, knife, cassette tape. Have them pass it among themselves, commenting upon how it is similar to pain or suffering. For example, someone could say, "When a flashlight has a new battery, it shines brightly. When the battery has been around a while, the light dims. So it is with pain. When a horrible situation first occurs, it's intensely painful. But time dims the sharpness of the pain."

After groups have shared these similarities, exchange items and let them compare the new item with suffering and pain. Exchange items a third time, following the same procedure.

Hand out pencils and copies of the worksheet What Do You Do When . . . Give the kids a chance to work through the questions on their own, and then have them share their answers with their small group.

Ask the group members to give you reasons why they think God allows us to suffer. Write these on newsprint. Some reasons might be:

> We suffer because we make a mistake
> We suffer because someone hurts us
> Suffering and pain just happen with no apparent reason
> God causes the pain to punish us
> God causes the pain to teach (or test) us
> We suffer so we can identify with others who suffer
> We suffer because there is evil in this world
> Satan makes us suffer
> Other _____

What Do You Do When . . .

Directions: Place a check mark (✓) in the boxes that indicate how you respond when you are hurt physically. Place an "X" in the boxes that indicate how you should respond when hurt physically. Circle those boxes that indicate how you respond when you are hurt emotionally. Underline those items that indicate how you should respond when hurt emotionally.

☐ I act myself into believing that it no longer hurts
☐ I pray about the pain
☐ I wait; time heals all pain
☐ I talk about it to other people
☐ I get angry
☐ I cry
☐ I throw a temper tantrum
☐ I ignore the pain
☐ other _____

Go down the list and have the kids vote for the reasons they think suffering exists. Allow time to discuss each possibility.
Then ask the kids these questions to try and further clarify reasons for suffering:

● Which reason do you not understand clearly?
● Which reasons are new to you?
● Which reasons seem empty? false?
● Which reasons do not seem consistent with your image of God?
● Which reasons are you most comfortable with?

Pass out copies of the Covenant to each person. Ask each person to sign his or her copy, and write his or her partner's name in the blank provided.

Read 2 Corinthians 1:3-5 and explain that you are asking each person to help support his or her partner long after this retreat is over. Ask each person to silently go to his or her partner, pray together concerning upcoming tough events in each other's lives and exchange covenants.

Bring the group back together in one circle. Ask everyone to place their arms on the shoulders of their neighbors. Sing a song like "Love Lifted Me" and close in another open-eye prayer, asking everyone to look around the circle as you thank God for each person present, as well as everyone's willingness to share grief, feel guilt and love others.

Covenant

"Remember those in prison as if you were their fellow prisoners, and those who are mistreated as if you yourselves were suffering" (Hebrews 13:3).

_____, I agree to be there when you need a friend; to support you through tough times; to listen to you when you want to talk; to pray for you when you need God's help. I love you, and want the best God has to offer.

_____   _____
(Date)   (Signed)

Section Four

Bible Study

17

Baptism

By Bruce Nichols

Baptism methods vary from church to church. Some believe in infant baptism; some believe in adult baptism; some believe in other forms of baptism. But we all believe that baptism is a gift from God; that God loves us and calls us his children.

During this retreat, the participants will:

● learn about Jesus' baptism;
● read about Bible references to baptism;
● talk about their own baptisms; and
● hear about different types of baptisms.

Before the Retreat—Advertise the retreat with posters and fliers that include pictures or drawings of water. Use blue posterboard and construction paper, aluminum foil and pictures from magazines.

Baptism Retreat

Time: March 14-15
Cost: Free!
Who: All youth group members and their friends
Where: Sky Ranch Camp

Let the church office know by March 1 if you plan to attend.

Ask the pastor from your church to talk about your service of baptism and invite a pastor from another church to talk about their service of baptism. (Be sure the types of baptisms are different.) Tell both pastors to anticipate questions from the kids. If the pastors are unable to attend, ask two adult sponsors to team up with two young people to research your church's service of baptism and another church's in town. Have them make the presentations. The purpose of this activity is not to argue which method is best, but to give kids an idea of the different ways of baptism.

Gather a cassette recorder; microphone; cassette tape; newsprint; markers; watermelon; several pitchers; food for all meals; refreshments; props such as hats, scarves, balls, bats and books; and, for each person, several 3×5 cards, a pencil, a paper cup and a handful of modeling clay. Ask kids to bring jackets for one of the games.

On separate sheets of newsprint, write the discussion questions for each session.

Retreat Schedule

Friday
    7:00 p.m. Arrive and unpack
    7:30 p.m. Shoes and Jackets
    8:30 p.m. What Is Baptism?
    9:00 p.m. Bible Baptisms
    10:30 p.m. Free time and
                   refreshments
    11:30 p.m. Lights out

Saturday
    8:00 a.m. Breakfast
    9:00 a.m. Water Relays
    10:00 a.m. Guest Speakers
    11:30 a.m. Servant's Lunch
    1:00 p.m. Free time
    2:00 p.m. Station Studies
    4:00 p.m. Closing Worship
    5:00 p.m. Head for home

Retreat Ingredients

FRIDAY

Shoes and Jackets—Welcome the participants and say that you'll begin the retreat with a fun, wild game called Shoes and Jackets. Divide into two equal teams. Ask each team to mix their shoes and jackets in one big pile (one pile for each team). Then have each team line up 20 feet away from its pile. At the word "Go" the first person in each line runs up to his or her team's pile, chooses two shoes and one coat (other than his or her own), puts them on, runs back to the line and tags the next person, who repeats the process. First team done (with members wearing different coats and shoes) is the winner.

Afterward, while everyone is still wearing their different outfits, talk about differences, and how it's okay to be different from others. Introduce the theme of the retreat by saying: "Just as people are different, so are our beliefs in baptism. At this retreat, we're going to talk about our baptisms, learn about different kinds of baptisms and see what the Bible has to say about baptism.''

What Is Baptism?—Post the discussion questions onto the wall. Gather the participants in small groups and have them discuss these questions:

● Have you been baptized? If so, describe it.

● How old were you when you were baptized? If you were baptized as an infant, what have your parents told you about that day?

● What does baptism mean to you?

● What does it mean to be a child of God?

● As a small group, come up with a definition of baptism.

After 15 minutes, discuss the answers as a large group. What are some of the definitions of baptism? Are any definitions the same? What are the differences?

Bible Baptisms—Gather the kids and tell them they're going to search the scripture for various references about baptism. Give the kids each a Bible Baptisms handout, a Bible and a pencil. Allow 30 minutes for them to answer the questions. Afterward, discuss the handout in the large group.

Enjoy free time and refreshments. Have the refreshments go along with the theme of baptism. How about serving watermelon and water? Or if it's cold outside, serve hot water with lemon slices.

SATURDAY

Water Relays—Divide into teams. Give each team a pitcher of water and one paper cup for each team member. Place the pitchers and cups on one side of the room; ask the teams to line up on the opposite side of the room. On the word "Go" the first person in each line runs up to his or her team's pitcher, fills a cup with water, drinks the water, then runs back and tags the next person. First team finished with their water wins.

Or you could play another water relay. Place a paper cup filled with water on the head of the first person in each team. These first-in-liners must walk forward 20 feet, then walk back to their line without spilling the water (no hands allowed). Then the next people in line try it, and so on. If anyone spills, he or she must start over.

Guest Speakers—Invite the pastor of your church to tell about your beliefs in baptism. Ask him or her to describe the service for baptism. Allow 15 minutes for this presentation. Then, ask the other pastor to tell how his or her church baptizes people, and their beliefs. Allow 15 minutes for this presentation.

After the presentations, distribute several 3 x 5 cards and a pencil to each of the kids. Give them 10 minutes to write down any questions they have about baptism. Collect the cards, then ask the guest

Bible Baptisms

Read Matthew 3:1-6. Describe what was happening here. How did John the Baptist baptize? Why do you think confession of sins goes along with baptism?

Read Matthew 3:13-17 and Mark 1:9-11. What do these verses tell us about Jesus' baptism? How are the verses similar? different?

Read these other references to baptism. Summarize each passage by writing a brief note to the side of it.

● Mark 16:16—
● Acts 8:12-13—
● Acts 16:14-15—
● Matthew 28:19-20—
● Acts 16:25-34—

How are these baptisms alike? different?

Were there any requirements to be baptized (such as age, belief, etc.)? Explain.

What is important for us to remember about baptism?

speakers the questions. Allow plenty of time for group discussion.

Close the session by having everyone gather in a circle. Ask the two guests to stand in the center. On the count of three, everybody moves in and gives them a massive squeeze. Re-form the circle, and make sure everyone is holding hands. Go around the circle and invite each person to say a one-sentence prayer thanking God for something he or she learned from the session.

Servant's Lunch—This activity is from *Building Community in Youth Groups* (Group Books). Set out the food and other supplies, then introduce this unique lunch time by saying: "Jesus lived the lives we live. He came to show us how we're to act as God's children. He was baptized, just as we are to be; and he helped and served others, just as we are to do. During lunch, we're going to play the role of servant. The rules are as follows: No person can prepare or ask for food for himself or herself. You *can* feed yourself if someone else prepares it for you."

After everyone has eaten, ask:

● Do you feel more comfortable in everyday life serving or being served? Why?

● Why does God want us to be servants?

● Why is it important for us to accept help from others?

● How does being a servant relate to baptism?

● What did you learn from this activity?

Station Studies—Set up three stations. Station 1 should include modeling clay; Station 2 should include a cassette tape recorder, cassette tape and microphone; Station 3 should include all kinds of props such as hats, scarves, balls, bats and books.

Divide the kids into three groups and assign them to each of the three stations. Give them these instructions: "Those of you at Station 1 are to each take a handful of clay and form a symbol of baptism. For example, you could shape the clay like a drop of water or a cross. Leave your symbols at the station when you're through.

"Those of you at Station 2 are to create a song about baptism and sing it to the tune of 'Row, Row, Row Your Boat.' Record the song in the tape recorder. For example, you could sing, 'We have been baptized in the church of God. He loves us very much and calls us all his own.'

"Those of you at Station 3 are to prepare a baptism skit using any of the props. For example, you could dress up like a mom, dad and child going to the church for a baptism service.

"You'll each get 30 minutes at these stations. Then we'll rotate three times so you all can experience each one."

Go ahead as planned and see all of the creative ideas the kids come up with.

Closing Worship—For the first part of the worship, let each person explain his or her clay symbol of baptism. Notice the similarities and differences of people's interpretations. Next, play the cassette recordings of baptism songs. Finally, let each small group present its baptism skit. Say: "Although there are many forms and beliefs about baptism, we know one thing for sure: God loves us and we are his children. We are the family of God."

Sing "We Are the Family of God," *Songs* (Songs and Creations, Inc.) Pass around a cup of water. Ask all participants to say, "You are a child of God," as each person dips in a finger and forms a cross on his or her forehead. Close with the Lord's Prayer.

Display the clay creations at church under a sign that says "Symbols of Our Baptism." Play the recorded songs and perform the baptism skits for younger Sunday school children.

18

Basic Training

By Ben Sharpton

People, like snowflakes, are all different. Because we are different and because we have diverse backgrounds, the way we each put our Christian faith into action is unique.

Use this retreat to help your young people:

- choose areas they want to study as they seek spiritual growth; and
- enjoy an intensive study of the basics of Christian faith.

Before the Retreat—Gather newsprint; markers; seminar sign-up sheets (you'll need one sign-up sheet for each session in each time slot); 3×5 cards; a ball of string; flashlight; candle; matches; communion elements (grape juice, bread, cup); scissors; and, for each member, Bibles, pencils, paper and all handouts.

Cut two three-foot lengths of string for each participant.

On newsprint, make a copy of the charts found in Sessions III and IV.

Retreat Schedule

Friday
4:00 p.m. Arrive at camp
5:00 p.m. Orientation
5:30 p.m. Supper
7:00 p.m. General Session I
7:45 p.m. Seminar Sessions (first time offered)
9:00 p.m. Snacks and recreation
11:00 p.m. In cabins, lights out

Saturday
7:00 a.m. Reveille

8:00 a.m. Breakfast
9:00 a.m. General Session II
9:30 a.m. Seminar Sessions (second time offered)
10:30 a.m. Free time
Noon Lunch
1:30 p.m. Seminar Sessions (third time offered)
2:30 p.m. Free time
5:30 p.m. Supper
7:00 p.m. Worship Session
8:30 p.m. Leave for home

Prepare 3×5 cards as described in Session IV.

The retreat site you choose should allow for small-group sessions. A separate room for each group is ideal for the seminar format.

Recruit at least one adult to lead each of the seminar sessions. Explain that the adults may lead a seminar as many as three times for three different groups depending on the interest among the young people.

Retreat Ingredients

FRIDAY

Orientation—After everyone has settled in their cabins, set the tone for a fun weekend with group singing. Briefly describe the seminar format and session topics. Introduce the leaders and give group members time to sign up for three sessions. Finally, explain camp rules and answer any questions about the retreat.

General Session I—Conduct games and activities that will help your members meet new friends. Play a get-to-know-you game such as Memory Lane from *Building Community in Youth Groups* by Denny Rydberg (Group Books). Gather the kids in a circle. Go around the circle and ask the group members to answer the following questions. Allow the participants to ask questions to clarify each individual's response.

● What is one of your first memories?

● What do you remember about the first house in which you lived?

● What is an incident you remember from the fourth grade?

● Whom did you have a crush on, or who was your hero in grade school?

● What is an incident you remember from seventh grade?

Review the seminar topics and remind everyone where each seminar will take place. Dismiss the group members and tell them to go to their respective classrooms.

Seminar Session I: Concepts of God—The goal is to help these young people formulate and clarify their own view of what God is like.

Pass out pencils and copies of the Getting a Handle on God handout. After everyone has worked through the sheet, discuss the responses. Be sure to note which items raise the most questions.

Give a Bible and at least one of the following scripture passages to each person. Tell the kids to read their passage and find a characteristic of God portrayed in that passage.

Getting a Handle on God

DIRECTIONS: In the box preceding each statement:
Place a plus (+) sign if that statement is very important to your beliefs.
Place an "X" if you have difficulty with the statement.
Place a question mark (?) if the thought is new and you want to discuss it further.
Place an exclamation point (!) if that statement is exciting.

☐ God is love
☐ God is our Father
☐ God is the Lord of all
☐ God is jealous
☐ God is the creator and he creates today
☐ God is the supreme Judge
☐ God hates sin
☐ God is invisible
☐ God is faithful

☐ God is changeless
☐ God is here
☐ God is all-powerful
☐ God knows everything
☐ God is holy
☐ God is just
☐ God is unsearchable
☐ God is eternal
☐ God is merciful

Omniscient—Psalm 33:13-15; Proverbs 15:3, 11
Omnipresent—Psalm 139:7-10
Omnipotent—Matthew 19:26
Invisible—John 1:18
Just—Deuteronomy 4:11-12
Jealous—Psalm 78:56-59

Now, share the following stories with your group. Ask each person to describe God's role in each case according to his or her passage. Use the questions following each situation to help your group members clarify their view of God.

Tanya had fallen asleep while studying for her final exam. She felt a great deal of pressure to make a good grade in this course in order to gain a college scholarship. During the exam, Tanya resorted to a "cheat sheet" that she had created at the last minute. Being a bit too careless, Tanya was caught and given an "F" on the exam for cheating.

● Did God tempt Tanya? Explain.
● Before Tanya fell asleep, did God know she would cheat? Explain.
● Did God cause Tanya to be reckless in her cheating? Explain.

● Did God cause the teacher to avoid being lenient in the grade he gave Tanya? Explain.

Bill, a prominent and respected businessman, was running for the school board. No one except his accountant knew he cheated on his income tax. The fact Bill cheated on his wife was also unknown. Bill assumed he would never get caught.

On election day the community was hit by the worst thunderstorm in its history. Tornadoes were sighted and one elderly man lost his life when a tornado hit his trailer. Only a few people made it to the polls and Bill lost his bid for election by a small majority.

● Did God tempt Bill? Explain.

● Was God concerned about Bill's unethical behavior? Explain.

● Did God cause the storm that kept the community's residents inside? Explain.

● If so, what about the elderly man who died in the storm? Did God know the man would be killed? Explain.

Brainstorm together and list on newsprint the possible ways to help a person grow in his or her understanding of God. Aim for quantity. Some examples are:

Worship	Bible study
Sharing	Singing
Witnessing	Prayer
Fasting	A retreat

Close by asking each person to praise God, in a sentence prayer, for one or more of God's attributes.

Seminar Session II: The Church—The purpose is to help young people to understand the concept of the church as the "body" of Christian believers, and to seek ways they can help build up the church.

Give each group member two pieces of three-foot lengths of string. Have each person tie one piece to his or her right hand and the other piece to his or her right foot. Then, with everyone sitting in a circle, ask the kids each to tie the other end of the string on their right hand to the left hand of their neighbor. Next, have them tie the string on their right foot to the left foot of the same neighbor. In this way, the entire group should be literally connected together, hand-to-hand and foot-to-foot.

Say, "If you could win $100 for the best definition of 'church,' what would you say?" Accept several definitions and discuss each one.

Ask a volunteer to read Ephesians 4:14-16. Discuss the passage to clarify its meaning. Brainstorm a list of attributes that are symbolized by the following parts of the body:

Hand	Eye
Foot	Heart
Ear	Legs
Mouth	Shoulders/arms

(Examples of attributes that may be symbolized by a hand are helping others, working hard, offering a handshake and giving support.)

Next, go around the circle and affirm each person in your group by asking members what part of the Christian body they feel that person exemplifies. For instance, one person may be said to be like the heart of the body because he cares for so many others. Another may be like an eye because she sees trouble ahead and warns others about it. Continue until each person has been affirmed in this way.

Pass a pair of scissors around the circle and ask each person to clip the string from his or her hands and feet. Have one person collect all the pieces and tie them together to form one long length of string. He or she should add this length on to the end of a ball of string, forming a much larger ball of string. As the string is being collected, ask for individuals to share how this session could be applied to their lives.

Take the ball of string and explain that you are going to state one thing that God has done for you (or that you are thankful for) and then toss the ball to someone in the circle. Each person should have a chance to receive the ball of string at least once and to toss it to another. Be sure to remind them to keep hold of their end of the string. Eventually your group will have formed a large web of string. Ask for volunteers to share how that web is similar to the church. Tell two or three people to drop their end of the string and notice how the web becomes distorted. Point out the symbolism demonstrated here that requires all of us to carry our load in being the church.

With everyone in the group holding the string web, close in prayer, thanking God for the church and for the love and support we can find there.

Seminar Session III: Prayer—Young people are taught how to deepen their commitment to God through prayer by clarifying its meaning, by sharing meaningful experiences of prayer and by praying together.

Quiz the kids on prayer by reading each of the following statements and asking for a show of hands for the answers.

● How many of you pray every day?

● How many of you find it easy to keep from daydreaming as you pray?

● How many of you pray for your church?

● How many of you really believe God answers your prayers?
● How many of you pray before every meal, even in public?

Hand out pencils and copies of the Prayer Squares worksheet. After the kids have completed the survey, have each person share his or her responses with a partner.

Prayer Squares

Shade in the square that best reveals your relative position on each issue.

Positive		**Not So Positive**
I know that God answers prayers	☐☐☐☐☐☐☐	I have serious doubts about how involved God may be in people's lives
When I pray, I often praise and thank God	☐☐☐☐☐☐☐	I always pray to receive something
An answered prayer strengthens my faith	☐☐☐☐☐☐☐	Answers to prayers are coincidental
God sometimes answers by telling me to wait	☐☐☐☐☐☐☐	God seems inconsistent in answering prayer
I pray often	☐☐☐☐☐☐☐	I don't pray very often
I feel comfortable praying at any time	☐☐☐☐☐☐☐	I won't pray in public
My prayer life is growing	☐☐☐☐☐☐☐	My prayer life needs serious help

---

Divide your group into several small groups. Show them the Jesus Prayed chart, then assign each group one of the passages of scripture. Explain that each passage mentions a time when Jesus prayed. Each group is to read the passages around its verse to find what circumstances preceded or followed Jesus' prayer, and the manner in which he prayed. Ask each group to write on the chart their observations so that all can see.

Jesus Prayed				
Passage	**What caused Jesus to pray?**	**What results occurred?**	**Where did this take place?**	**Observations**
Mark 1:35				
Mark 14:32				
Mark 6:46				
Luke 3:21				
Luke 5:15-16				
Luke 6:12				
Luke 9:18				
Luke 9:28				
Luke 11:1				

Ask for suggestions from your group on ways they can improve their prayer time. Write these on newsprint. Pass out paper and pencils and encourage everyone to jot down any suggestions they like as a reminder to put that suggestion to practice. Some you may suggest are: be honest with God, pray regularly, be positive in your prayers.

Close in sentence prayers. Holding hands, you begin the process, saying one or two sentences of prayer. Then, squeeze the hand of the next person in the circle and give him or her a chance to pray. If someone wishes to pass he or she may do so by squeezing the hand of the next person. Continue until all have had an opportunity to pray.

Seminar Session IV: Praise—Young people will gain a clearer understanding of the meaning of praise while having opportunities for expressing praise to God.

On a sheet of newsprint, write the following directions. As people arrive, point out the definitions and give them a 3×5 card and pencil to use for the assignment.

Define "praise"
Define "thanks"
Give a synonym (meaning is the same) of "praise"

Give an antonym (meaning is the opposite) of "praise"
List three things we can praise God about
In your own words, write a prayer or poem of praise to God

Display the Praise chart and assign one of the scripture passages to each young person. Have the kids read the passage and be prepared to write answers on the chart. Work through the chart as a large group.

Praise			
Scripture	**Definition of praise**	**Who is praising God?**	**Why is God praised?**
Psalm 7:17			
Psalm 71:5-6			
Psalm 145:1-6			
Psalm 21:13			
Ephesians 1:12-14			
Psalm 100:4			
Ephesians 5:19			
1 Peter 2:9-10			
Acts 2:46-47			

Divide your group into two smaller groups. Give each member from the first group a 3×5 card containing one of the scriptures listed below. Give each member in the second group a 3×5 card with one of the attributes of God as listed next to the scripture. Have the two groups mingle together to try to match each scripture verse with the appropriate attribute. When they find their match have them sit down together and determine why that attribute is worthy of praise. Give each pair a chance to share their findings with the rest of the group.

Psalm 7:17	God is just
Psalm 71:5-6	God is trustworthy
Psalm 148:3-5	God is the Creator
Psalm 138:2	God is love
Psalm 21:13	God is powerful
Psalm 100:4-5	God is good, loving and faithful

Close in a "praise" litany. Ask group members to state out loud an attribute of God. After each volunteer's statement, the entire group should respond with, "We praise thee, Lord." Continue until several attributes are shared, then close in prayer.

Seminar Session V: Witnessing—The purpose is to introduce the concept of witnessing as a way of life, encouraging kids to reach out and share their faith with others.

We all are witnesses. Some of us are better examples of the Christian lifestyle than others. Non-Christians often view our actions to learn about the Christian faith and its degree of importance in our lives. Encourage your young people to intentionally and honestly share their faith with others. Stating in everyday language what Christ has done for them can be more effective than a 45-minute sermon of an ordained minister.

Explain to your group that you are going to say several words or phrases. They should respond by giving a "thumbs up" sign if that word or phrase evokes positive feelings, a "thumbs down" sign if it has negative connotations. If they don't understand what that term means, or they have no feelings about the phrase, ask them to cross their arms.

Sunshine	Confession
Cancer	Evangelism
Salvation	"Be saved"
The beach	"The Elect"
Justification by faith	Restitution
Washed in the blood	Born again

Ask for volunteers to explain why they think the words elicited the responses they did.

Ask the young people each to share the name of the person who had the greatest impact on their spiritual life and how that person influenced them. Give everyone the chance to pass, and you begin the process.

Divide your group into four small groups. Assign each group one of the following passages and ask everyone to find as many reasons as they can in their verses for sharing their faith with other people: Matthew 28:19-20; Luke 10:2; John 3:3; 15:8.

Read Matthew 5:14-16. Pass a flashlight and a candle around the room and ask each person to share how that object is similar to being a Christian.

Go around again and ask group members to affirm the person sitting on their right by describing him or her as a light (caution light because the person warns us of approaching danger; searchlight because the person seeks us when we're lost; spotlight because the person highlights the good in others without glorifying himself or herself).

Ask for volunteers to participate in a role play. One person in each situation will play the part of a friend who is concerned about leading his or her friend into a relationship with God. The other person will play one of the following roles which you will assign:

- A young person troubled about his or her parents' relationship.
- A young person who has everything and is bored.
- A young person who has everything and is not bored.
- A person afraid of heights who must take an airplane trip tomorrow.
- A person who has just decided to give up a cocaine habit.
- A person who is everyone's friend.
- A person who never feels accepted by anyone else.

You may choose to do these role plays as "telephone role plays" in which the people are talking to one another on a phone.

Wrap up the discussion by talking about the importance of establishing a good relationship prior to witnessing. Recent research indicates that the majority of people come to know Christ through the invitation of a *friend*. Ask the kids to each think of a friend they can invite to church or to a youth group activity the next week.

Close by having everyone join hands and bow their heads. Read Acts 1:6-9 as a closing benediction.

SATURDAY

General Session II—After breakfast, lead a few exercises to get everyone's blood flowing. Lead the exercises "basic-training-style." For example, shout, "Attention! Stretch tall, then bend over and touch your toes." Shout "At ease" when you're finished exercising.

Remind retreat participants of classroom locations and other upcoming activities. Review the sign-up sheets and let everyone know what sessions they signed up for; dismiss the participants to the sessions.

Worship Session—Begin by singing worshipful songs such as "Jesus My Lord" from *Songs* (Songs and Creations).

Ask for volunteers to share aloud sentence prayers. Ask them to focus on what they've learned during the retreat.

Make sure everyone has a Bible, then read responsively Psalm 100. Ask members on one side of the room to read verses 1, 3 and 5 and members on the other side of the room to read verses 2 and 4.

Ask volunteers to share how God is working in their lives right now.

Share in a communion service. Ask a young person to read Luke

22:17-20. In a prayer, thank God for the communion elements. Invite the group to come to the table, where you will hand them the loaf of bread. They should tear off a piece of the bread and dip it in the cup before eating it.

Close the service by passing the peace to one another. This is done by approaching a young person, shaking his or her hand and saying, "The peace of God be with you." The person responds with, "And with you." Then the two of you go to two other young people and the process repeats itself. Continue in this way until everyone is sharing God's peace with each other.

19

The Bible Adventure

By Arlo Reichter

If you're ready for an adventure in Bible study, this is the retreat for you. This retreat requires you to be adventurous yourself. You won't know which areas of the Bible will be studied during the retreat until you arrive and begin the adventure.

Don't let this unknown keep you from trying this retreat. The co-learning and co-adventuring which this design sets up between the leaders and the young people is a good learning technique. Share the adventure. Share the study. Share the excitement of learning together. The teamwork which grows out of such an approach provides foundations for future positive experiences with your group.

The Bible Adventure lends itself well to a group of people who have a variety of backgrounds with the Bible. There is no basic requirement of a biblical understanding, though such understanding is definitely helpful to the retreat.

Use this retreat to:

● expose young people and leaders to different areas of scripture through Bible research and study;

● teach young people to use Bible research materials; and

● provide an opportunity for young people and leaders to share biblical findings and insights.

Before the Retreat—Since the retreat deals with exploring the Bible, use the Bible as a symbol in the publicity; for example, design a display around an open Bible, or create a poster using an illustration of an open Bible. Using a Bible as a visual aid when promoting the event is a constant reinforcement of the centrality of the Bible to the retreat.

Prepare a brief overview of the Old and New Testaments. You'll also have to prepare a brief presentation which will help your young people understand the concept of "Word" as presented in John 1:1-5. (See the retreat for more details.)

Gather several copies of the Bible (Today's English Version—TEV), Bible commentaries, topical Bibles, Bible dictionaries, concordances, a variety of Bible translations, candles, matches, 3×5 cards, paper, newsprint, markers and pencils.

On separate 3×5 cards, write these verses and names of parables: The Hidden Treasure—Matthew 13:44; The Pearl—Matthew 13:45-46; The Laborers in the Vineyard—Matthew 20:1-16; The Sheep and Goats—Matthew 25:31-46; Lamp Under a Bushel—Mark 4:21-25; New Wine, Old Wineskins—Mark 2:22; The Sower—Mark 4:3-9, 13-20; The Lost Coin—Luke 15:8-10; The Prodigal Son—Luke 15:11-32; The Dishonest Steward—Luke 16:1-13. These cards will be used during Bible Charades.

Retreat Schedule

Friday
7:00 p.m. Arrive at retreat site
7:30 p.m. Getting Acquainted
8:00 p.m. Bible Portrayal
9:00 p.m. Giving Thanks Through Prayer
9:30 p.m. Group Bible Adventure
11:00 p.m. Announcements and snacks
Midnight Lights out

Saturday
8:00 a.m. Breakfast
9:00 a.m. Worship
9:30 a.m. Bible Exploration
10:30 a.m. Finding the Meaning
11:30 a.m. Sharing
Noon Lunch
1:30 p.m. Creative Expressions

3:00 p.m. Free time
5:00 p.m. Dinner
6:30 p.m. The Bible Show
8:00 p.m. Break
8:30 p.m. Bible Charades
10:00 p.m. Refreshments
10:30 p.m. Candlelight Devotions
11:30 p.m. Lights out

Sunday
7:30 a.m. Breakfast
8:30 a.m. Review
9:00 a.m. Presentation
9:30 a.m. Small Groups
10:30 a.m. Bible Sculpture
11:15 a.m. Closing
11:30 a.m. Clean up, pack and head for home

Retreat Ingredients

FRIDAY

Getting Acquainted—Take 15 minutes to warm up; set a tone for the weekend. Select songs which include references to the Bible, Bible stories and Bible personalities.

Take five minutes for participants to learn the middle names of 10 other people. Then have the kids find the person who has a birthday the nearest theirs and the person who has a birthday the farthest from theirs.

Bible Portrayal—Form small groups by asking the young people to select one person whom they'd like to get to know better this weekend. Each pair should link with another pair. The group of four should include both guys and gals.

Have each small group select a Bible character to act out. Give them five minutes to develop their brief academy award-winning portrayals. Have the groups share their portrayals.

Giving Thanks Through Prayer—Ask each group to think of three reasons they are thankful for the weekend retreat. After several minutes, have each group share its reasons for thanks with the total group. Once a group has shared, have the total group respond in unison: "We join in your prayer of thanks." After all the groups have given their reasons, do a threefold amen (repeat "amen" in unison three times).

Group Bible Adventure—Invite everyone to begin the Bible adventure. Explain that this event is an adventure for the leaders, as well as the youth group members. No one knows the Bible passages which will be studied.

Instruct each group to choose a leader—either an adult or a reliable young person who'll help keep the group on track and who can ask questions as their process develops. Let the adventure begin!

● *Choose*—Direct one person in each group to close his or her eyes. Hand him or her a Bible. Allow him or her (with eyes closed) to open the Bible to any place—wherever the Bible opens is the book the group will study.

● *Select*—Find the beginning of any chapter in that book. Select eight to 12 verses which appear to be a logical grouping to study.

● *Outline*—Give each group a copy of the Bible (TEV). Ask a group member to read aloud the opening material relating to the book of the Bible the group is to study. Have another group member write the outline of contents from the TEV on newsprint along with the name of the book and the author (if known). After the outline, write the chapter and verses of the scripture portion randomly selected for study.

● *Read and write*—With the group members following along in their own Bibles, have someone read aloud the portion selected for study. Encourage group members to write down key words, names or feelings which they are getting from this scripture portion.

● *Arrange*—Have the small groups arrange themselves along a line representing the Bible—beginning with Genesis, ending with Revelation. This will give the members a sense of what other books of the Bible have been selected and the relationship of their book to the others.

Announcements—End the day's experiences by giving announcements and directions for the next day. Encourage private Bible reading, especially relating to the scriptures selected by small groups. Solicit prayer concerns and invite different group members to join in a prayer.

SATURDAY

Worship—Begin with exercises, singing and prayers. Invite several groups to read the scripture portions they selected last night. Make announcements as necessary.

Bible Exploration—Give a brief overview of the Bible by presenting the major sections of the Old Testament and the New Testament. It is important that this not be a lengthy and detailed presentation; it is an overview.

Have the kids divide into the small groups they formed last evening. In these groups they will now begin to explore the various Bible study resources which are available.

Have several Bible commentaries available for each group. The group members should look at the book to see the kinds of information available. Allow 10 minutes for this exploration. Then have the kids list on newsprint the various kinds of information available in their commentaries. Post this newsprint where they can refer to it.

Ask the group members to look up their scripture in the commentary and review the materials they find. Again have this written on newsprint and posted.

Finding the Meaning—Now it is time for each group to determine the "meaning" of the passage for their faith journey. Have group members individually write some words or sentences in response to these questions:

● What is there in your group's scripture passage which encourages you as a person of faith?

● What words mean something to you personally?

● What meanings in the scripture are helpful to you?

● Does the scripture point to something you need to deal with in your life? If so, what is it?

Sharing—Have each small group join with another group. Ask each group to read its scripture passage to the other group and share some of the things they've listed on the newsprint.

After all participants have shared, applaud the group for their adventures in the Bible.

Creative Expressions—Have the groups once again line up according to their scripture passage order in the Bible. (This will be the order of the presentations which are about to create for the evening session.) Ask each group to choose one of the following creative mediums to develop a presentation which communicates the meaning of their Bible passage.

- *Drama*—Act out the passage silently or with words which may be the actual scripture lesson. Or do a contemporary version to express the passage's meaning.

- *Sculpture*—Create a sculpture with things found around the camp (without destroying natural surrounding or property). Try to represent some of the meaning the group has found in the scripture passage.

- *Human sculpture*—Create a sculpture using the bodies of the group members to create a representation of the meaning found in the scripture.

- *Song*—Write a song which the group can sing to communicate the meaning of the scripture.

- *Poem*—Write a poem which the group can recite together to share the meaning of the scripture.

- *Other expressions*—Try other expressions such as soap opera, newscast or games. Give anything a try.

The groups should work for the hour doing their creation. Encourage them to review their learnings as they develop their expression.

The Bible Show—Have the groups share the creative expressions they developed in the afternoon session. Remember to have them share in the order that their scripture passages appear in the Bible. (Take these ideas back home and present them to your congregation.)

Bible Charades—Divide into small groups; give each group one 3×5 card with a parable on it. Allow 10 minutes for the groups to think of how they can pantomime their parable. One at a time, act out the parables. All observers try to guess the teaching. After the parables on the cards have been acted out, have the kids try acting out teachings in Proverbs.

Candlelight Devotions—Close with brief moments of discussion using the theme from Hebrews 11—the great cloud of witnesses to faith who have gone before us. Talk about all we can learn from the early Christians. Discuss the impact these "witnesses to faith" have had on our world today. Give the young people "alone time" to think about this passage. Light the candles and darken the room. Allow no speaking during this time.

SUNDAY

Review—Open the session with music and prayers. Read John 1:1-5. Ask each small group to identify three key words from the

scripture which they have studied this weekend. Then ask each group
to recite in unison their three key words to the total group.

Presentation—Prepare a brief presentation which helps your
young people understand the concept of ''Word'' as presented in John
1:1-5. Ideas:

● The Word has been with us this weekend and active in our
lives, in our group.

● God's Word continues to say things to us through our interac-
tions with scripture, with each other and with God in moments of
prayer and meditation.

● Three words were selected by each group which have key
meanings. These words probably have different messages for each of
us and we can grow in faith if we seek their meaning in our lives.

● This weekend of looking at the Bible can help to light our path
of faith. Let us be open to that light and be willing to follow it.

Small Groups—This step begins the closure of the groups. The
following moments should be spent with the small groups completing
the phrase, ''This group has been helpful to me by . . . '' Ask each
person to complete the sentence. After a person has shared have the
entire group say, ''That's great.''

Ask each individual to write down the three words their group
listed as key words. Quickly have the individuals write five additional
words for each of the three words. An example might be:

Hope—needed, faith, God, future, helpful
Grace—free, love, confusing, a gift, amazing

These word lists are for brief sharing with one other person and
meant to be helpful in encouraging the young person to continue to
reflect on the retreat after the event is concluded. Encourage them to
take these lists home.

Bible Sculpture—Begin a Bible sculpture by putting your
opened Bible in the middle of the room. Now invite all the participants to add their Bibles—opened or closed, flat or standing to this
developing Bible sculpture. When the sculpture is complete, form a
circle around the sculpture and have the group repeat after you (in
short phrases) John 1:1-5.

Closing—Remain in the circle. Sing a favorite song and say a
closing prayer. Ask the participants to remove their Bibles in silence
and in a worshipful attitude. Invite the participants to hold their Bibles
and meditate silently for five minutes.

20

Creative Bible Study

By Mitch Olson

This retreat will expose the youth and leaders to creative Bible study. The intent is not to help participants become perfect Bible scholars or professors, but to demonstrate that their approach to Bible study is what makes it fun.

In this retreat, the participants will:
- complete several Bible studies;
- know more about the scriptures;
- create their own Bible study; and
- begin a foundation of study skills that they can build on after the retreat.

Before the Retreat—An important step in preparation is for the leader to examine his or her study habits. What kind of Bible study

---

Retreat Schedule

Friday
8:00 p.m. Arrive at camp and settle in
8:30 p.m. Get-Acquainted Time
9:30 p.m. Wild Bible Stuff
11:00 p.m. Go over camp rules (If it's cold, sing around a warm campfire and drink some hot chocolate)
Midnight Lights out

Saturday
8:00 a.m. Breakfast
9:00 a.m. The "I Hate Bible Study" Bible Study

10:30 a.m. Free time
11:30 a.m. Sense Scriptures
Noon Lunch
1:00 p.m. The Inspector in Samuel
2:00 p.m. Free time (Try playing softball using a kickball—you don't need baseball gloves and it is a lot easier to catch)
4:00 p.m. Create Your Own Bible Study
5:00 p.m. Dinner
6:00 p.m. Worship
6:30 p.m. Head for home

habits do you have? Do you need a fresh approach to Bible study? Do you need to get excited about the Bible? Once you've examined your study habits and noted areas of strength and weakness, then you can help others improve their study habits.

Another important point to remember is to get away from a "teacher-to-learner" setting. Rather than telling the kids what they should do to improve their Bible study skills, share your experiences with Bible study, and what motivates you. Try to help the kids develop a love for personal devotions and time with God.

Gather pencils, Bibles, newsprint, markers, two carrots, handouts and game equipment. Read the retreat, then on newsprint write the Bible study steps found in the session titled The "I Hate Bible Study" Bible Study.

—————— Retreat Ingredients ——————

FRIDAY

Get-Acquainted Time—After everyone has settled in at the retreat site, gather and play some fun crowdbreakers. For example, you could play Pass the Carrot from *Try This One . . . Strikes Again* (Group Books). Have everyone form a circle. Place a carrot between the knees of the tallest person; he or she must pass the carrot to the knees of the person to the left, without using hands. This continues until the carrot has traveled around the circle. Then break off a piece and send it around again. If a person drops the carrot, he or she is out of the game. The last person left is the winner. Give him or her a fresh carrot to eat.

Wild Bible Stuff—Begin by asking the question, "Did you know . . . ?" before each of the following statements (these facts are from the *King James Open Bible*—Thomas Nelson). Keep your enthusiasm high so the kids are excited about this list of Bible facts: Did you know . . . ?

● the entire Bible has 66 books, is divided into two testaments, the first containing 39 books, the second 27 books?

● the entire Bible has 1,189 chapters, Old Testament with 929 and the New with 260?

● the entire Bible has 31,173 verses—23,214 in the Old and 7,959 in the New?

● the entire Bible has 773,692 words—592,439 in the Old and 181,253 in the New?

● the entire Bible has 3,566,480 letters—2,728,100 letters in the Old and 838,380 letters in the New?

● the word "gnat" only appears one time in the entire Bible (Matthew 23:24) yet the word "and" is found 46,227 times throughout the Bible?

Distribute pencils and Believe-It-or-Not Bible Search handouts. Divide the kids into small groups, then give them 15 to 20 minutes to find out these unusual facts. The purpose of this activity is to take a closer look at the scriptures and find out some funny things. After the kids complete the handouts, discuss the answers in the large group. Close the meeting with prayer and petition for God's presence during the retreat.

Believe-It-or-Not Bible Search

Find the following "unusual" facts. Write the answers in the space provided.

1. Oldest man in Bible (Genesis 5:27) _____

2. How many total toes and fingers did this guy have? (2 Samuel 21:20)

   _____

3. Awful dinner item! (2 Kings 6:29) _____

4. Figure out how many "mothers-in-law" this guy had! (1 Kings 11:3)

   _____

5. A fact sure to tickle your "funny bone" (Ezekiel 37) _____

6. An interesting "Breakfast of Champions" (Matthew 3:4) _____

SATURDAY

The "I Hate Bible Study" Bible Study—Write these Bible study steps on newsprint and post it in front of the group. Explain to the kids this new method of Bible study:

1. Read a favorite Bible story, Psalm or parable, etc.

2. Divide it into small sections of three to four verses.

3. Summarize each of those few verses in "up-to-date" terms to help you remember the message; for example, "Jesus Meets a Strange Character," "Jesus Heals This Strange Character," and so on.

4. Apply the story to your life by answering a few questions:

● What is the setting of this passage (time, place, occasion, people)?

● What is the context of this passage (who is speaking, to whom is he speaking)?

● Can you identify with someone in the text (who would you like to be)?

● What is the message (how can you apply it to your life)?

Distribute Bibles, pencils and the Prodigal Son handouts. Say: "On your own, complete the handout and answer the questions as best you can. Notice how the Bible study follows the steps posted on newsprint. After you finish your handout, we'll get in pairs to discuss the answers."

Give the kids 20 minutes to write their answers. Instead of "num-

---

Prodigal Son

Turn to Luke 15:11-32. This section is often referred to as the parable of the prodigal son. Read each section of scripture, then read the brief summary. Think of a different way to summarize each section of verses, and write it in the space provided.

● Luke 15:11-16 "The Younger Son Takes Off" _____

● Luke 15:17-21 "The Younger Son Comes to His Senses"

_____

● Luke 15:22-24 "The Father Accepts His Son's New Heart and Attitude" _____

● Luke 15:25-30 "The Older Brother Is Mad" _____

● Luke 15:31-32 "The Father Reassures Older Son" _____

Answer these questions concerning this story:

1. What is the setting (time, place, people)?

2. What is the context (who is speaking, to whom is he speaking)?

3. Can you identify with someone in the text? If so, who?

4. What is the message? Apply it to your life.

bering off," get into pairs by "sounding off" with two words: "Bible
. . . study . . . Bible . . . study . . ." Have the kids each say one of the
two words. All people who said "Bible" must find a partner who said
"study." Let them discuss answers with their partners.

Sense Scriptures—Help the Bible touch the kids' senses as well
as their intellect by trying this activity from *Try This One . . . Strikes
Again* (Group Books). Select a Bible passage such as Mark 4:35-41
where Jesus calms the sea. Tell the participants they are to use their
imaginations to sense the story. They are to try to set themselves in
the middle of the story and see, hear, smell, taste and feel it.

Ask the kids to close their eyes, then read the story. Afterward,
discuss the sensations. Some examples:

See—darkness; big, black clouds; lightning; huge waves

Hear—thunder; splashing; men screaming; boat creaking

Smell—rain; salty, wet people who didn't smell good anyway

Taste—water; salt; cottonmouth caused by fear; lunch coming up

Feel—seasick; the boat rocking; humidity; fear; anger; confusion;
helplessness

This process sets the mood for digging into the meaning of the
text. The Bible is easier to understand if you can imagine yourself in
the middle of it. Try it again reading a different passage.

The Inspector in Samuel—Distribute Bibles, pencils, the story
of The Inspector in Samuel, and the handouts. Divide the kids into
two groups. Where the story says "A" one group reads, where the
story says "B" the other group reads. After the story, have them complete the handouts. Then find a partner and discuss their answers.

Create Your Own Bible Study—Gather the kids and review the
last two Bible studies. Did they discover anything different about the
stories of the prodigal son and David? Go over the list of steps to Bible study which you have printed on newsprint. Then divide into four
smaller groups. Give each group a sheet of newsprint, a marker and
several Bibles. Have them choose a favorite Bible story, divide the passage every three to four verses, summarize each section in "up-to-
date" terms, then list and try to answer the follow-up questions. After
about 30 minutes, take turns having the small groups lead their Bible
study for the large group.

Worship—Divide into groups of three. Give each group a sheet
of newsprint and a marker. Have the kids write a list of things they
learned or discovered about the Bible this weekend. Highlight similarities and encourage their positive responses to the weekend's activities.
Use the lists as a praise portion of the worship. After you read each
item, have the kids shout, "We praise you, Lord."

For the meditation, say to the kids: "The story of David is a good
example of how even the worst sin can be forgiven by the grace and

love of God. This doesn't mean that we should find excuses for our sin, but we should always turn to God in total submission and he will forgive us. Turn to Psalm 51. David wrote this to ask forgiveness after he had committed adultery with Bathsheba. Try and see the true sorrow and regret David felt. This psalm points out the understanding that 'law' isn't as important as knowing that you have a personal relationship with God.''

Divide into two groups. Have one group read Psalm 51:1-2, the second group read Psalm 51:3-4, and so on. Close with a one-word prayer of thanksgiving. You begin with: ''We thank you Lord for . . . '' Then kids each add one thanksgiving. After everyone has contributed, have everybody shout ''Amen!''

David's Story

Turn to 2 Samuel 11. This is a story similar to the one you just heard. Read each section of scripture, then read the summary. Think of a different way to summarize each section.

- 2 Samuel 11:1-5. ''Watch Out for What You Watch Out At''

  _____

- 2 Samuel 11:6-9. ''David's Plan'' _____
- 2 Samuel 11:10-13 ''Uriah Won't Go Home''_____
- 2 Samuel 11:14-24 ''Sent to Battle''_____
- 2 Samuel 11:25-27 ''David Moves In—God Displeased''

  _____

Our story continues in Chapter 12 with the meeting of the prophet Nathan and David. Nathan is disappointed in David's great sin and delivers judgment upon him. David then repents, and asks the Lord's forgiveness. Read 2 Samuel 12:1-25. Then answer these questions.

1. What is the setting (time, place, people)?

2. What is the context (who is speaking, to whom is he speaking)?

3. Can you relate to anyone in this passage? If so, who?

4. What is the message? Apply it to your life.

The Inspector in Samuel

A. It was more than just being able to overlook the city. Sure it's nice to have the penthouse suite when you're king; I guess even the best face temptation. I'm an inspector. I was hired by Nathan, the prophet, when the story of David's adultery with Bathsheba and murder of her husband was still just a rumor. After all, you don't just go into your king's office and accuse him of adultery and murder you know!

B. I usually don't pry into the affairs of political dignitaries, but this case was different. David isn't your average, every-day, run-of-the-mill king. Were talkin' Psalm writer, composer (Top 10), musician; even a sort of hero—kinda like Moses in the *Ten Commandments*. But hey, I went into this thing hoping to find him innocent (and maybe even earn a little money). I wanted to clear the slate. Wipe it clean. I just can't accept all the stories I've heard so far—you know, David seems so good, so perfect; he's got the perfect alibi—I guess only time will tell in a case like this.

A. As an inspector, I usually don't interview my clients as suspects, but I still can't figure out the relationship between Nathan and David. They have a weird sort of relationship. I know, I know. David is king—but the spiritual connection in their relationship scares me.

B. Usually I rule out the butler in a case real early (the butler is always the murderer in a cheap novel), so I kept searching for my first clue. What I found was difficult to prove, but it made sense. Why was David so interested in the war all of a sudden? Everyone and his brother knew David would rather sing and dance than lead an army. But lately David had taken personal interest in a certain commander Joab. Why the sudden change? Then it dawned on me. The first sign of trouble is always a cover-up. At least that's what Joab led me to believe.

A. Joab. Respected, trustworthy, pure class. Morning inspection is like a visit to the ark of the covenant, in this guy's mind. He followed David's guidance like it was chipped in stone. Claimed that questioning the commander in chief was like questioning God. Joab did mention a letter from David concerning Uriah. I guess I did kinda "pry" it out of him. The minute Joab mentioned the letter—he changed the subject. A slip that aided my next clue. Who is Uriah? Why is this guy haunting the mind of Joab? You know— Uriah never finished even basic academy training, much less officers training school. What's the connection? You know?

B. My next clue cost me a few friendly dollars. You know, a servant is always the first to tell—and the last to lie. At least when it concerns the truth. And that depends on who pays them the most. Aw heck. This guy had no reason to lie. I knew I should have waited . . . I heard the same story five times later for free. Well, the information dealt with the victims whereabouts and activities before his death. (The fact that Nathan knew first, bothered me—but not anymore.) What kept Uriah away from his wife? Seem's funny to me. Especially after seeing his wife!

A. Uriah. One hundred percent, pure Judean—rugged build, dark hair, moustache. To say nothing of the thousands of women he's melted with his smile. I guess we average guys were thankful for his devotion to the king's army. It put the chances of losing our own girl's hearts to him a bit farther away. But none of us worries about that anymore. Uriah is dead. In a way, Uriah was lucky. A beautiful wife, good job, respected by all, dedicated soldier; maybe he was too lucky . . .

21

The Grace of God

By Suzanne E. Zobel

G od's grace is a difficult concept to explain to young people or to help them understand. We seldom recognize grace or experience it in our daily relationships, except with God. But does this limit grace to simply a God, church or religious concept?

It is essential to share the grace, love and forgiveness of God with young people as they struggle daily with their self-worth. They need to be surrounded with grace and experience it, not only from God, but from others within their Christian community. Adult leaders need to model their own experiences of grace. This is the challenge of this retreat.

Use this retreat to:
- help young people clarify what the grace of God is;
- offer examples of grace as it was experienced in the Bible;
- share personal experiences of grace; and
- model a "grace-filled" relationship as you work with your own young people.

Before the Retreat—Encourage youth leaders and other adults to prepare themselves for this retreat by reading Romans 1—8 and Galatians. Ask them to think about the objectives of the retreat and how they can help to make this a "grace-filled" experience.

Games and activities are important to building a sense of community and relationship among participants. Keep all activities non-competitive and enjoyable, while helping the participants get to know more about each other. Recreation should include both structured and non-structured options. Excellent sources for games are the *Try This One* series and *Building Community in Youth Groups* (Group Books). Try to use music that reflects a tone of celebration. Include lots of familiar favorites as well as new songs.

Gather volleyball equipment; several umbrellas; newsprint; markers; different-colored construction paper; stiff white paper; glue; scissors; yarn; masking tape; magazines; and, for each person, a Bible, pencil, safety pin, shoebox and copy of each handout.

Read the retreat and prepare the following items according to the directions given: the "question/feeling" walls; name tags made from 4×8 pieces of stiff white paper; blessing circles; and green and brown leaves for evaluation.

On separate sheets of newsprint, write the quotation found in the G.R.A.C.E. session; write the scripture found in the His Love Endures session; and draw a tree for the evaluation.

Retreat Schedule

Friday
7:00 p.m. Arrive and get settled
7:30 p.m. Who Are You?/Who Am I?
8:00 p.m. G.R.A.C.E.
8:50 p.m. Break
9:10 p.m. Box Collages
10:10 p.m. We're Surrounded
10:30 p.m. Snacks and recreation
Midnight Lights out

Saturday
7:45 a.m. His Love Endures
8:00 a.m. Breakfast
9:00 a.m. Volleyball Challenge
10:00 a.m. Under God's Umbrella
Noon Lunch

1:00 p.m. How Can I Know? (As a "grace" gift, cancel this activity for free time and recreation)
5:30 p.m. Dinner
7:00 p.m. Keeping in Step With the Spirit
7:30 p.m. Fruits of the Spirit
10:00 p.m. Snacks and games
Midnight Lights out

Sunday
8:00 a.m. Breakfast
9:00 a.m. Worship Preparation
10:00 a.m. Celebrating Grace
11:30 a.m. Evaluation
Noon Lunch and departure

Retreat Ingredients

FRIDAY

Who Are You?/Who Am I?—As participants assemble, ask them to complete their name tags. Provide a sample since the format of the tags is necessary for the first Bible study. On the front of a 4×8 piece of paper, ask the participant to write his or her first name down the left side. On the back each participant should note the following: an unexpected gift he or she received, a favorite Christmas carol, and the last time he or she sang "Jesus Loves Me."

When everyone has arrived and name tags are complete, instruct the participants to locate three people they don't know well. With the first person, they should tell their stories of the unexpected gifts. With the second person, they should each sing the first verse of their favorite Christmas carol. And with the third person, they should exchange stories about the last time they sang "Jesus Loves Me." Encourage your participants to share their stories and songs with at least three other people, but to listen to the stories and songs of others so they can meet as many people as possible during this experience.

Continue with other community-building games and exercises until it is time for the Bible study. End this get-acquainted session with a relay which puts participants into small groups of five to seven people. If you have designated Bible study leaders, be sure one leader is a member of each group.

G.R.A.C.E. (God's **R**iches **A**t **C**hrist's **E**xpense)—The purpose of this first Bible study is to define grace and to begin to see grace as part of each person's relationship to God. Write this purpose on newsprint and post it for everyone to see.

Ask each participant to use his or her name tag to write a word associated with grace for each letter of his or her name. For example, Sue could write:

S(alvation)
U(nconditional)
E(xtra special)

After about 10 minutes ask participants to share these words within their small groups. If individuals have difficulty finding a word for a specific letter, they can ask for help from the group. Some may want to include an explanation about why these grace words are special for them.

After the name tag activity, read Romans 3:21-26. Encourage individuals to reflect on this passage. On a large sheet of newsprint, list all of the grace words in this passage. Participants may want to add other words too.

Have the following quotation written on another sheet of newsprint. Read it together and discuss what it means:

"God's grace is that he gives us what we do not deserve.
God's mercy is that he does not give us what we do deserve."
—Charles Mueller

After the discussion give each small group banner-making materials such as newsprint, markers, magazines, construction paper, scissors and glue. Ask each group to create a banner defining grace. Have individuals arrange words, colors and pictures on a large sheet of newsprint to be displayed at the end of this session. Allow about 20 minutes for this activity.

Box Collages—After the break participants should return to their small groups. Ask them to think of a time in their lives when they experienced God's grace. This may have happened during worship, a time alone with God or through the response of another person. Offer an opportunity for sharing these experiences within the small groups, but be sensitive to those who are not willing or ready to share. Try to limit this part of the session to about 10 to 15 minutes.

After participants have thought about and shared experiences of grace in their own and others' lives, they should use the shoe boxes they brought with them to create box collages. Using the materials provided, individuals should personalize their boxes. Say: "The outside walls of the box should reflect how you think *other people* view you. The top of the box should reflect how you think *God* views you. And the inside of the box should reflect how *you* feel about yourself." Allow at least 30 minutes for participants to create their collages since these creations will play a major role in the worship experiences at this retreat.

When participants are finished, have them meet with their small groups and discuss their boxes. Encourage people to share as much or as little information as they feel comfortable. After everyone has shared within the small group, seal the boxes with tape and prepare for the final session. Make sure the group is prepared to share both its banner and boxes with the total group.

We're Surrounded—Unite the large group with some singing. Allow participants to select songs they enjoy. Begin this final session by having each small group come forward to post their banner. After sharing the significance of their banner, group members should use their box collages to build an altar. Remind everyone to build the altar with the box tops visible, so the altar reflects God's view of us. Use this altar throughout the retreat for devotions and times for worship.

Ask one of the young people to read Romans 6:3-4. Discuss the relationship between baptism and grace. The outcome of this discussion should be reassurance that the gift of life is offered by virtue of the faith relationship. Encourage participants to react by sharing "Something I learned tonight . . . " or "Something I feel tonight . . . "

Ask the participants to look around them. Each wall around the main meeting area should be covered with large sheets of newsprint. Point out that these "question/feeling" walls are there to write questions, reactions or thoughts about the retreat. Invite every person to write, read and react to the questions and comments of others.

Move the group into a prayer circle and close by singing a quiet song in a whisper, such as "Alleluia."

SATURDAY

His Love Endures—Begin singing to gather participants around the altar. End the singing with "I Love to Tell the Story." Have the following scripture written on newsprint for all to see and repeat in unison:

Give thanks to the Lord for he is good.

His love endures forever!

He frees us from our enemies.

His love endures forever!

Give thanks to the God of heaven.

His love endures forever!

(Psalm 136:1, 24, 26)

Call the group to worship and thanksgiving by saying: "These words come from Psalm 136. This psalm relates the history or story of God's love and gracious action on behalf of the people of Israel. After each phrase, the psalmist would respond: 'His love endures forever!'

"Each person has a story to tell about God's love and grace. We began telling some of our stories last night, but we have lots more to share. We are beginning to realize just how much we are surrounded by God's grace. God gives us opportunities to tell the story again and again by both our words and our actions. Let's use today to spread the word that 'His love endures forever!' "

Close with a prayer of thanksgiving and praise, especially for the blessings of God that surround us and the food everyone is about to share.

Volleyball Challenge—An organized game, like volleyball, can serve a dual purpose. It provides a means to put new energy back into participants and offers an opportunity to demonstrate grace. Mix the Bible study groups and break them into teams. Set up a mini-tournament, playing each game to five points. Encourage teams that aren't playing to select another team and cheer for them.

Before the tournament begins, inform the teams that the champions will receive a special reward of extra free time during the afternoon. (Write a neutral activity into the schedule following lunch. Then "gracefully" cancel this activity during the Bible study to award the extra free time.)

Under God's Umbrella—Try this session outside under large umbrellas or shelters. Use the same Bible study groups that were formed yesterday. Remind participants they will need their Bibles and a pencil.

The purpose of this Bible study is to discover God's grace as it surrounds us and empowers us in this world to a life dead to sin and alive in Christ. Write this purpose on newsprint for everyone to see.

Begin this session by making the following announcement: "Good news! Our 1:00 p.m. session has been cancelled! *Everyone* gets extra free time whether you won or lost the volleyball tournament!" Allow time for the participants to react to the announcement and then encourage a discussion by asking the following questions:

- If you were one of the "losers," how did you feel about losing? How do you feel now?
- If you were one of the "winners," how did you feel about winning? How do you feel now?
- What can we learn about grace from this volleyball tournament experience?

After individuals have had a chance to share their feelings and thoughts, ask them to return to their small Bible study groups. Pass out the first handout on Images and ask participants to answer the questions. When they are finished, they need to gather as a group to discuss their answers.

Images

Read Romans 5:20—6:14. Notice the images, or pictures, of sin and the law versus grace, as they are presented by Paul. Draw some of these images below.

Images of Sin and Law   **Images of Grace**

Circle the image that most accurately represents your life right now. Share this with the group and explain why you selected that image.

Reflecting on the scripture you just read in Romans, what words would you use to describe the following relationships?
- The relationship between sin and grace.
- The relationship between faith and grace.

In what ways do you abuse God's grace in your life?

Share your responses with the rest of your small group.

After the small groups have talked about their Images handout, pass out the second handout on The Umbrella of God's Grace. Have each participant complete the handout, then discuss it within the small group.

The Umbrella of God's Grace

In Romans 6:14, Paul re-emphasizes the fact that sin will not have power over us since we are under God's grace. Picture grace as a large umbrella.

In the left-hand column, write about a time when someone you know needed to "find shelter under God's umbrella," or needed to hear of God's grace.

Then, in the right-hand column, write about a time you needed the shelter of God's umbrella.

Someone else   **Me**

Share these times within your small group.

Something to think about: If someone needed grace, but did not experience it at the time he or she needed it, what can be done now to share God's grace with that person?

As the morning session ends, remind participants to take a few moments to explore the "question/feeling" walls. Ask them to add their own comments about the retreat, their experiences with God's grace or their reactions to others' comments.

Keeping in Step With the Spirit—After dinner bring the total group together to sing around the altar. Review some of the general observations you have noted on the "question/feeling" walls, not mentioning specific names or comments. Ask participants to move into their small groups and pass out the Keeping in Step With the Spirit handout. Ask them to complete the handout and discuss it in their small groups. Allow 20 minutes for this activity.

Fruits of the Spirit—Distribute a Fruits of the Spirit handout to each participant. Explain that this handout contains the discussion questions for the next activity.

Divide the large group into exactly five small groups. Have one

---

Keeping in Step
With the Spirit

Read Galatians 5:13-25. Take 10 minutes to individually develop two lists from this passage: a list of acts of a sinful nature and a list of fruits of the Spirit.

Acts of sinful nature   **Fruits of the Spirit**

Share your lists with your group, adding those items you missed. Discuss the scripture you just read:
● Where do you see grace in this passage?
● What is the relationship between the Spirit and grace?

---

leader assigned to lead a discussion on each of the following sections of fruits of the Spirit: love; joy and peace; patience and kindness; faithfulness; gentleness and self-control. Explain by saying: "Each small group will spend a short time (10-15 minutes) with each leader, discussing one topic. At the end of the time period, the small group will rotate to a new leader. In this way each of your small groups will experience five different discussions, but the leader will direct the same discussion five times." Move your groups from one discussion group to another by singing one verse of a familiar song.

After each group has moved through the five discussion sessions, it should remain at its last station. Tell each group to use the next 30 minutes to develop a short dramatization or role play for the last fruit of the Spirit discussed. If a group's last study session was on faithfulness, they could role play what it means to be faithful by pantomiming going to church, reading the Bible or praying. These short dramatic productions should be based on the continuing discussion, "How do I use the fruit of the Spirit to communicate grace?"

Fruits of the Spirit

LOVE (Matthew 5:43-48)
1. Describe the kind of love Jesus challenged us to show.
2. How difficult or easy is it to model this kind of Christian love? Why?
3. Using this fruit of the Spirit, how can we as sons or daughters communicate grace to our parents? Give specific examples.
4. Using this fruit of the Spirit, how can we expect our parents to communicate grace to us as their children? Give specific examples.

JOY AND PEACE (Philippians 4:4-7)
1. Describe the joy and peace that Paul mentions. What is the source of this joy and peace?
2. How do we show this in our lives? What is the most difficult thing this passage asks you to do?
3. Using this fruit of the Spirit, how can we as students communicate grace to our teachers? Give specific examples.
4. Using this fruit of the Spirit, how can we expect our teachers to communicate grace to us? Give specific examples.

PATIENCE AND KINDNESS (James 1:19-20, 5:7-8)
1. How are patience and kindness related?
2. How do we demonstrate patience and kindness each day?
3. What special kind of patience does James discuss in 5:7-8? Give examples of how we express that hope daily.
4. Using these fruits of the Spirit, how do we communicate grace to our brothers and sisters? Give specific examples.
5. Using these fruits of the Spirit, how do we expect our brothers and sisters to communicate grace to us? Give specific examples.

FAITHFULNESS (Luke 12:35-40)
1. What point does this parable make about faithfulness?
2. Identify the things that get in the way of our daily faithfulness.
3. Who is always faithful and good? How does that knowledge encourage our faithfulness?
4. Using this fruit of the Spirit, how do we communicate grace to our friends? Give specific examples.
5. Using this fruit of the Spirit, how do we expect our friends to communicate grace to us? Give specific examples.

GENTLENESS AND SELF-CONTROL (1 Peter 4:7-11)
1. Explain which words in this passage help us describe gentleness and self-control.
2. What relationship does Peter point out between gifts (fruits) and God's grace?
3. What is the ultimate purpose of the gifts (fruits), i.e. the special abilities that God has given us?
4. Using these fruits of the Spirit, how can we communicate grace as one friend to another? Give specific examples.

When all groups are ready, ask them to gather in a circle and share their role plays. Close this session by asking participants to think about a particular fruit they would like more of in their own life. Encourage them to think of a particular relationship in which they need more help communicating grace. Close with a circle prayer which allows each participant to pray for a special concern.

SUNDAY

Worship Preparation—Explain that this time will be used to prepare for the worship service. Distribute an Evidence of God's Grace handout to each person. Divide into the Bible study groups and have individuals complete and discuss this handout. (Allow about 30 minutes for each group to prepare its demonstration and find a visual aid appropriate for this activity.)

When the groups are ready, they should return to the large group

---

Evidence of God's Grace

We can discover God's grace all around us, even in our sinful world. Select one of the following Bible passages and find a way to demonstrate its message during our Sunday morning worship.

Read the passages below and decide which one your group wants to demonstrate. After you decide which scripture to use, discuss what it says about our sinful selves and God's grace in our lives.

Your demonstration may take the form of drama, music or some other creative method. Part of your demonstration should also include sharing some visual object or sign of God's grace within his creation.

Lamentations 3:22-23	Matthew 5:43-48	Luke 15:1-7
Luke 15:8-10	Luke 15:11-32	John 1:6-18

- Plan your demonstration.
- Explore God's creation for some visual sign of his grace; for example, select a blade of grass as a sign of God's grace. Say that God loves us and doesn't want us to worry. "If that is how God clothes the grass of the field, which is here today and tomorrow is thrown into the fire, will he not much more clothe you, O you of little faith. So do not worry . . . " (Matthew 6:30-31a).
  - Prepare your sharing for this Sunday morning session.

to plan the rest of the worship arrangements by discussing these
questions:

- How will our group gather around the altar?
- What will be the focal point for our worship?
- What items from previous sessions and Bible studies do we
need to include as part of our celebration?
- Are the paper banners securely hung?
- Does our altar of box collages need any changes?
- Is our Bible study group ready to present and explain its visual
sign of grace?
- Do we need to include any special music that has become es-
pecially meaningful to our group?
- What else needs to happen to provide an atmosphere for
worship?

After this discussion, involve the group in setting up the worship
area and preparing themselves for their roles in worship.

Celebrating Grace—Begin your worship by sharing greetings
from several epistles. Participants should be scattered around the room
to read these opening verses (each verse builds on the previous verse):
1 Timothy 6:21; 1 Corinthians 16:23; Galatians 6:18; 2 John 3; Revelation 1:4-5; 2 Corinthians 13:14.

Following this scriptural call to worship, lead the group in singing
a song that reflects the spirit of the retreat like "Amazing Grace." Between each verse the Bible study groups will share their Evidence of
God's Grace demonstrations developed during the preparation session.
After each group shares, it should explain its visual aid and leave it on
or near the altar. When all the Bible study groups have shared, the
group should move into a circle around the altar. In this way everyone can see the others' offerings and contributions to the fruits of the
Spirit. Use spontaneous prayers to celebrate and focus on special concerns individuals have experienced within the retreat.

Following this prayer time, provide participants with an opportunity to share a blessing of grace with each other. Pass each participant
a marker and a paper circle with a yarn loop and safety pin attached.
Instruct participants to write a blessing on this circle for the person to
their right. This can be done in words or pictures. They should include the person's name in their blessing. For example, "May God
bless you, Sandy, with strength during the next week at school." Go
around the circle one by one and ask each person to share the blessing with the person on his or her right. The yarn loop and safety pin
can be used to attach the blessing to the person for whom it is intended.

Invite everyone to hum "Amazing Grace" while individuals
throughout the room read the following scriptural benedictions: Reve-

lation 22:21; 1 Timothy 1:2; 2 Peter 3:18; Galatians 1:3-5; 1 Peter 5:10-11; Numbers 6:24-26. Have the group stand where they are and celebrate with a song like "Great Is the Lord" from *Songs* (Songs and Creations, Inc.). Then close with a group hug.

Evaluation—Participants should have an opportunity to share their responses to the retreat, facilities, leadership, etc. This may be done with a short written form or in other creative ways.

One suggestion is to draw a tree with bare branches on a sheet of newsprint. Give each participant several green and brown leaves. Encourage participants to write on the green leaves ways they have grown, new insights they have gained and things they have especially enjoyed about the retreat. Tape the green leaves on the branches. Ask participants to write on the brown leaves things that need improvement. Tape these around the base of the tree.

Take the "question/feeling" walls home and post them in your youth room. Read the comments for additional insights into the participants' retreat experiences.

22

A Water Weekend

By Mitch Olson

The Bible is full of stories about water: creation, Noah and the flood, Jesus changing water to wine, Jesus and the woman at the well, Jesus washing the disciples' feet, and so on. A Water Weekend focuses on these stories, as well as gives everyone a fun, refreshing time together.

During this retreat, the participants will:

● enjoy all kinds of water activities;

Retreat Schedule

Friday
8:00 p.m. Arrive and take luggage to cabins
8:30 p.m. Welcome and Gargle Games
9:30 p.m. Water Collage
10:30 p.m. Devotions
11:00 p.m. Refreshments
Midnight Lights out

Saturday
8:00 a.m. Breakfast
9:00 a.m. Camp Explorations
10:00 a.m. Exploration Conversation
11:00 a.m. Water: Creation, Destruction, Promise
Noon Lunch
1:00 p.m. Water-skiing, swimming, canoeing, fishing and suntanning

3:00 p.m. Planned group water games such as water volleyball, water balloon fights, water polo, etc.
5:00 p.m. Dinner
6:00 p.m. Water: Strength, Compassion, Celebration
7:00 p.m. Television Topics
8:00 p.m. Meet with whole group to go view sunset together. Eat watermelon afterward
11:00 p.m. Lights out

Sunday
8:00 a.m. Breakfast
9:00 a.m. Baptism and Living Water
10:00 a.m. Footwashing Service
11:00 a.m. Pack and leave for home

- learn about various Bible references and stories which include water; and
- relax and enjoy this refreshing resource God has given us.

Before the Retreat—Schedule this weekend at a camp that is near a lake. This retreat is written as if you would do it in the summer. So plan activities such as water-skiing, swimming, canoeing, fishing, and so on. If you plan to water-ski and swim, recruit experienced adults to help drive the boat and lifeguard. Prior to the retreat ask a nurse or doctor to come to youth group and teach kids the basics of first aid and water safety.

Ask kids to bring swim suits, towels, suntan lotion, sunscreen and a canteen filled with water. Gather several bottles of mouthwash (for prizes), a piece of posterboard, markers, large bowl, towel, watermelon and garden hose. Each person will need a Bible, concordance, sheet of blue construction paper, aluminum foil, glue, scissors and copy of the handout.

Activities in this retreat can be varied according to the season. For example, in the winter, plan to ice skate, build snowmen, have snowball fights and cross-country ski. Ask kids to dress warmly and bring along some skates.

_____ Retreat Ingredients _____

FRIDAY

Gargle Games—Start off the evening by playing a few crowd-breakers. Try to play games that go along with the theme of "water." For example, give everyone a glass of water and have gargling contests. See who can gargle the loudest, the softest, or the longest. Then gather in groups of threes and give each group a few minutes to think of a familiar tune. Rather than singing the tune, they must "gargle" it. One at a time, let each small group gargle its melody. Let the others try to guess the tune. Award bottles of mouthwash for the best garglers.

Water Collage—Tell the group members that since the theme of the retreat is water, they're going to decorate the room with pictures of water. Give the group members each a sheet of blue construction paper, aluminum foil, glue and scissors. Have them each create a water picture; for example, the blue construction paper could represent a lake and the aluminum foil could represent waves. While they are working away on their artistic endeavors, make a sign from posterboard that says "Water—God's Gift to Us." Hang it on the wall. When the kids are finished, hang their water pictures around the sign. The Water Collage will be a weekend long reminder of the retreat theme.

Devotions—Sing songs about water; for example, "Deep and wide, deep and wide. There's a fountain flowing deep and wide."

Gather the kids in a circle. One at a time have them tell one of their first memories of water (like swimming lessons, getting caught in a rainstorm). Say: "Water affects our lives in so many ways. We use it for recreation, we use it to clean, we need it to survive. Water was also a major theme throughout the Bible."

Give everyone a Bible and a concordance. Have them find as many places as they can where water is mentioned. When someone finds a passage, have him or her read it. Let everyone have a chance to participate. Tell them they will be learning more about some of these stories throughout the retreat.

Gather in a circle and have the kids each complete this sentence: "Water is . . . " Answers could be "Water is refreshing," "Water is life-giving" or "Water is thirst-quenching." Close with a prayer thanking God for water. Then serve ice water for refreshments!

SATURDAY

Camp Explorations—Gather in small groups of three or four participants. Tell them they have one hour to hike and explore the area. Ask them to notice anything that has to do with water; for example, the lake is water, trees depend on water, clouds are filled with moisture, etc.

Exploration Conversation—Gather around the lake side and discuss the explorations. Ask:

● What sights did you discover during your hike?

● What things did you notice that have to do with water?

● What areas do you want to enjoy during your free time at this retreat?

Water: Creation, Destruction, Promise—Meet by the lake for this session. Make sure all participants have their canteens filled with water. The kids will learn about water as it was first seen in creation, during the flood, and as a promise. Have the kids open their canteens and be prepared to drink the water during the reading.

Creation—Ask a person to read Genesis 1:1-27. Have the listeners count the number of times the word "water" is read. Each time the word water is read, the kids all take a gulp of their water from their canteen. Ask: "Were you surprised at the number of times water was mentioned? What do you think the water represents in the creation story?"

Destruction—Ask several people to read Genesis 6—8. Relive the flood experience by "making rain" with everyone. While Genesis 6 is read, have the kids brush the palms of their hands back and forth; while Genesis 7:1-10 is read, have them snap their fingers; while Genesis 7:11-24 is read, have them clap their hands loudly; while Genesis 8:1-5 is read, have them snap their fingers; while Genesis 8:6-11 is read, have them brush their palms back and forth; while the rest of Genesis 8 is read, have them listen.

After listening to the stormy story, discuss these questions:

● Why do you think water was used to destroy creation?

● What sins and evil preceded the flood?

● How do you think Noah felt when God told him about the upcoming flood?

● How do you think the people felt when they saw Noah building the ark? Did the people take Noah seriously? Did they take God seriously? Do we take God seriously today?

Promise—Take the kids by the garden hose. Ask someone to read Genesis 9:12-17. As the verses are read, spray a light mist with the hose to create a rainbow. First spray the water mist in the darkness of shade (where no rainbow appears); then make a rainbow in the light of the sun. After the reading, contrast how Christ's love is like the sun on the mist. His warm presence comforts us in cloudy, sad times. Ask these questions:

● When was the last time you saw a rainbow?

● Why did God make this covenant?

● Is God holding his part of the bargain today? Explain.

● Compare today with the time of Noah. How are things the same? different?

Water: Strength, Compassion, Celebration—Gather in small groups of four to five participants. Give each group a Bible, and give each person a pencil and a Strength, Compassion, Celebration handout. Have the participants each complete the handout, then discuss the answers in their small group.

Television Topics—Divide into small groups; assign each one of the passages discussed so far during the retreat. Give the group members 30 minutes to think of how they can present their stories television-style in the form of a commercial, news bulletin, soap opera or western. An example of a news bulletin on the flood could begin, "There is a flash flood warning for all areas. Repeat. There is a flash flood warning for all areas. Climb to safety . . ." Let each group present its TV topic.

SUNDAY

Baptism and Living Water—Ask two volunteers to read John

Strength, Compassion, Celebration

Strength—Read Psalm 1:1-6, then answer these questions:
● How does the "tree planted by streams of water" show strength?

● Does God's Word flow through you like that? Explain.

● Trees need water to grow fruit and leaves. How does God's Word affect your growth and your decisions?

Compassion—Read Matthew 10:40-42, then answer these questions:
● When have you shown compassion like the one in the text who offered a cup of cold water?

● Has someone shown compassion to you this weekend? last week?

Describe the experience.

● Why does Christ want us to treat others with compassion?

● Fill in the blanks: "I will show compassion to (name of a person)
_____, on (date)_____, by
(action) _____.

Celebration—Read John 2:1-11, then answer these questions:
● Why did Jesus attend the wedding?

● How did Jesus happen to be asked for a miracle?

● Why do you think he changed water to wine? Why not change milk to wine?

● Is Jesus concerned with our recreation time like he was with the bride and groom's? Explain.

3:5; 4:10-15. Ask:
● Why does Jesus say that we should be born of the "water" and the Spirit? Why not just "Spirit"?
● Do we observe this in our church? When? How?
● What did Jesus mean by "living water"?

● Do we seek "living water" today? Explain.

Pass around a bowl of water. One at a time, have the kids dip their fingers in it and touch their foreheads. Say: "Remember your baptism. Remember Jesus is the living water."

Footwashing Service—Bring the towel, and gather everyone by the lake side. (If you are unable to meet near a lake, gather around a large bowl of water.) Read John 13:1-20. Then explain: "Jesus used water to demonstrate servanthood by washing the disciples' feet. This is a special opportunity to do as Jesus did. Remember how Peter responded in verse eight when he saw no need for washing his feet. But Jesus said we all must be washed if we are to be with him. I will now wash your feet."

Wipe off excess water with a towel. Ask a volunteer to wash your feet. Gather in a circle and link arms. Close with this prayer: "We thank you Lord for your example of the servant lifestyle, that you humbled yourself and washed your disciples' feet. Thank you for the gift of water, for the role it plays throughout history and throughout our lives. Help us go home from this retreat refreshed and ready to love and serve one another, as you did. Amen."

Section Five

Faith

23

CROSSroads: A Retreat and a Journey

By Nancy Going

Reflections: Who am I? What do I think? How do I feel? How does God operate within my life?

In our fast-paced lives, many everyday events and decisions simply rush past us. We don't take time to recognize God's action around us. We need quiet time alone, and time with just a few friends, to make ourselves thankful for the gifts God has given us.

Use this retreat to help your young people:

● experience the journey to which Christ calls us;

● develop a faith that grows, moves and stretches as they seek to follow the one who calls himself "the way, the truth and the life";

● recognize the impact of the cross on the decisions they make; and

● recognize that their maturity, freedom and decision-making affects the rest of their lives.

This retreat is written for a camp weekend or a retreat setting; however, it would be especially effective as an accompaniment to a trip. The journey would become real.

As leaders, we need to recognize the difficulty of activities like journaling, reflecting and just being alone. Help your young people enjoy life's journey!

Before the Retreat—During this retreat each person will be using a Journey Book in which he or she records reflections and thoughts. You should provide each person with a cardboard file folder and a set of Journey Sheets, prepared from the Journey Book outline shown at the end of this retreat. (Allow at least one page for each Journey Sheet.)

This retreat calls for young people to spend time alone with their Journey Books and then to share within groups of three or four.

These groups (or Road Crews) will spend most of the weekend together. Very little of the weekend's activity is done with the total group. To assist the grouping process, structure events during the first evening to build community within the smaller groups.

Assign individuals to Road Crews of three or four people. Consciously structure the crews around age and personality factors. Assign yourself and other adult leaders to crews as well. Since the youth group will spend most of the weekend working in these crews, look for the most optimal pairings possible.

At the retreat center, you could incorporate the element of "journeying" by arranging a series of field trips. Expose kids to new sights or experiences. Don't let their experiences run right by them. Provide additional pages in their Journey Books and allow time for reflection on what they've seen and heard.

If you limit the journey to the retreat center, arrange to meet at different locations for each group session. Help the group experience the movement that goes with a journey.

Each participant should bring a Bible, plus pencils or a pen. Each crew will need a copy of the Problem Situations sheet to be used in Pit Stop 2. In addition, you will need to gather old magazines, glue, scissors, posterboard, markers, pins, a stapler for each crew and sticks for signs.

Retreat Schedule

Friday
5:30 p.m. Journey Preparation
6:00 p.m. Journey
7:00 p.m. Arrival and unpacking
7:15 p.m. Road Crew Preparation
8:30 p.m. Break
8:45 p.m. Pit Stop 1
9:45 p.m. Touring the *ways* of
each Road Crew
10:15 p.m. Snacks and free time
11:30 p.m. Journaling in Journey
Books
Midnight Lights out

Saturday
8:00 a.m. Breakfast
9:30 a.m. Pit Stop 2

11:30 a.m. Free time
Noon Lunch
1:00 p.m. Crew Activity Time
5:30 p.m. Dinner
7:00 p.m. Pit Stop 3
9:30 p.m. Free time
11:30 p.m. Journaling in Journey
Books
Midnight Lights out

Sunday
8:00 a.m. Breakfast
9:30 a.m. Pit Stop 4
11:00 a.m. Journey Worship
Noon Lunch
1:00 p.m. Pack up and return
home

The beginning activity in Journey Preparation will require your creativity in providing materials for the crews' uniforms. Some suggestions include miscellaneous clothing (hats, bandannas, T-shirts), newspaper, construction paper, safety pins, straight pins, staplers, etc. Your imagination is your only limitation!

Retreat Ingredients

FRIDAY

Journey Preparation—After the vehicles are packed, ask the group to meet in the youth room. (Be sure the items for uniform preparation are already in place.) Briefly explain the purpose of the retreat and how most of it will take place in Road Crews.

Pass out Journey Sheet 1 with crew assignments and directions for the activity. Allow 15 minutes for the crews to create their uniforms. When everyone has finished, meet again as a total group to share each group's creativity. Ask all participants to enter their vehicles and hand Journey Sheet 1 to the driver as a ticket. Begin your journey.

Road Crew Preparation—Provide each retreat member with a cardboard file folder. Tell the group this will be the cover for their CROSSroads Journey Books that they will be working in for most of their time together.

Ask participants to spend the next half-hour decorating these covers with the materials provided (magazines, scissors, glue and markers). Each person should create at least 10 pictures or designs that describe characteristics of his or her personality. These pictures or words should describe how the individual spends his or her time, not just what he or she likes to do. They should also describe the role that faith plays in the individual's life.

At the end of the time period or when most are finished, send crews to different areas of the room or building. It is important for crews to spend this time alone, with no distractions from members of other crews. Instruct crews to share their covers in detail.

Pass out Journey Sheet 2 and complete. While the crews are still in small groups, pass out Journey Sheet 3. Ask the small groups to work together on this sheet and be prepared to share their creation.

After 30 minutes or when most are finished, ask the crews to return to the total group and have fun sharing their Crew Theme Song.

Use a few minutes to clarify any plans or details of the weekend with the group. Encourage the group to reflect on what they saw happening that evening. Read Genesis 12:1-9. Then close by saying, "Just as God called Abraham out of his home to a new land, he calls us to trust him, and be on the road with him. We want to spend this weekend discovering what it means to be traveling with God.''

Ask individuals to place all of their Journey Sheets in their Journey Books in order. Then pass out packets containing the remainder of the Journey Sheets so individuals can add to their Journey Books before the rest of the retreat goes on.

Pit Stop 1—All participants should have their Journey Books, Bibles, and a pencil or pen. Crews should have posterboard, markers, staplers, pins and sticks available.

This activity is designed to help participants reflect on the roads they travel. It should describe their journey of faith, and how they have learned from the Savior who calls himself ''the way, the truth and the life.''

After participants return from their break, take some time for singing and solving any large-group concerns. Then send crews off to work on Journey Sheets 4-8. Some crews may finish earlier than others. Let them know that's okay, but stress the importance of staying together and away from other crews until every group is finished.

Close the evening by having each crew progressively tour the ways of the other crews prepared from Journey Sheet 8. Each crew should end their tour at their own site and close the evening with prayer. Youth leaders should remind their group members to read and journal with Journey Sheet 9 before going to sleep.

SATURDAY

Pit Stop 2—Individuals should bring their Journey Books, Bibles, and pencils or pens. Each crew should have a Problem Situation sheet.

Tell the group, ''Today is our day at the CROSSroads. Today we look at decisions and how we make them. We will look again at important events in our lives and investigate the impact the cross has had on those times.

The psalmist wrote his poems as he struggled with himself, God and his personal decisions.'' Ask one of the group to read Psalm 130.

Continue by saying, ''Now is the time for each of us to spend some time alone. Complete Journey Sheets 10-12 and return to your crew sites at 10:15 a.m. or when you hear the signal.

''Each crew will have a Problem Situations sheet. Follow the directions on your sheet. Return to the large group at 11 a.m. or when you hear the signal.''

Crew Activity Time—During the first two hours each crew must make a group decision about how they want to spend their time. The only requirement is that each crew must arrange an activity for the to-

Problem Situations

1. Spend about 15 minutes sharing personal responses to Journal Sheets 10-12.
2. Read through the situations below and decide which of the three your group would like to discuss.
3. Come to a group decision about the problem you choose.
4. Appoint a spokesperson to report on your group's struggle and final decision.
5. Return to the total group and share with the other groups.

Situation #1
You are a high school senior, trying to decide where you will go to college and what your major will be. You have just completed a battery of tests which reveal a natural aptitude for a degree in engineering. You know that being an engineer can take you places and provide good money because your dad is an engineer. He has encouraged and supported your studies, and you have enjoyed all the technical courses you have taken in high school. You recently visited your state's technical college and found it to be a great place with an excellent reputation. In fact, you have just received your notice of acceptance, and your father is very proud.

You've also been active in your youth group throughout high school. You have participated in the outreach program of your church, and you've experienced a deep sense of commitment to God as you've reached out to serve others. You feel drawn to a profession directly involved with the lives and needs of other people. And you know the Lord has called you to share with others the gifts you have been given. At a recent youth convention held at your church-related college, you visited with some professors about their social work program, and it sounded interesting. You have to decide soon, but you feel torn. What would you do?

Situation #2
Your friend has become an alcoholic. It was hard to see at first, but you know it's true. You've been friends a long time. She always seemed to be a

tal group to experience something they've never done before. (Skydiving anyone?) Offer a series of choices. Suggestion: One crew might plan a mini-olympics with unique events where the crews will compete against one another.

Be realistic, using resources available. The last hour and a half will be used for the crews' planned activities. Encourage a positive attitude with your own enthusiastic participation.

Pit Stop 3—Participants will need their Journey Books, Bibles, pencils or pens. For this session it is important to move the whole group to a new location. Choose a peaceful environment, perhaps a normal kid with normal problems, even though she was never too sure of herself. About a year ago she started dating a guy, hanging around with all his friends and going to lots of parties. You could understand her drinking once in a while at parties, but it got to be every weekend, all weekend, then during the week.

Several months ago this guy broke up with her, and now she's drinking even more. She tries to hide it from you, but you know when she's been drinking, and she's drinking a lot. You've tried to talk with her. But she keeps saying it isn't a problem—and she's got it under control. You know her parents pretty well, but you don't want to squeal. Her grades are slipping, and she doesn't seem to care about anything. A lot of her other friends have stopped calling and seeing her, but she's a special friend to you. What should you do?

Situation #3

It's your family. You really love them, but they are doing it to you again! They're moving, and it's your senior year! You and your friends started planning for this year three years ago when you moved here as a freshman. You've become extremely close to these friends, and you've looked forward to the things you want to do together.

Your mom and dad are really understanding about your feelings. That's what makes it so difficult. They called your best friend's parents who volunteered to let you live with them for your senior year. But your parents have also let you know they're having a hard time. They know this is the last year you'll be at home, and they really would like to share your senior year with you. You get along great with your family, and you know you'd miss them a lot. The city where they are going also sounds fun and exciting. They say the decision is yours. What will you do?

graveyard, a closed restaurant or a large auditorium. You want a place in which individuals can quietly look at their lives in perspective. Perhaps they can think of themselves in relation to nature. Perhaps they can look at the lives of friends and relatives who have gone before them.

Introduce this session by saying, "As we struggle with our own lives at the CROSSroads, as we strive to make decisions, we need to ask, 'What is the will of God for me in this particular situation?' We may wonder how we can know. Yet there are ways that help us feel confident about the decisions we make. We can also assure ourselves that God is walking with us through this process.''

Ask participants to turn to Journey Sheet 13, and read silently as you list the suggested "ways" we can get help in our decision-making. Inform the group they will spend the next couple of hours working through this process, both alone and together.

Explain that individuals should separate themselves from each other for 15 minutes. They should take their Journey Books and pencils so they can record their personal thoughts. Ask them to focus on an issue in their life about which they have been trying or needing to make a decision. This struggle does *not* have to be a big one. It could be any situation in which a decision needs to be made and this process can be used. Ask them to work through Journey Sheets 14 and 15. After their time alone, each crew should meet at their designated positions and share their reflections.

When this sharing is complete, ask the crew members to move away from each other again and work through Journey Sheets 16-21. After 30 minutes all small groups should meet again to discuss these Journey Sheets. This meeting is critical for sharing specific corcerns, struggles and needs for support.

SUNDAY

Pit Stop 4—Each participant will need a Journey Book, a Bible and a pencil or pen. Ask Road Crews to work together through Journey Sheets 22-24 and plan their part of the Journey Worship. (Each crew will be given its assignment at this session.)

Journey Worship—Close your weekend with a total group Journey Worship. Assign each Road Crew to prepare a part of the worship: the scripture lessons, music, prayers, communion, confession and absolution or the benediction. Ask each crew to pick a different location for their part of the worship. The whole group should journey from place to place as you worship.

You may want to construct your Journey Worship for along the way home. Choose different sites along the way for each part of the worship. For example, you could read the scripture lessons at a gas station. Reflect on how God's Word can fill us and our lives. You might testify to God's healing power by doing confession and absolution in front of a hospital. You could also stop for prayers at a telephone booth and talk about our connection to God.

Encourage your group to use Journey Sheet 25 sometime during the next week.

The CROSSroads Journey Book

Use 8½×11 paper for the Journey Sheets. When there is more than one activity on a page, allow space in between for writing.

Journey Sheet 1

Name
Crew Number

1. The number for your crew is at the top of the page below your name.
2. Each crew member should autograph the other crew members' Journey Sheet.
3. Make or find crew uniforms from the materials on the table. When your crew is dressed in its uniforms, return to the total group to share your creativity.
4. After everyone has shared, enter your vehicle for the journey. Your uniform and completed Journey Sheet are your ticket for your ride to the retreat site.

Journey Sheet 2

Write the name of each crew member across the top of your page. Reflect on five new things you have learned about each of your crew members. Identify these new things by writing them underneath their names.

Journey Sheet 3

Together, write a Crew Theme Song to a familiar tune. Each person should write the words on this sheet.

Journey Sheet 4

Try to reflect on what you're seeing and feeling here at this place. How is it different from what you see and feel at home? How do you feel about those differences? Write your observations and feelings here.
(Add extra paper.)

Journey Sheet 5

Take time this evening to share with your fellow crew members about the road you travel. Begin by completing the following statements:
For me, the toughest thing about school is: (circle three)

a. getting up early
b. hassles from my parents
c. boredom
d. homework
e. getting along with teachers

f. making friends
g. feeling lonely
h. popularity
i. grades
j. pressure

*Place a star next to the one that is toughest!

When I go to new places, I am usually: (circle three)

a. afraid
b. excited
c. unsure of myself
d. shy
e. pretty worried
f. wishing I were home

g. feeling lonely
h. taking everything as it comes
i. crazier than I am at home
j. acting tough
k. happier

*Put a star next to how you feel now.

Share this sheet and Journey Sheet 4 with your crew.

Journey Sheet 6

1. Make a continuum of your life, where you've been and where you're going. (See example below.) You'll want to note at least 10 milestones or important events along the way.

2. Go through your continuum a second time and mark places where your faith has had a special impact.

3. Share this continuum with your crew.

Journey Sheet 7

In many Roman Catholic cemeteries or churches, you see "stations of the cross." These are stopping points where you can pause and reflect on scenes from Jesus' last days. Some of those scenes are:

Jesus before Pilate
The Last Supper
The betrayal in the Garden
Peter denies Jesus
Joseph carries Jesus' cross
The Crucifixion
Jesus is buried

1. Choose at least two of these scenes that have a special impact on you. Take time to write about them here. (Add extra paper.)

2. Share your thoughts with your crew.

Journey Sheet 8

1. What does it mean to follow Jesus? He calls himself "the way, the truth and the life."

What was that "way" for him?

What does it mean for us?

2. Divide these passages from Luke among your crew. Read and respond to what each one says about Jesus' way or the way to follow him.

Luke 3:21-22   Luke 9:1-6
Luke 4:1-13   Luke 9:23
Luke 4:16-19   Luke 10:29-37
Luke 6:12   Luke 19:28-44
Luke 7:11-17   Luke 23:26-56
Luke 8:1-3   Luke 24:1-12

3. Now as a crew, make a path or a way from the group's central meeting place to where your crew has been meeting. Fill the path with road signs and symbols of Jesus' way, and what it means to follow him.

Journey Sheet 9

Before going to sleep, read Ephesians 4:1-6 to yourself. Reflect on what it means to be "one" with others along the journey. Write your thoughts here.

Journey Sheet 10

Describe two difficult decisions you've had to make lately: Try to think of one that turned out to be a "good" decision and one that was a "bad" decision.
Were your decisions based on feelings, facts or both?
What made your decision "good"?
What made your decision "bad"?
Can you think of any way you could have altered the manner in which you made your decision?

Journey Sheet 11

Draw a cartoon to help you reflect on and describe how you go about making a decision. What kind of process is it for you? Try to be as specific as possible.

Journey Sheet 12

Read Psalm 130 again. What were some of the feelings the psalmist seemed to struggle with in making his decisions? List them here.
*Put a star next to the feelings with which you struggle.

Journey Sheet 13

There are several ways to know the mind of God when we make decisions.
(These suggestions are taken from the January 1, 1986 issue of The Lutheran. The article is "God's Will for My Life?" written by Herbert W. Chilstrom.)
Read scripture.
Pray.
Talk to friends.
Write out your options.
Go to a place where you can look at yourself in perspective.
Use common sense.

1. Which of these ways appeals to you?
2. Which of these ways do you use?
3. Do you have any additional suggestions or revisions to this list?
4. How do your additions work for you?
(Add extra paper.)

Journey Sheet 14

Decision making: Take five minutes to answer the following questions individually:
When I make decisions, I usually struggle with . . .
To what or whom does the psalmist turn to find strength?
To what or whom do you turn when making a decision?
Share your findings with the rest of your crew.

Journey Sheet 15

Discoveries: Fill in these sentence stems. Share them with your crew.
When it comes to making a decision, I've learned that I . . .
When it comes to making a decision in a group, I . . .
When I am standing at a CROSSroads, God is usually . . .
Something I learned from the situations this morning is . . .

Journey Sheet 16

Read some scripture. Rather than open your Bible, point to a verse and expect it to speak to you or your situation, start with a favorite passage or a story. Don't expect flashes of instant wisdom! Use your reading as a basis for further reflection.
1. Share with your crew the scripture you read.
2. What response(s) did you have to your reading?
3. Were there any surprises or new understanding in the familiar?
4. Did you discover anything of which you weren't already aware?

Journey Sheet 17

Pray. Do that now. Go off by yourself and talk to God about a decision you need to make. Make this the beginning of your conversations with him on this subject.

Journey Sheet 18

Go where you can see yourself in perspective. That's why we're here.
Take a walk. Go sit on a rock. Curl up on a blanket. Reflect on your need to make a decision and fill in these sentence stems:
When I look around me now, I think . . .
When I think about this decision, I . . .
Right now, I sense God's presence in . . .
When I look at my whole life and this decision, I think . . .
Share these reflections with your crew at the end of this session.

Journey Sheet 19

Write out your options. List all the possible pluses and minuses for each side of your decision.

———— (+) ————   ———— (-) ————

Be prepared to share your options with the rest of your crew.

Journey Sheet 20

Talk to friends. When you're back together with your crew, spend time with each crew member sharing Journal Sheets 18 and 19. At this point it is extremely important

not to tell other crew members what you think they should do. Each person needs the freedom to make his or her own decision—with God's help. This is a good time to:
- help an individual think of additional options,
- bring up things he or she might have missed and
- help an individual examine the decision he or she must make in the perspective of the rest of his or her life.

Journey Sheet 21

Use common sense. Rely on what feels right after you have done all the suggested activities and feel confident that God is with you.

My decision is:

Pray for each person in your crew and the decisions that have been made.

Journey Sheet 22

What do you want to tell your family and friends about this trip? Why?

Journey Sheet 23

Autograph sheet. Sign one another's Journey Books. Write something you'd like to tell each one before you go home. Take time to respond to each other's messages, especially if some are unclear.

Journey Sheet 24

You have spent this time on a personal journey. Like most journeys you may have mixed feelings about its beginning and its end. Now is a good time to reflect on what this particular journey meant to you.
1. When do journeys end?
2. When does this journey end?
3. How is this an ending?
4. How is this a beginning?

Share your final reflections with your crew.

Journey Sheet 25

Take time after you are home again to think about your weekend and your decision. Record your thoughts and feelings about how your decision is going. Think about what you need to do to make your decision work for you.

24

Day by Day

By Ben Sharpton

Being a Christian is a daily process involving three specific areas of growth: understanding, love and service. Sometimes being a Christian seems like hard work, but if we trust God as we live one day at a time, we can do it.

Use this retreat to help participants:

- deepen their faith and commitment;
- realize that being a Christian is a day-by-day process; and
- develop understanding, love and service in their lives.

Before the Retreat—Learning does not take place in a vacuum. For this reason, several community-building strategies are offered at the beginning of each session to help your group members get to know one another. These are great opportunities to let your young people know and trust you better and for you to learn more about your kids.

An excellent theme song to use with this retreat is "Day by Day" from the musical *Godspell*. The words to this song and the words to all suggested songs for this retreat are found in *Songs* (Songs and Creations, Inc.).

Be creative and informative as you publicize the retreat in your church newsletter, bulletin and mailers. You could announce the retreat during the Sunday morning worship session in your church. Have your youth choir sing the song "Day by Day," then hum it as a young person announces the retreat. Request people to pray for this retreat, asking for God's guidance and power in the participants' lives.

Gather pencils, paper, markers, 3×5 cards, newsprint, tape, Bibles, construction paper and copies of all handouts. You also will need a few current calendars.

Read the retreat and write all designated discussion questions and the Love Chart on newsprint.

On separate sheets of construction paper write each of these letters: A,B,C,D,E.

An optional activity for Friday night is to show the movie *God-*

spell. Bring a film projector, screen and popcorn if you decide to do this!

Ask the kids to come prepared to have a lip-sync contest with their favorite Christian song. Have them supply the music and costumes. Bring a prize for each singer like throat lozenges or gargle.

Retreat Schedule

Friday
7:00 p.m. Arrive at camp and settle in
7:30 p.m. Day by Day
9:00 p.m. Show the movie *Godspell*
11:00 p.m. In cabins
11:30 p.m. Lights out

Saturday
8:00 a.m. Breakfast
9:00 a.m. See Thee More Clearly: Reason to Live
11:00 a.m. Free time
Noon Lunch
1:00 p.m. Planned recreation (softball, volleyball, etc.)

3:00 p.m. Putting on the Gospel Hits
5:30 p.m. Dinner
7:30 p.m. Love Thee More Dearly: Reason to Love
9:30 p.m. Snacks and free time
11:30 p.m. Lights out

Sunday
8:00 a.m. Breakfast
9:00 a.m. Follow Thee More Nearly: Reason to Give
10:30 a.m. Clean cabins and pack
11:30 a.m. Lunch, then leave for home

——————— Retreat Ingredients ———————

FRIDAY

Day by Day—During this session you will concentrate on knowing what it means to establish a day-to-day relationship with God. This is the foundation for the rest of the retreat.

Along the walls of the meeting room, tape the five construction-paper sheets which each contain a letter. These will be used during the last part of this session. Also post several sheets of newsprint on which you have written the discussion questions needed for this session.

Sing some lively songs like "Walkin' in the Light," "Country Roads" or "Sing Alleluia." Make announcements and explain the rules for the weekend.

Pass around the calendars and ask the participants to figure out what day their birthday will fall on this year. If you have enough young people, divide them into seven groups according to these days (Mondays, Tuesdays, etc.). If you have less than 30 in your group, combine the weekdays (all Monday and Tuesday people in the first group; all Wednesday and Thursday people in the second group, etc.). Make sure that there is at least one adult in each small group.

Have each small group form a circle, then find the person whose birthday is closest to today. Starting with this person, ask everyone to share their answer to the first question. Then ask the next question, and allow everyone time to share, and so on. Here are the questions:

- What is your name? grade? favorite fast-food restaurant?
- What is your favorite amusement park?
- What is your favorite time of day?
- What is your favorite holiday?
- If you could vacation any place in the world, where would you go?

Pass out pencils and copies of the Daily Schedule Sheet to each person. Give kids time to answer the questions, and then find as many similarities as they can in each group. (How many people wake up at 6:30 a.m.? How many people brush their teeth with Colgate?) Give each small group time to complete and share the answers.

Daily Schedule Sheet

In the space provided, write a time when you usually participate in that activity.	In the space provided, write the name of the product you use.
Sleep:	Alarm clock:
Wake up:	Toothpaste:
Brush your teeth:	Breakfast cereal:
Breakfast:	Deodorant:
Lunch:	Pop or soda:
Supper:	Shampoo:
Bathe/shower:	Hand lotion:
Watch television:	Toilet paper:
Talk on the phone:	
Go to sleep:	

Compare your answers with the others in your group!

Lead the kids in singing "Day by Day." Now, instruct all participants to share their answers to each of these questions in their small groups:

● What color best describes the *feeling* you received while singing this song?

● Which line do you like the most?

● What time of day comes to mind when you think of this song?

● Have you ever heard this song? If so, can you remember when you first heard it and where?

Pass out copies of the Personal Survey to each individual. Ask the young people to fill out the survey, and tell them *not* to place their name on their paper. When everyone has finished, collect these surveys. After this session is over, tally the surveys and prepare the percentages for the Sunday session.

Personal Survey

Do not sign your name. Complete the following questionnaire by checking the appropriate boxes or by filling in the blanks.

A Christian is:

☐ Someone who is good and goes to church
☐ Someone who believes in God
☐ Someone who is born again
☐ Someone who reads the Bible and prays a lot

What is the best reason for someone to be a Christian?

☐ To help others	☐ To go to heaven
☐ To love God	☐ To avoid hell
☐ To join a church	☐ To make God happy
☐ To find happiness	☐ Other _____

List as many reasons as you can that explain why people don't become Christians:

_____   _____

_____   _____

Are you a Christian?   ☐ yes   ☐ no   ☐ I don't know

Why? _____

_____

What difference should a day-to-day relationship with God make in one's life?

_____

_____

Gather all small groups. Explain: "I'm going to ask you to share your opinions by answering a few multiple choice questions. (Point out the five letters you have hung around the room.) After I read a question, you are to go and stand under the appropriate letter, indicating your answer."

1. My opinion of the camp facilities:
   a. Great
   b. Good
   c. Okay
   d. Fair
   e. Ugh

2. My opinion of the camp food:
   a. Great
   b. Good
   c. Okay
   d. Fair
   e. Ugh

3. My opinion of what it is like to begin a daily relationship with God:
   a. Like a sunrise: gradual, almost imperceptible
   b. Like a bolt of lightning: electrifying
   c. Like a flowing stream: no beginning or end
   d. Like the Rocky Mountains: lots of peaks and valleys
   e. Like the Grand Canyon: breathtaking

4. Now, read Mark 8:22-25. Ask the members of your group to compare their spiritual pilgrimages with the blind man in the story. Where do they see themselves right now?
   a. Still groping around in the darkness
   b. Vision is blurry
   c. See clearly
   d. Don't know
   e. Choose not to say

Ask each person to share what it means to be a Christian. Close in prayer, asking God to become more real to each person on this retreat.

SATURDAY

See Thee More Clearly: Reason to Live—Young people will

learn how a deeper relationship with God provides a purpose and meaning to life.

Post the lists of Sentence Philosophies and discussion questions in a place where everyone can see.

Your group may be tired, so work to keep them awake. Sing songs like "Ah-la-la-la-la-la-la-la-le-lu-jah," "Look All Around You" and "I Am the Resurrection." Share any special announcements.

Play the Sit-Down Game. Instruct everyone to stand up. Say that you will read the following statements. If one applies to them, have them sit down.

—Your nose is crooked
—Your socks don't match
—You have a bottle opener with you
—You're ticklish
—You believe in kissing *on* the first date
—You believe in necking *before* the first date
—You wear flannel pajamas in the winter
—You have dandruff
—You walk funny
—Your nose is running

Divide your group into the same small groups you formed last night. Form a circle and ask each person in your group to share something good that has happened to him or her since coming on this retreat. Answers may be serious or humorous. Always give participants the right to pass.

Next, go around the circle and ask each person to share "something good" about the person sitting to his or her right.

Distribute pencils and paper. Draw the group's attention to the list of Sentence Philosophies; read these one at a time. Then instruct the kids each to create their own Sentence Philosophy, indicating their outlook on life. Have them share these with their small group. Here are some Sentence Philosophies:

"Live and let live"
"Go for all the gusto you can get"
"Do unto others as you would have them do unto you"
"Do unto others before they do unto you"
"Give and it shall be given to you"
"Play your hand close to yourself"

Read John 15:1-5. In your own words briefly compare the similarities between the Christian life and a vine, plant or tree. Pass out several sheets of newsprint and markers to each group and ask the kids each to draw a plant that symbolizes their spiritual pilgrimage. If some people are stumped, give examples of what you mean: a pine tree reaching toward the sky; an oak tree with strong roots; a fragile flower. Post these newsprints around the room.

Read Micah 6:6-8. Have each group explore the meaning found in these verses by answering the questions which you have posted on newsprint.

● What does this passage indicate that God is least concerned with?

● What is God most concerned with?

● What does it mean to act justly, to love mercy and to walk humbly with your God?

● How would your life differ if you obeyed this passage?

Have small groups brainstorm to list items that help promote spiritual growth. Call these ideas Spiritual Fertilizer and describe them in terms that might be associated with horticulture. For instance, someone might suggest that we need "Proper PH Prayer" or "Balanced Bible Study." After creating their lists, have each group rank them in order of importance. Finally, have each group share their lists with the rest of the group.

Ask volunteers to tell how a personal relationship with God can give purpose and meaning in life. Close by having the entire group form one large circle, arms on one another's shoulders. Read Micah 6:6-8 aloud.

Putting on the Gospel Hits—Provide time for this fun activity from *The Return of Try This One* (Group Books). Divide the kids into small groups. Tell them that they will be participating in a lip-sync contest. They have 45 minutes to choose a favorite song, dress in costume and practice. Have a "Christian concert" and award prizes for originality, appearance and "lip-syncability."

Love Thee More Dearly: Reason to Love—During this session you will help young people identify what loving God means and encourage them to show love to others.

Post the Love Chart on the wall at the front of the room with masking tape. Recruit a young person to read the passage from Romans at the end of the session.

Open up the session with more songs and announcements. Choose songs with "love" themes like "They'll Know We Are Christians by Our Love," "We Are a Circle" or "Love Lifted Me."

Pass out 3×5 cards and pencils and ask the kids each to write their name (first and last) on the left side of the card, and their best definition of love on the right side. Ask the participants each to tear their cards in half, handing in the right side (containing their definition of love). Pass these out again, and give everyone time to try to match the definitions with the appropriate person. If the cards fit together perfectly, then you know you've got the right match.

Copy the Love Chart onto newsprint and post it in front of the group. Distribute a pencil, a Bible and a Love Chart to each person. Have kids work in pairs to read the passages and to determine what they say about dealing with God, others or ourselves. After everyone has had sufficient time, ask for volunteers to share their answers. Write their responses in the appropriate boxes on the newsprint Love Chart.

Love Chart			
How should we respond:	**to God?**	**to others?**	**to ourselves?**
Matthew 5:43-47 John 15:5-10 Romans 13:9-10 1 Corinthians 13:4-7 Philippians 2:1-4			

Ask volunteers to tell why it's so hard to accept and show God's love. Have everyone gather in one large circle and place their arms around each other's shoulders. Ask a volunteer to read Romans 12:9-21.

SUNDAY

Follow Thee More Nearly: Reason to Give—During this session you will lead your young people to identify areas in which God is leading them, sharing what their next step of faith will be.

Be prepared to share the percentage statistics from the Personal Surveys used in the first session. Since this session is on Sunday morning, give it a more worshipful atmosphere by singing songs like "Amazing Grace," "Follow Me" or "Jesus My Lord."

Break into small groups and ask each person to share something special that happened to him or her in the last 24 hours. The answers may be humorous or serious, and each person should be allowed to pass.

Supply newsprint, markers, paper and pencils. Distribute a Bible to each small group, ask each group to read Matthew 25:14-30. Give each group one of the following tasks to perform based on this passage:

- Create a short skit depicting this passage
- Rewrite the passage in "modern slang"
- Write a newspaper story about this passage
- Draw a cartoon strip (on newsprint) about the passage
- Write a poem about the passage

Come back together in one large group and share in a litany. After each small group presents its passage interpretation, ask the large group to say, "Help us to give, Lord." Close in a brief prayer.

Share the information from the Personal Surveys given in the first session. Focus on percentages instead of numbers (What percentage said a Christian is someone who believes in God? What percentage said they were Christians?)

"Sketch" an imaginary football field in the front of the room. Show where the 50-yard line, bleachers, bench, showers, cheerleaders, snack bar and goal lines are. Now ask everyone to go and stand on one of the spots indicating where they considered themselves in the "game of faith" before this retreat. Were they involved in the game? Were they sitting on the bench or in the stands? Had they gone to the showers, or were they cheering on other teammates? After everyone stands on the appropriate spot, ask for volunteers to share why they chose that place.

Now ask everyone to stand on a spot that demonstrates where they see themselves right now in the game of faith. Ask for volunteers to share why they chose these places.

Finally, ask for everyone to stand in a place depicting where they would like to be in their faith. Give everyone time to move to the appropriate place, and then ask for individuals to share their reasons for choosing these spots.

Bring the group back together; give the kids each a 3 x 5 card and pencil and ask them to go to a spot by themselves to think about their relationship with God. Ask them to consider where God is leading them right now, and to write that information down on the 3 x 5 card. Tell them *not* to sign their names to the cards, because you will post these responses on a bulletin board when you return home.

After everyone returns from their brief time alone, collect the cards, and close by singing "Day by Day." Round up the kids and head for home, remembering all the meaningful experiences of the past few days.

25

Discipleship—Costs or Rewards?

By Susan Wilke and Cheryl Rude

Jesus calls us to be his disciples. He changes us from ordinary sinners to extraordinary forgiven people. As extraordinary forgiven people we must take up our cross daily and follow Jesus.

Use this retreat to help your kids:
- understand the sacrifices that come with following Jesus;
- understand the rewards that come with following Jesus; and
- know more about God's free gifts of love and forgiveness.

Before the Retreat—Gather paper, pencils, candles, matches, an offering plate, masking tape, a 15-foot piece of string, Bibles and copies of all the handouts.

Retreat Schedule

Friday
7:00 p.m. Arrive at site and settle in
7:30 p.m. Pingpong Plunge
8:00 p.m. Show the movie *The Hiding Place*
10:00 p.m. Discussing the Movie
11:00 p.m. Free time
Midnight Lights out

Saturday
8:00 a.m. Breakfast
9:00 a.m. Cost of Commitment?
11:00 a.m. Free time
Noon Lunch

1:00 p.m. Growing in Commitment
3:00 p.m. Free time for volleyball, softball, football, kickball, hiking, etc.
5:30 p.m. Dinner
7:00 p.m. Counting the Cost
9:00 p.m. Evening Events
11:00 p.m. Free time
Midnight Lights out

Sunday
8:00 a.m. Breakfast Celebration
9:30 a.m. Pack, clean and head for home

For the Pingpong Plunge, you'll need a ladder, several paper cups and five pingpong balls.

For the Breakfast Celebration, tell the adult sponsors they will play the role of servant. They'll serve the kids, clean up afterward, and treat them like royalty. Bring decorations, a cassette tape of Christian music and a tape player. A song that goes along with the theme of this retreat is David Meece's "Count the Cost" from his album of the same name.

Rent *The Hiding Place* from your local video store. Bring video equipment and popcorn for the movie time.

Retreat Ingredients

FRIDAY

Pingpong Plunge—Here's a crazy crowdbreaker for your group members to try once they're settled in at the retreat site. Pingpong Plunge is from *Try This One Strikes Again* (Group Books).

Set up the ladder in the middle of your meeting area, place a cup on the floor in front of it and line up the balls on top of the ladder. Divide your group into pairs and let the fun begin.

Choose one pair to go first. Have one partner kneel on the floor facing the ladder and put the cup in his or her mouth. The other partner climbs the ladder so that his or her face is even with the top of the ladder where the five pingpong balls are lined up. He or she then blows the balls, one at a time, off the ladder and into the cup below. The partner with the cup may freely move about to catch the balls, but must remain kneeling and continue holding the cup in his or her mouth. No hands allowed.

Let all pairs have a try. Keep score. See who can get the most pingpong balls in the cup. Award the pingpong balls to the winners!

Discussing the Movie—After you show the movie *The Hiding Place*, lead a discussion using these questions. Be prepared to handle a mixture of emotions the kids will experience after viewing the movie.

1. Share reactions and feelings about the film.

2. What do you think the Jews were feeling as they lined up to get the stars? How would you feel?

3. In the movie, a Christian pastor said, "We could lose everything for the sake of the child. Christians must obey the law. Think of what you are risking for the sake of one Jewish baby."

What do you think about the preacher's reaction to smuggling the baby? Do you think it would have made a difference to him if the baby was not Jewish? What would you do if you were in his place?

4. While Corrie is giving her nephew numbers that could lead to someone's death, she asks the question, "For Holland, does that make it right?" What do you think?

5. When Corrie is the first imprisoned, the lady who feeds her tells her "The only way to live here is to hate." After the prison guard beats Corrie's sister, her sister says, "Don't hate, Corrie." How do you handle your feelings of anger and hate?

6. Have you ever felt like you would not survive something? What are those feelings like? Where and what is our strength for those times?

7. Corrie and her sister treasured and cherished God's Word so much that they took tremendous risks for it. How do we show that we cherish and treasure God's Word?

8. Are there things in life that you do not understand? If so, what? How do you accept those things?

Close by praying: "God, help us to rejoice always. Comfort us in trying times, and give us your peace that passes all understanding. Amen."

SATURDAY

Cost of Commitment?—Begin by praying for God's guidance during this time. Then say: "Dwight L. Moody, a 19th-century evangelist, was once standing outside a church inviting people to come in to the services. When an 11-year-old boy came along, Moody invited him to the service. The boy looked up and asked, 'How much will it cost me to get in?'

"Moody said, 'Nothing.'

"After a long pause, the boy asked, 'Well, how much will it cost me to get out?'

"This is what we're talking about when we discuss the cost of discipleship. The gift of Christ is free, no strings attached. All we must do is accept him. However, the depth of our commitment is our choice. How much do we want to grow in our commitment?"

Ask a volunteer to read Matthew 19:16-26. Ask the kids these questions:

● What does Jesus tell the rich young ruler he must do to be complete?

● Although the rich man was willing to follow the Ten Commandments, what was he not willing to do?

● Why did he decide not to pay the price?

● What are things Jesus asks us to do when we follow him? Why is it difficult for us to pay the price?

Give kids each a pencil, Bible and an Accountable Christianity handout. Divide them into pairs by saying, "Find a partner with the same color eyes as yours." Have the partners complete the handouts together.

Accountable Christianity

Passage	What are the costs?	rewards?

Matthew 6:14

Matthew 6:25-33

Matthew 10:16-23

Matthew 10:32

Matthew 11:28-30

Matthew 20:26-28

Matthew 24:13

Luke 6:35-36

Luke 21:10-19

John 3:16-21

John 14:27

John 15:16

What are costs we have to pay today to be a Christian? (For example, worship regularly, care for each other.)

The Bible tells us there are many costs to believing in God, yet we also will receive many gifts. An important point to remember is that we are saved by God's grace. We can't earn our way to heaven by "paying" more than others. Read these verses and write them in your own words.
Ephesians 2:8-9

Romans 4:1-5

Romans 5:6-8

Close this session by distributing an I Will Always Remember . . . handout to each person. Have the kids fill in their names and keep the handouts as reminders of God's free gift of forgiveness.

I Will Always Remember . . .

Jesus paid the price for me

_____
(name)

He freely died for me, a sinner.
I am forgiven, a child of God.

Growing in Commitment—Ask a volunteer to read Matthew 4:18-22. Then ask kids to describe the type of people Jesus asked to be his disciples. How are we similar? different? Say: "Jesus made ordinary men extraordinary. The disciples' faith in Christ and their willingness to receive the power of the Holy Spirit changed them from ordinary fishermen to extraordinary witnesses for God. There are many ways God can use us and teach us. Let the Holy Spirit direct you to what he wants you to do. Challenge yourself to be extraordinary."

Distribute a pencil and a Growing in Christ handout to each of the young people. Have them complete the answers. After they finish, have them discuss their answers with a partner. Form pairs by asking kids to find someone with a birthday close to theirs.

Close this session by having kids join hands in a circle, then have them step back as far as they can—stretching the circle, yet still holding on. Say: "Absolutely nothing separates us from God's love." Then have everyone take 10 quick steps to the center of the circle and give a huge hug. Say: "God's love is free. So we should freely love others."

Counting the Cost—Begin by praying for God's guidance in your thoughts during this time. Say: "Everything in life costs something. For example, if you play on a soccer team or in the band, it costs you time, energy and concentration. Think of an activity you participate in, then complete this statement: Right now in my life I 'pay' a lot to . . .''

Growing in Christ

There are many things we can do to grow in our commitment to Christ. Read the following characteristics of a disciple:

_____ 1. A disciple believes in Christ.

_____ 2. A disciple is a learner, an open and teachable person.

_____ 3. A disciple puts Christ first in all areas of his or her life.

_____ 4. A disciple is committed to a pure life—he or she really tries not to sin.

_____ 5. A disciple has regular devotional times and a regular prayer life.

_____ 6. A disciple shares his or her faith.

_____ 7. A disciple learns everything he or she can from the Bible.

_____ 8. A disciple worships God.

_____ 9. A disciple fellowships with other disciples.

_____ 10. A disciple serves and helps others in practical ways.

_____ 11. A disciple gives to God's work and honors him with his or her finances.

_____ 12. A disciple demonstrates the fruit of the Spirit: love, joy, peace, patience, self-control, kindness, goodness, faithfulness and gentleness.

Check the characteristics that are already true in you. Now pick two or three you would like to begin working on. Write down three things you want to do this week to help you move toward these goals:

1.

2.

3.

Let everyone have a chance to complete the sentence. Then say: "What Jesus did for us cost him his life. We know that God's love is free, but following him and living for him involves a cost. In Luke 9:23, Jesus tells us to deny ourselves and take up our cross daily. What does that mean to you?"

Let everyone answer the question, then ask someone to read Luke 14:27-33. Say: "Jesus taught us that there is a cost required in living out the Christian life. We have to sit down and count the cost before we tackle the job. Just like a person who builds a tower, or a person who lays a foundation must count the cost to see if he or she can complete the project. Many people begin the Christian life, but don't finish. Why do they give up? What might following Jesus cost you?"

After everyone answers the questions, distribute Costs handouts and pencils. Have the kids fill in three things they want to do to grow in their faith. For example, be brave and tell others about Christ, worship regularly, etc.

Costs

Three things I want to do to grow in my faith:

1.

2.

3.

Once everyone has completed the handouts, dim the lights and light a few candles. Pass around the offering plate and ask each person to fold his or her handout and place it in the plate. Pray: "We offer our costs to you. Help us to grow in faith each day. Give us the courage to serve you. We thank you for your free gift of love, we thank you for your free gift of forgiveness, and we thank you for the free gift of your Son. Amen."

Evening Events—After the seriousness of the past sessions, plan some activities to lighten the atmosphere. Play all kinds of games and relays. Try some like these from *Building Community in Youth Groups* (Group Books).

Climbing the Walls—Divide into groups of six to 15 people, and give each group a piece of tape. Give the group members eight minutes to see how high a mark they can make on the wall. Instruct the young people about the importance of using "spotters" to soften the landing if someone takes a tumble. Tell them that they only can use the wall and others in the group for support.

Electric Fence—Tie a 15-foot piece of string about 5 feet off the ground between two objects that are at least 10 feet apart. Use the same groups. Tell the kids that their goal is to get their whole group over the string without touching it. It is illegal to use the objects the string is tied to for support. Have the group members visualize an "electric field" extending from the string to the ground. If they touch the string or cross beneath it they become "electrocuted." The "shocked" individual must try again. Use spotters for this one also. Don't allow individuals to make uncontrolled leaps over the fence. To make this exercise more difficult, don't allow participants to talk.

SUNDAY

Breakfast Celebration—This celebration is designed to help sponsors give the kids a large dose of affirmation. Set a mood of celebration by decorating the dining area and playing a tape of contemporary Christian music. Sponsors take the role of humble servants and treat the kids like royalty. Have fun with this! Have sponsors seat the kids, make sure they're comfortable, serve them food, offer second helpings, clean up after them, and so on.

A "servant's heart" is catching. After the breakfast everyone will be in a mood to help each other out with the tasks of packing and cleaning!

26

Finding Solitude in Our Lives

By Catherine Simmering

S olitude. Silence. Listening to God. All are difficult to fit into our personal lives. The purpose of this retreat is to create space where these things can happen.

Use this retreat to help young people:

● begin to understand what solitude is and how to incorporate it into their lives;

● discover their personal worth and value as they experience the presence of God;

● find untapped resources within themselves; and

● see how involved God is in their daily lives.

By spending time in personal listening and reflection, young people will return to their group with a greater awareness and appreciation of each other.

This retreat is structured around six worship experiences beginning with Friday's worship at 6:00 p.m. and ending with Holy Communion at noon on Saturday. This schedule will allow you to use your own church building, eliminating travel time and extra expense.

Let quiet and reflection be the focus of your retreat. Worshiping together often, especially getting up in the middle of the night, will create a real bond within your group.

Before the Retreat—Most of the preparations for this retreat will be done ahead of time. All plans should encourage kids to spend as much time as possible alone in personal meditation and reflection. Set aside at least one area to be used as a "quiet room." Plan all worship experiences and discussion groups to emphasize solitude.

Create numerous interest centers with as many suggestions for activities as you have time and space. These centers can be as simple as a corner with a poster on the wall or a table with materials for an arts and crafts activity. Ideas for interest centers include:

A nature center—This could be simply a small table with a single rose in a vase or a small collection of plants, rocks and shells. Include a magnifying glass for added interest.

An arts and crafts project—Create either a wire or clay sculpture. Obtain colored wire from the telephone company and self-hardening clay from your nearest craft store. Suggest to participants that their creations could represent any biblical character or scripture passage which has particular meaning or significance for them. Working with their hands while focusing on a particular scripture can be an exercise in learning how to meditate.

Journal writing—Provide a handout with suggestions on how to begin a journal. Include numerous suggestions and examples of topics to stimulate their thinking and writing. Remind participants that journals are personal; therefore, it's impossible to do anything wrong.

A drama center—Offer suggestions for acting out biblical stories. Some may want to create interpretative dances or charades of familiar scripture passages or religious music. Others may design various relaxation methods to allow for more effective meditation.

Plan your interest centers carefully and then allow free time for kids to take advantage of the opportunities available. Provide folders so the kids can organize their materials and keep them together.

Plan worship experiences carefully. Use songs that fit the spirit of the worship experiences. You can find all of the songs listed in this retreat in *Songs* (Songs and Creations, Inc.). Make sure Psalm 4:1-8 and Psalm 100 are written on newsprint prior to the event. Assign the scripture readings to various participants. Ask two of your young people to meet ahead of time to record Psalms 46:1-3 and 63:1-8 on tape. Bring the ingredients and objects to be used for Holy Communion on Saturday.

Write the retreat schedule on newsprint so all participants can follow along. You might also prepare an additional handout for the worship experiences which will include the Psalms, scripture passages and hymns. These materials could be used after the retreat for personal devotions.

Gather materials you will need for the "quiet rooms," including Bibles, small lamps or candles (don't forget the candleholder and matches) and a small plant or flower. Make these rooms as conducive to worship and as free from distraction as possible.

Ask participants to bring a Bible and a pencil. Even though this retreat requires a lot of preparation *before* the event, there should be little to do later. Your time as a leader would be spent best in a supportive role as your teenagers struggle with this little-known experience of solitude.

Retreat Schedule

Friday
- 6:00 p.m. Evening Prayers
- 6:30 p.m. Supper
- 7:15 p.m. Community-building activities
- 7:30 p.m. Introduction
- 7:45 p.m. Empty Your Cup 1
- 8:15 p.m. Why Solitude?
- 9:00 p.m. Free time for interest centers
- 11:00 p.m. Evening Worship
- 11:30 p.m. Sleep

Saturday
- 2:00 a.m. Night Worship
- 2:30 a.m. Sleep
- 6:00 a.m. Morning Prayers
- 6:30 a.m. Breakfast
- 8:00 a.m. Empty Your Cup 2
- 8:30 a.m. Learning to Listen: Finding That Quiet Place
- 9:30 a.m. Free time for interest centers
- 11:30 a.m. The Gift of Solitude: A New Awareness of Each Other
- Noon Lunch, cleanup and leave for home

Retreat Ingredients

FRIDAY

Evening Prayers—The theme of this early-evening worship is light and repentance. This is a time to quietly wait for the Lord and meditate on the scripture. Light one candle to represent the light of Christ.

Begin your worship promptly at 6:00 p.m. Sing a hymn celebrating Jesus as the light such as "Pass It On." Ask four different individuals to read Psalm 141, followed by a few moments of silent meditation. To close the meditation, ask participants to turn to Isaiah 55 and read the verses responsively. After you read the first verse, direct the participants to follow with the second verse. When you have completed the 13th verse, ask participants to turn to 1 John 4:7-21. Read verses 7-12 and ask the participants to respond by reading verses 13-21.

Conclude this scripture reading with time for silent meditation. Ask everyone to concentrate on how Christ is the light in their own lives. Request prayers for others who need Christ's light in their lives.

Ask the group to form a circle. Have each individual introduce himself or herself to the people on both sides by sharing a concern or need for which he or she needs prayers. When individuals have shared their concerns with each other, ask everyone to join hands and pray for:

- the person on their left,
- the person on their right,
- individuals in their lives who need help or guidance, and
- themselves.

After these guided prayers, stretch the circle as far as it will go and then ask participants to let go carefully. Talk about each individual's need for space and the opportunity available this weekend to spend time alone with God. Remind the group to support each other during this time for personal reflection.

Close your worship with a hymn like "Beautiful Savior" to ask for God's presence during this weekend.

Introduction—Take time to explain the purpose and schedule for this retreat. Explain the worship experiences, the interest areas and the quiet reflective atmosphere you want to maintain during this time period. Ask the kids to be considerate of each other's attempts to find time for quiet and reflection.

Hand out the retreat folders and review the schedule posted on the newsprint. Ask each person to choose a scripture verse on which to focus during the retreat. Someone might choose Psalm 46:10 where the psalmist asks us to "Be still and know that I am God." Another might select Matthew 26 which describes Jesus in Gethsemane. Give individuals an opportunity to share their choice with the entire group at the closing worship.

Since silence can be threatening and frightening, be sure to let participants know you are available should they need to talk about what is happening to them.

Empty Your Cup 1—Open your discussion session with this relaxation exercise. Inform participants that the purpose of this activity is to empty oneself of all distractions, worries and thoughts of the day in order to fill up again with new information. Have everyone get comfortable by relaxing in their chairs or reclining on the floor. Begin by having everyone close their eyes. Ask them to relax step by step: first, their toes; then, their feet and so on until their whole body is relaxed. After everyone is relaxed, play soft music in preparation for your small group discussions. Don't rush this time; allow plenty of time for silence and relaxation.

Why Solitude?—Ask individuals to read the following scripture passages to the total group: Mark 1:32-39; John 14:10 and 1 John 5:3. Discuss the following questions:

- How can we apply the example of Jesus' life to our own lives?
- Are we any busier than Jesus was? Explain.

Divide into small groups of three to five people and discuss the questions on the handout for this session. After this session spend the rest of the evening at the interest centers. Remind participants to work quietly to allow others the space they need for personal reflection.

Why Solitude?

These are hard questions, but be patient and loving with each other as you reflect on these issues.

1. Do I have a lonely place where I go to listen to God?
2. Do I want to have a lonely place? Is that an important priority for me?
3. Is it possible that my actions are meaningless and my words and care for others are empty if I don't first listen for God's direction?

Evening Worship—The theme for this late-evening worship is confession. This time is set aside to bring a quiet end to the day. Since participants have been actively involved at the interest centers, bring them together as a group by playing a familiar song of confession like "Seek Ye First."

Have Psalm 4 written on a piece of newsprint. Ask the group to read responsively. You should start by reading first and dividing the responses as follows: verses 1, 2-3, 4-5, 6-7, 8. Reassure the participants of God's availability when we call on him, even when we have done things that disappoint him. Suggest that each person examine his or her own life for a time when God's presence was evident, even when he or she failed to acknowledge it. Ask each participant to confess this failure to God and use this silent time to think about God's continuing presence.

Have two young people prepared to read scripture from both the Old and New Testaments. One should read Isaiah 43:1-7, followed immediately by another young person reading 1 Peter 5:7. Emphasize the reassurance of both passages. Remind participants, "God thinks of each person as precious and honorable. He loves and cares for everyone he has created. He invites all of us to release our cares to him and depend upon him." Ask the group to pray silently for a few minutes and then repeat the Lord's Prayer together to close this session.

Remind the group of their scheduled worship at 2:00 a.m. Recognize the difficulty this schedule presents, but encourage everyone to share this rare opportunity.

SATURDAY

Night Worship—The theme of this worship is the assurance of being watched and cared for during the night. Wake the group with recorded music that celebrates God's presence. When the group is together, sing a song like "Father We Adore You" to acknowledge God's continuing care.

Have the reading of the Psalms recorded ahead of time and play the tape at this time (Psalms 46:1-3; 63:1-8). As soon as the recording is finished, have two young people read Isaiah 41:10 and Ephesians 3:16-21. Ask the group to pray silently for a few minutes. Thank God for his continuing presence. Then quietly begin singing "Alleluia" to praise God as participants return to their sleeping area.

Morning Prayers—The theme for this worship is the Resurrection and praise for a new day. Celebrate this theme by singing a song of praise like "Love Him in the Morning." This kind of music offers both exuberance and a message of newness that alert us to God's presence and power.

Have four participants scattered throughout the group prepared to give the readings from the Psalms. Ask them to begin their reading as soon as the music ends and to follow each other immediately in this order: Psalms 98:4-6; 24:1-2; 24:7-10; and 67:4-5. Have Psalm 100 written on a sheet of newsprint and posted at the front of the room. Ask everyone to read it together in a spirit of celebration. Make sure your own spirit is joyful and contagious so this reading will be a true celebration.

Encourage participants to take a few moments for silent reflection and observation. Ask them to:

● look around them for things that celebrate newness like the dew on the grass or the rays of the sun peeking over the horizon;

● think about their own lives and the personal observations they have made during this retreat;

● consider any revelations that are new to them; and

● think about the results of their decision to spend some time being with God in a new way.

After a few minutes of meditation, ask two participants to read Lamentations 3:20-24 and John 15:12-17. Remind the group, "God's love never ceases. It is new with every morning. And once we have known that love, we are no longer servants to God, but companions with him, ready to offer to others the love that was given us."

Close this morning prayer time with an "eyes-open" prayer. Ask everyone to look around them and celebrate the new life and growth they see:

● in the world of nature around them;

● in the individuals around them; and

● in the group of which they are a part.

Celebrate this newness as a group by singing a song like "This Is the Day That the Lord Has Made." Ask the group to continue to hum the melody as they move away to prepare for the rest of the day.

Empty Your Cup 2—Open the morning discussion session with another relaxation exercise. Direct individuals to empty themselves of all distractions, worries and thoughts to fill up with new information. Use the same body-relaxation exercise, but delete the music. Once everyone is relaxed, ask individuals to use their imagination to go on a trip. Ask them to choose a favorite place and imagine themselves there. It could be a trail in the woods, a special beach, a rock next to a rushing river or a favorite room in their grandparents' house. Enhance their trip by asking leading questions to be answered silently in individuals' minds:

● What do you see?

● What do you hear?

● Is anyone with you? If so, do you recognize the person?

● How do you feel?

● What do you want to do now that you're here?

Do not rush this activity; allow plenty of time. When you are ready to stop, be sure to slow the trip gradually. Direct participants to think about leaving. Remember to ask if there's anything they need to take care of before they leave. And then slowly talk them back to the present.

Learning to Listen: Finding That Quiet Place—To begin this discussion, remind participants of the numerous clues God provides to guide us in finding ways to be with him, even with our busy schedules. Divide into new small groups of three to five people and read the following scripture passages. See what God has to say about finding moments for solitude: Ecclesiastes 3:1, 7; Psalms 1:1-3; 5:1-3; 27:4, 7-9, 11, 13-14; 46:10; Lamentations 3:22-24. List the suggestions of the scripture for finding a place to be alone with God and then discuss the following questions:

● Should we simplify our lives and schedule time for solitude on a regular basis?

● Is that kind of scheduling feasible with our busy lifestyles?

● Do we need to make it possible?

Give participants a reminder: "Take advantage of the little solitudes we all have—the time right after we first wake up in the morning, taking a shower, walking or riding to and from school, waiting for the bus, standing in line, waiting for class to start. There are *many* ways we can find solitude even in the midst of our busy days."

Pass participants the handout that goes with this session. After the

Learning to Listen: Finding That Quiet Place

Reflect on the following questions within your small group. These are difficult questions, but they touch areas many of us need to talk about in relation to God.

1. Do I have a need to be a deeper person? Explain.

2. Am I tired and bored by my own superficiality? Do I sense a needed change in my life? Explain.

3. Am I afraid of silence, of solitude, of being alone? Does silence make me feel helpless? Do I worry about who will be in control? Explain.

small groups have discussed these self-searching questions, spend a few moments talking about the various interest centers you have set up. Encourage your kids to take advantage of them during the free time.

Ask participants to bring some object or statement of personal discovery to share during the final session. It could be the wire sculpture they made at the interest center or a written statement about how the "eyes-open" meditation helped them realize how many times they fail to "see" or "look at" what is actually there.

Move into free time for using the interest centers again. Remind participants that this is still a time for quiet reflection and meditation. Play some quiet music as the groups return to the interest centers.

The Gift of Solitude: A New Awareness of Each Other—The theme for this closing worship is the fellowship of believers and unity for all Christians. Begin this worship by singing a song that celebrates the joy of being Christians together like "Blest Be the Tie That Binds." After singing, celebrate the success of the weekend. Recognize the gift of solitude as a new awareness of each other.

Say: "When we experience God's presence within our solitude, we realize just how much we are accepted and loved. We begin to see ourselves as worthwhile and valuable. When we finally learn to listen to God, we realize we are free to love others. We experience a new gentleness and peace. We no longer have to protect ourselves; we are free to care."

Ask participants to open their Bibles and read Psalm 145:1-13 responsively by verses. You begin by reading the first verse. After the 13th verse, ask the participants to move into a circle around the room and place their objects or statements of personal discovery in front of them.

Have two individuals prepared to read Micah 6:6-8 and Philippians 4:4-9 as soon as everyone is settled. After these passages are read, ask the group to prayerfully consider the following question: "If solitude gives us freedom to be ourselves, to reach out to others in new ways, then could the greatest gift we offer each other be to take time in our busy lifestyles to listen to God?" Allow a few minutes for silent meditation. Close this time of silence by singing a familiar song that reflects unity like "Bind Us Together."

At this point ask individuals to share any new insights or experiences they have had during the retreat. Some may want to share their objects or statements of personal discovery at this time. Others may want to share the scripture they concentrated on throughout the retreat. Encourage but don't force participation in this sharing.

Close this final worship session by celebrating with the elements of Holy Communion. Lead participants in singing "They Will Know We Are Christians by Our Love."

27

Spirituality—A Relationship With God

By Arlo Reichter

S pirituality is a tough topic for many people. We have so many misconceptions about it; we imagine spiritual people as being superhuman saints. So spirituality often becomes a topic that teenagers avoid or think is too far beyond their reach to ever be a part of their lives.

In his book *Reaching Out* (Doubleday), Henri Nouwen shows how spirituality can be an integral and enriching part of our everyday lives. He describes how our relationships to ourselves, to each other and to God are interrelated parts of our spirituality.

We grow in our spiritual lives, Nouwen says, by growing in all three of these kinds of relationships. He challenges us to move from loneliness to solitude, from hostility to hospitality, and from illusion to prayer.

Using Nouwen's framework as a reference, use this retreat to help the participants:

● see that spirituality is a part of a Christian's everyday life;

● know that a relationship with God can turn their loneliness into meaningful solitude;

● draw connections between their personal relationships with friends and family, and their relationship with God; and

● develop a prayerful relationship with the one true God.

Before the Retreat—Gather a roll of butcher paper, 3×5 cards, Bibles, paper, pencils, newsprint, markers, songbooks, tape, communion elements and an offering plate. Copy the handouts for each session.

Make banners to represent each of the three spiritual movements: solitude, hospitality, prayer. Display the banners after their particular movement has been presented at the retreat. All three banners can be brought together for the closing worship.

Choose a retreat location where the group will not be distracted by noise or activities. A spiritual growth retreat needs and deserves a setting with time and space available for quiet reflection.

Plan a pre-retreat session with adult and youth leaders to introduce them to Nouwen's thinking and to the retreat structure. Since the theme is a deep one, it will help for group leaders to be familiar with the retreat material. Encourage some of the adults to read Nouwen's book *Reaching Out* before the retreat.

Recreational activities are especially appropriate at several points in the retreat. Use your own ideas or consult with resources such as the *Try This One* series and *Building Community in Youth Groups* (Group Books).

Retreat Schedule

Friday
- 8:00 p.m. Arrive and get settled
- 8:30 p.m. Getting-acquainted games
- 9:00 p.m. What Is Spirituality?
- 10:00 p.m. Devotions
- 10:30 p.m. Free time—games, night hike, singing
- 11:30 p.m. Head to bed
- Midnight Lights out

Saturday
- 7:00 a.m. Rise and shine
- 8:00 a.m. Breakfast
- 9:00 a.m. Loneliness to Solitude
- 11:00 a.m. Afternoon Planning Time
- Noon Lunch
- 1:30 p.m. Afternoon events (as planned in the morning)

- 5:30 p.m. Dinner
- 7:00 p.m. Hostility to Hospitality
- 9:00 p.m. Free time—games, snacks
- 11:00 p.m. Devotions
- 11:30 p.m. Head to bed
- Midnight Lights out

Sunday
- 7:00 a.m. Rise and shine
- 8:00 a.m. Breakfast
- 9:00 a.m. Illusion to Prayer
- 11:00 a.m. Worship
- 11:30 a.m. Evaluation
- Noon Lunch
- 1:00 p.m. Pack and depart for home

Retreat Ingredients _____

FRIDAY

What Is Spirituality?—Post a long sheet of butcher paper on the wall and distribute markers. At the top of this "graffiti wall" write: "What does the word 'spiritual' mean to you?" Ask the participants to write quickly on the graffiti wall the first 20 words that come to their minds.

Discuss the variety of words, then divide into groups of three. Give each group a sheet of newsprint. Have the groups each write a definition of "spirituality." Share these definitions. Which ones are similar? different? Did the kids find this activity to be difficult or easy? Post the sheets around the graffiti wall. Affirm that all their definitions of spirituality are valid. Say: "It's not easy to understand the spiritual things of life because they cannot easily be located, quantified or seen."

Distribute a Bible to each small group. Ask them to read Romans 8:1-18, then discuss how this passage might change their definition of spirituality. Ask each small group to pair up with another group and create a TV commercial based on this scripture for "the life in the Spirit." The commercials must involve everyone in their group. For example, each member of a group could take turns saying this commercial: "Now . . . for an unlimited time . . . there is no condemnation for those who are in Christ Jesus . . . Through Christ Jesus . . . the law of the Spirit of life . . . can set you free!" Allow 10 minutes for the development of the commercials and then have each group share its commercial with the total group.

Distribute a songbook to each small group. Ask each group to look up hymns which deal with "spirit" or "spirituality." Ask each small group to pick one hymn to read to the entire group, or if it is a familiar hymn, you may want the whole group to sing it.

Devotions—If your retreat is in a nature setting, have devotions outside in a secluded spot. Ask the teenagers to lie on their backs and look at the stars throughout the devotion.

Ask someone to read Psalm 8 which talks about the grandeur of creation and how, in the midst of all this beauty, God relates to us individually in our solitude. Ask the young people to think about when and where they feel closest to God. Do they feel closest to him in church? on a city street? in the mountains? in their room? by themselves? Help them see the importance of silence and personal reflection.

SATURDAY

Loneliness to Solitude—Tell the kids: "This retreat is based on Henri Nouwen's book *Reaching Out*. During this retreat we will be learning about three 'movements' to spiritual growth. Nouwen says that to increase in faith we must move from loneliness to solitude, hostility to hospitality, and illusion to prayer. The first movement we'll learn about is 'loneliness to solitude.' We'll work on improving our relationship with our 'selves.' "

Give each person a pencil and a handout on Thoughts About Solitude. Instruct them to answer the questions on the handout. Give them time to complete their sentences, then divide them in different groups of three to share their responses.

Thoughts About Solitude

When I was a child, I liked to be alone by:	My favorite place to spend time alone is:
When I find time to be alone, I like to:	I hope this weekend can:

On the opposite side of their handout, have the participants each write about a time when they felt lonely. You may want to begin by sharing a lonely experience you had. Say: "Everyone feels lonely sometimes. We should not feel guilty about it but rather welcome it as an opportunity to confront and discover more about ourselves.

"Because we fear loneliness we often try to avoid being alone. We may avoid being alone by turning on a radio or television when we come home to an empty house. We avoid lonely time at home by calling friends after school who we just saw 20 minutes earlier. We avoid being alone by going shopping, going to the park or to a ball game.

"Yet time alone can be very creative and meaningful. In fact, if we want to grow spiritually we must embrace time alone so that we can get in touch with ourselves and our lives. This quality alone-time is called solitude."

Post a sheet of newsprint in front. Have the participants complete the phrase "Solitude is . . . " as many times as they can in five minutes. Record the answers on newsprint.

Write the following verses on newsprint: Matthew 4:1-17; Mark 1:35-42; Mark 6:1-12; Mark 6:30-45. Assign one of the verses to each group of three. (More than one group can have a scripture, or you can add other verses to aid this study.) Have them read the scripture and write the answers to the questions on the opposite side of their handout:

- What is the situation?
- Who is involved?
- Does anyone experience loneliness or solitude? If yes, who?
- What happens after a person is alone?
- What does this say to you about loneliness and solitude?

After 15 minutes, ask each group to share its answers with the entire group.

Have the groups join to make groups of six. Each group is to make a body sculpture to illustrate the movement from loneliness to solitude. Each person must be a part of the sculpture; the sculpture may move, but it cannot speak or make any sounds. For example, the group members can stand with their backs to each other and a forlorn look on their faces; then they can all kneel and raise their arms with a look of joyful praise on their faces. Give the groups 10 to 15 minutes to prepare, and then have them present their sculpture to the rest of the group.

Afternoon Planning Time—Divide the group into teams of four or five. Each team is to plan an afternoon activity for the entire group. The activity should take 15 to 20 minutes, and it can be active or quiet. Encourage the groups to be creative! Ideas include: a scavenger hunt, a water balloon fight, a relay or a hike. Plans should be complete by lunch time. Each group needs to tell you its plans so you can schedule the activities appropriately.

Hostility to Hospitality—Tell the kids: "To grow spiritually we must move from loneliness to solitude, and we must move from hostility to hospitality. This session will help us improve our relationships with others."

Give the kids each a Relationships handout, a Bible and a pencil.

Ask them to answer the first three questions to help them focus on their relationships with others. Say: "On the part of the handout that asks you to list three times when you have experienced hostility, you could include experiences such as moving to a new community and having to make new friends; or experiences with cliques in school, church or community; or times adults have treated you as young children, not as teenagers.

"After you have listed three times when you have experienced hostility, list three times where you were hostile toward someone else. It might not have been physical hostility, it might have been much more subtle—maybe you are in a clique.

"It is important to remember that we all are 'hostile' at times. The purpose of this exercise is not to make you feel guilty, but to help you realize how we can grow spiritually by becoming more hospitable.

"Complete the rest of the handout, then we'll share answers in a large group."

Relationships

1. In my relationship with others I am like:
2. My best friend is like:
3. As a friend I am like:

● Three times I have felt hostility:
1.
2.
3.

● Three times I was hostile:
1.
2.
3.

● Search the Gospels and find a time when Jesus was hospitable (for example, in Mark 10:13-16 where Jesus said to let the children come to him).

1. With whom was Jesus hospitable?

2. Were other people hospitable to these people? Why or why not?

3. What does this passage tell you about hospitality?

On the opposite side of their handout, have participants draw a square and label it "my space." Inside this square ask them to list the names of six people whom they have allowed into their "space" (or into their personal lives) within the last week. Say: "In his book *Reaching Out*, Nouwen observed that hospitality must be inclusive. Our life is enriched through relationships with a variety of people."

After the kids fill in the square with six names, have the participants review how inclusive they are by answering these questions:

● Did you admit someone into your space who is younger than you?

● Did you admit someone into your space who is older than you?

● Are there males and females on the list?

● Are there people from an ethnic group different from yours? (This may not be possible in your community.)

● Were there "new" people admitted to your space last week?

Challenge the participants to reach out and include a wider variety of people in their relationships in the future. Ask them to list beside their "space" the names of three people they will reach out to in the month ahead to bring a greater variety of relationships into their life.

Based on the input and exercises of this session, ask each participant to write a one-sentence sermon about the movement from hostility to hospitality. For example, "Let us move from ignoring newcomers to our school, to welcoming them in our activities." Give them five to 10 minutes to prepare their sermons and then have each one read their sermon. Affirm each one by having the group say in unison "Amen" after each has shared.

Devotions—An excellent passage to emphasize the theme "hostility to hospitality" is Luke 19—the story of Zacchaeus. Ask several people to read the passage out loud. Encourage the kids to see the difference between the hostility of the people toward tax collectors, and the hospitality and acceptance of Jesus toward Zacchaeus. Have them compare the passage to experiences they've had.

SUNDAY

Illusion to Prayer—Review briefly the first two movements of the spiritual life: loneliness to solitude and hostility to hospitality. Refer to things posted on newsprint and certain exercises they have completed so far during the weekend. Then say: "The final movement in spiritual growth is from illusion to prayer. We discuss ways to appreciate our relationship with God."

Distribute paper and pencils. Ask the participants each to make an acrostic with their first name. The theme of the acrostic is faith. An acrostic is made by writing the name vertically down a page, then using each letter of the name as the first letter of a descriptive term about their faith. For example, an acrostic for someone named Sandy might be:

Sincere

Alive

New

Dedicated

Young

Have each person share his or her acrostic with the entire group. After each person shares, have the entire group repeat: "May your faith continue to grow."

Ask group members to think of five "safe gods" in their lives—gods they rely on in place of relying on the one true God. Examples are: money, clothes, status, car, being in the "popular" crowd, etc. After 10 minutes, compile on newsprint a master list of safe gods. Ask each person to pick one safe god in his or her life, write it down and answer the following questions in the small groups:

● How does this safe god keep you from a closer relationship with the one true God?

● How can you overcome the safe gods of your life?

Another way to review our commitment to God is to look at how much "space" we give God. Ask group members to list the days of the week on their sheet of paper. Then tell them to note how much time they spend directly involved in faith-related activities such as devotions, worship, church school, service projects, etc. Next, tell them to note how much time they watch non-religious TV programs and how much time they spend in recreation. After they have completed their charts, ask them these questions:

● Is God really a priority in your life?

● How could someone else tell by looking at your time study?

Post the following questions on newsprint, then read the story of Mary and Martha (Luke 10:38-42) to the entire group. In small groups, have them discuss the questions:

● What safe god did Martha cling to?

● What did Mary do that pleased Jesus?

● How are you like Martha?

● How are you like Mary?

● Is our youth group made up of more Marthas or more Marys? (A group of all Marys might not get many projects done, a group of all Marthas might get lots of projects done but miss connecting with God in the midst of it.)

● How do we balance the Martha and Mary aspects in our personal lives and in our group?

Worship—If a small chapel is available, have the young people go there. Otherwise, meet outside if the weather is nice. Place the offering plate and communion elements in the center of the space and ask the kids to sit in a circle around it.

Distribute a 3×5 card and pencil to each of the kids. Ask them to think again about the safe gods in their lives. Would they like to "give up" any one of these gods so that it will not distract them from their relationship with the one true God? After giving them time to think about the question, tell them that God can help them overcome the safe gods in our lives.

Ask the young people to write their safe god on the 3×5 card. Assure them that nobody will look at it. Tell them to fold the card, then pray silently that God will accept it as an offering. Ask the young people to place their card in the offering plate. Tell them that this act symbolizes that they are turning over that safe god to God.

Retreat Evaluation

1. The best thing about this retreat was:

2. The most difficult thing about the retreat was:

3. Can you remember the three movements of the spiritual life studied this weekend? If so, name them.

4. We needed more time for:

5. We should have spent less time on:

6. The most enjoyable activities were:

7. One thing about this retreat I'll never forget is:

8. Other comments about the retreat:

Once the offering is completed, assure the kids that God accepts their offerings and welcomes them into a closer relationship with him.

Explain that communion is a Christian symbol that describes all three movements of the spiritual life. It symbolizes that God cares for us individually (solitude). Because communion is taken as a group, it symbolizes the importance of our relationships with each other (hospitality). And it symbolizes our relationship with God (prayer).

Distribute the communion elements. Offer a closing prayer in which you ask God to be with the young people as they seek to deepen their spiritual lives by enriching their relationships with themselves, others and God. Close by asking the group to join hands for a closing hymn such as "We Are One in the Spirit."

Evaluation—Distribute the Retreat Evaluation forms to the kids. Have them answer the questions, then give the forms to you.

When you get home, tally the responses and decide which activities went well and which activities need to be adapted. Evaluations are a great way to determine the effectiveness of a retreat. Use them for each retreat you plan!

28

Spiritual Life

By Kathi Finnell

Many young people live hectic, over-scheduled lives that leave little time for reflection. This retreat offers an alternative to the usual fast-paced, activity-filled event. It is for teenagers who are ready to get serious about spiritual growth.

Use this retreat to help participants:
- think about their activity-packed lives;
- spend time alone with God; and
- develop daily habits of spiritual discipline.

Retreat Schedule

Saturday
- 1:00 p.m. Arrive and unpack
- 1:30 p.m. Thinking of God
- 2:00 p.m. Opening to God (Group Time)
- 3:00 p.m. Opening to God (Alone Time)
- 4:00 p.m. Group reflection (share thoughts from the previous two sessions)
- 4:30 p.m. Free time (swimming, hiking, volleyball, reading books about spiritual growth)
- 6:00 p.m. Dinner
- 7:00 p.m. Prayer (Group Time)
- 8:00 p.m. Prayer (Alone Time)
- 9:00 p.m. Group reflection (share thoughts from the previous two sessions)
- 10:00 p.m. Night Hike and Worship
- 11:30 p.m. Lights out

Sunday
- 8:30 a.m. Breakfast
- 9:30 a.m. Growing in Faith (Group Time)
- 10:30 a.m. Growing in Faith (Alone Time)
- 11:00 a.m. Group reflection (share thoughts from previous two sessions)
- Noon Lunch
- 1:00 p.m. Worship
- 2:00 p.m. Pack and depart. Eat pizza on the way home. Celebrate!

Before the Retreat—Reserve a site where your group may be alone, away from interruptions and noise. Choose a location rich with the beauty of nature, including a stream or a lake and plenty of space for people to be alone.

Prepare a reading table full of books about spiritual growth to be available to young people during free time. One excellent resource is *Great Devotional Classics*, a set of 29 booklets. The booklets are excerpts by writers such as St. Francis of Assisi and Dietrich Bonhoeffer (Discipleship Resources, Box 840, Nashville, TN 37202.)

Inner preparation is crucial. One week before the event, call or write each young person and adult sponsor encouraging them to pray for the retreat. Pray that God will use you as a channel of love and encouragement.

Gather several stacks of newspaper; markers; butcher paper; several rolls of masking tape; candles; matches; scissors; and, for each person, a sheet of construction paper, Bible (with a concordance), notebook, pencil, flashlight, 12-inch piece of yarn and copies of the handouts.

_____ Retreat Ingredients _____

SATURDAY

Thinking of God—This following activity is from *More . . . Try This One* (Group Books). Use this time to help the kids think about God and to help them get to know each other. Distribute a Thinking of God handout and a pencil to each person. Give the kids 10 minutes to answer the questions, then discuss the questions in a large group.

Opening to God (Group Time)—Gather the kids, then introduce the retreat by saying: "This event is a time for becoming quiet and knowing God within us. God is not 'out there' somewhere. God is as close as our breath, waiting to share love and communicate with us. However, we must be willing to receive God.

"Each person has the responsibility for what he or she will gain from this retreat. No one person can make it meaningful. We must trust God to overcome our fear of closeness to him and each other. We must be willing to let go of our distractions and look at ourselves honestly."

Give each of the young people a sheet of construction paper. Say that the paper represents them as a complete person: physically, intellectually, emotionally, socially and spiritually. Have them tear or crumple the paper to represent the things that keep them from being happy. For example, a person who's wound up with worries and real-

Thinking of God

Place an "X" on the line which represents your thinking on each issue.

1. Using human years, how old do you think God would be?

_____

1 year   100 years

2. How do you think God would dress today?

_____

Casual   Formal

3. In your mind, God's mood with you is mostly . . .

_____

Critical   Accepting

4. How involved is God in the affairs of people today?

_____

Passive   Active

5. If God would speak to you today, what would be the tone of his voice?

_____

Soft   Forceful

6. God's work load is . . .

_____

Very busy   Very laid-back

ly frustrated with school could crumple the paper into a tiny wad. A person who feels relatively happy but somewhat busy could simply tear off a corner to represent a need for a daily devotion time with God. Discuss the construction-paper symbols.

Distribute a My Spiritual Life evaluation form and a pencil to each of the kids. Tell them to check the space for "before the retreat." Have them follow the directions. Collect the evaluations. Explain that you'll be saving these forms for the end of the retreat. At the end of the retreat you will give the kids a chance to re-evaluate their spiritual life and see if there has been a change.

Divide into small groups and give each a stack of newspapers and masking tape. Instruct the small groups to each build a barrier that keeps us from opening ourselves to God. For example, one group could tape sheets of newspaper together to form a gigantic blanket. All

My Spiritual Life

Name: _____

Before the retreat: _____

After the retreat: _____

My spiritual life right now is like (circle one):

a candle

a search beam

a burnt matchstick

an underground tunnel

not sure

a budding plant

a full-grown flower

an old weed

Explain your answer: _____

_____

_____

To enrich my spiritual life, I want to: _____

_____

_____

group members could lay under it and say, "A barrier that keeps us from opening ourselves to God is relaxing in the comfort of day-to-day living—taking for granted all of our blessings." After the small groups create their barriers, discuss each one.

Opening to God (Alone Time)—Distribute a Bible, notebook, pencil and Breaking Down Barriers handout to each of the young people. Tell the kids they have one hour to be alone and reflect on how they can open themselves to God. Have them answer the handout questions in their notebook.

Dismiss the kids with this prayer: "God, be with us in our quiet time. Open our eyes so we can see ways we can let you into our lives. Amen."

Breaking Down Barriers

● What are five barriers in my life that keep me from being open to God? (For example, a busy schedule, not even thinking about it, being afraid of what others will think, etc.)

1.
2.
3.
4.
5.

● How can I break down these barriers and open myself to God? (For example, schedule an hour of quiet time each morning, pray each night, etc.)

1.
2.
3.
4.
5.

● What does Psalm 46:10 tell me about being open to God?

Prayer (Group Time)—Post a sheet of newsprint in front. Then ask kids to help list all types of prayer they can think of; for example, silent prayer, singing prayer, eye-open prayer, one-sentence prayer, etc. Next, have them list all kinds of positions in which we pray; for example, lying down, kneeling, sitting, etc. Note the many different types and positions of prayer.

Divide into small groups and assign each group one type of prayer. Ask each group to take 15 minutes and create an example of its prayer. After the time is up, gather and have each small group lead the others in the prayer.

A group assigned to silent prayer could write a prayer on newsprint, place it in front of the large group and have them pray silently. A group in charge of a one-word prayer could gather the large group in a circle and tell the members to each say one thing they're thankful for. After all small groups have presented their prayers, have everyone shout an enthusiastic "Amen."

Prayer (Alone Time)—Ask the kids to bring their notebooks and pencils. Make sure everyone has a Bible. Tell them that their assignment for the alone time is to search the scripture for all references to prayer. (Have them look in the concordance for references.)

Ask the kids to choose their favorite verse and write it in their journal in the form of a prayer. For example, a prayer for Matthew 21:22 could be, "God, help me to have faith that you hear and answer my prayers."

Invite kids to try different positions while praying during their alone time. Find one that works especially well for them, whether it be walking, sitting, lying down or kneeling.

Night Hike and Worship—Take your group on a night hike. (If it's nice outside, great! If it's cold, have kids bundle up in warm coats.) Encourage them to use flashlights as little as possible so they can be aware of their senses other than sight. Remind them that God is present in the darkness. They can be at peace without fear.

Hike to a stream or lake. Try to convey a sense of wonder. This can be a very special time for your group. Once you arrive at the worship location, try some of the following ideas:

Praising God—Sing a song of praise such as "Alleluia" that your group knows by heart so songsheets are not needed. Ask one person to use a flashlight and a Bible and read Psalm 8.

Receiving forgiveness—Ask kids to silently confess any sins to God. Confess times we have been too busy to enjoy the beauty God gives us. Confess times when we have forgotten to be thankful for all our blessings. Tell the kids that God forgives all of their sins.

Invite group members each to pick up a stone. Say that these stones symbolize things they're clinging to that keep them from being open to God and to others. Ask them to let go of these things by throwing the rock in the stream or lake.

On the way back to the cabins, sing songs that everyone knows like "Kum Bah Yah" and "Jesus Loves Me."

SUNDAY

Growing in Faith (Group Time)—The purpose of this session is to brainstorm for ways to grow in faith. Divide into four small groups; give each group a piece of paper and a pencil. Allow two minutes for each group to brainstorm for ways to grow in faith. (For example, worship in church every Sunday, visit people in need, take time to be alone, etc.) Have them write the ideas on their paper.

Call time after two minutes, and have the small groups fold their paper into an airplane. On the count of three, have them "fly" their ideas on to another group. Once the groups get another paper, give them two more minutes to brainstorm more ways to grow in faith and add these ideas onto the sheet. Ask them to think of different ways from the ones they had listed before.

Call time after two minutes. Ask groups to refold the planes and "fly" them on to another group. Continue this process until each group receives its original paper.

Tape a long sheet of butcher paper onto the wall. Label it "Ways to Fly in Our Faith." Give the kids markers and have them write on the butcher-paper banner all of the ideas they accumulated. Encourage them to add cartoons, drawings or other sayings to the banner.

Growing in Faith (Alone Time)—Ask the kids to bring their notebooks and sit in front of the butcher-paper banner. Have them copy in their notebooks 10 ideas they'd like to use to grow in faith.

Encourage them to think about these areas and decide how they can incorporate them in their lives. Have them write concrete, realistic steps for incorporating them. For example, a person may choose "Read the Bible daily" as a way to grow in faith. He or she could then decide to read one chapter of the Bible each morning before breakfast.

Worship—Make this a time of warm sharing to conclude this event. Gather your group and sit in a circle around a lighted candle. Invite each participant to share one thing from his or her alone time. How will each person try to grow in faith?

Distribute another copy of the My Spiritual Life evaluation. Give the kids some time to complete it. Then pass out their evaluations they completed at the beginning of the retreat. How have people changed? How have people stayed the same? What are areas kids want to work on? Let them keep these evaluations and take them home as a reminder to continue growing in the faith.

Give kids each a 12-inch piece of yarn. Have them lay it on the floor and shape it to symbolize their faith right now. For example, a person could form the shape of a leaf. She could say her faith is green and growing. Another person could form a circle and say his faith has grown from a circle of family and friends and the love they've shown him.

After all have shared, tie the pieces of yarn together to form one large circle. Leave this lying on the ground. Ask the group members to symbolize their care and support for each other by standing in a circle around the yarn and placing their arms around the people next to them.

Close by saying: "You are a circle of support for each other. Continue to care for each other and help each other in your lives as Christians. Remember all you've learned at this retreat. Keep your journals and continue to use them during your quiet time with God. God bless this circle of friends."

29

Take Me By Surprise!

By Joe Richardson

Just when you thought all winter retreats were the same, along comes an unforgettable weekend full of surprises! This stimulating and exciting retreat can renew your group's enthusiasm and battle the "ho-hum" attitude young people can develop toward God and their Christian life.

The Take Me by Surprise! retreat is designed to:

● involve the congregation, group members' families and community in the pre-retreat buildup;

● teach each young person that Christianity can be as exciting as a weekend full of surprises;

● give group members, as "secret servants," an opportunity to affirm and encourage each other; and

● help young people appreciate Christ's ultimate sacrifice on the cross, and the ultimate "surprise"—the Resurrection.

Before the Retreat—Invite a contemporary Christian musician or group to appear at the retreat. Surprise your group by choosing someone who's never performed for your youth group. An important reminder: Begin searching for your band or singer at least one year in advance. Also, make sure you or an adult leader meets with the musician(s) personally prior to the retreat, and that the music style is compatible with your ministry. (You want no surprises here!)

Choose a camp or retreat center the group has never attended. Keep the location a surprise too. (Tell kids' parents the retreat location, but ask that they help you keep it a secret.)

Begin publicity at least six weeks in advance. Take a picture of all the adult youth leaders together, hamming it up and displaying a comical look of surprise on their faces. Make 8 × 10 color photos and put these on posters. Place these posters around the church.

For another effective publicity tool, make portrait badges. Take photos of each adult sponsor looking surprised. Make badges with these photos. Have each sponsor wear someone else's badge. Wear a badge whenever you're at church. They make great conversation starters.

When publicizing the retreat, give only enough information to keep the enthusiasm high. Suspense will build automatically as people continue to hear about the Take Me by Surprise! retreat—that it'll be held at a mystery camp with a mystery musical guest.

Place a small advertisement in your local newspaper. It'll generate excitement—not only in your church, but also in the community.

Send eye-catching personal invitations to every young person on your mailing list. For example, on the front of the invitation, have a cartoon character (designed just for the retreat by a talented group member) shaking a gift-wrapped box. Above that, print in bold letters, "Take Me by Surprise!" Inside the invitation, give only the retreat date, leaving and returning time and a list of things to bring. For an added surprise, stuff each invitation full of confetti. Mail the invitations one month before the retreat.

Gather festive party favors (confetti, balloons and streamers); party noisemakers; small slips of paper, each with a group member's name written on it; small gifts for the Surprise Boxes (candy, cut-out cartoons, toys); a prerecorded cassette of popular television theme songs; a cassette player; a cassette featuring upbeat contemporary Christian music; the clues for the Treasure Hunt activity; a large commercial popcorn popper; popcorn; tape; and, for each group member, a large Styrofoam sandwich box from a local fast-food restaurant (for the Surprise Boxes), the Sign-Up Mixer handout, a piece of paper, a pencil and an envelope; plus the supplies listed below for each special session.

● For the Big Send-Off: Fill the Surprise Boxes (Styrofoam boxes) with confetti, balloons and streamers.

● For Bible Surprise Session #1: enough pipe cleaners, foot-long pieces of string, sheets of construction paper, small scissors, paper clips, crayons, modeling clay and foot-long ribbons for each group member to get one of the items; and an Expecting the Unexpected handout and a 3×5 card for each group member.

● For Bible Surprise Session #2: darts; newsprint; and, for each group member, a small slip of paper and a balloon.

● For Bible Surprise Session #3: the newsprint with the questions on it; markers; and paper.

● For Bible Surprise Session #4: a cassette recording of an instrumental version of the song "Via Dolorosa"; and the communion elements.

● For the Ice Cream Surprise: three or four 8-foot-long chicken-feeding troughs or rain gutters; ice cream; bananas; nuts; and topping.

● For the War game: strips of red and black cloth, enough for half the group to have red and half black; 50 small plastic pill containers; 50 jelly beans (25 red and 25 black); two coffee cans; and two flashlights.

● For Friday evening: a film of your choice and a film projector.

A Big Send-Off—Throw a rousing bon voyage party just before departure. Invite all the group members' families. Serve surprise snacks; for example, normal-looking hot dogs filled with chili sauce. Provide streamers, horns and noisemakers to add to the merriment.

If the weather is wintry, add a surprise tropical twist to the party. Decorate the departure area to look tropical. Play beach music and have the adult sponsors wear loud flowery shirts and shorts, leis and

---

Retreat Schedule

(All Times RST—Retreat Standard Time)

Friday
8:30 p.m. Arrive at the mystery camp
8:45 p.m. Unload and relax
9:15 p.m. Icebreakers and Secret Servants
9:45 p.m. Singing
10:15 p.m. Bible Surprise Session #1
10:45 p.m. Name That Tune and Ice Cream Surprise
11:15 p.m. Game time: War
12:15 a.m. View the film
1:15 a.m. Go back to cabins/rooms
2:00 a.m. Turn out lights

Saturday
10:00 a.m. Rise and shine
10:30 a.m. Eat breakfast and play Name That Tune
11:15 a.m. Aerobics
11:30 a.m. Singing
11:45 a.m. Bible Surprise Session #2
1:00 p.m. Treasure Hunt
2:30 p.m. Eat lunch and play Name That Tune
3:15 p.m. Singing
3:30 p.m. Bible Surprise Session #3

4:15 p.m. Free time
7:30 p.m. Eat dinner and play Name That Tune
8:30 p.m. Rehearse for Saturday Night Spectacular
9:00 p.m. Have a concert featuring a special guest
10:00 p.m. Participate in Saturday Night Spectacular
11:30 p.m. Eat snacks
Midnight Fireside Sharing
1:00 a.m. Go back to cabins/rooms
1:30 a.m. Turn out lights

Sunday
10:00 a.m. Rise and shine
10:30 a.m. Eat breakfast and play Name That Tune
11:15 a.m. Aerobics
11:30 a.m. Singing
11:45 a.m. Bible Surprise Session #4
12:30 p.m. Take communion
12:45 p.m. A Letter to Myself
1:00 p.m. Free time
2:30 p.m. Eat lunch and play Name That Tune
3:30 p.m. Pack up
4:15 p.m. Depart

straw hats. This will heighten the suspense about the retreat location. As you leave the church, give the parents envelopes that contain all the retreat information.

Introduce the Surprise Boxes at the conclusion of the bon voyage party. Have each group member label his or her own box. Explain that kids can keep the party favors but not destroy the boxes, because they'll be used later. Then collect the boxes.

You can arrange a police escort out of town. The kids will love it! Allow them to throw their confetti and streamers from the bus while the police car—sirens screaming and lights flashing—leads the bus on its way. (Ask some parents to clean up the confetti and streamers after the kids leave.)

Switch to "Retreat Standard Time." While on your way to the retreat site, stop the bus and instruct group members to set their watches two hours forward. Explain that the entire retreat schedule will be based on "Retreat Standard Time." When you arrive at the camp, be sure to set all the clocks ahead two hours. Now the young people can stay up until 1:30 a.m. and sleep in until 9:00 a.m. (This really works! No one will be late for breakfast, and the young people will comment on feeling more rested because of sleeping later. It's amazing what a change of time can do.)

—————— Retreat Ingredients ——————

FRIDAY

Icebreakers—Begin by having members stand in a circle and give backrubs. Next, do this Sign-Up Mixer: Give each group member a list of statements such as "I use mouthwash regularly"; "I was born 1,000 miles from here"; and "I eat raw oysters." Each group member must get the list signed by people who've done the items. (A person can sign his or her name only once on another person's list.) To help group members meet the newcomers, include "This is my first youth group retreat" on the list.

As an added surprise, give one of the newcomers a dollar bill. Instruct him or her to give that dollar bill to the seventh person who asks the newcomer to sign an item. Have the newcomer yell "Surprise!" before awarding the dollar bill.

Surprise Boxes—Use the Surprise Boxes for giving the young people small gifts and surprises: candy, cut-out cartoons, little toys or a personal note from an adult leader. Set the boxes on the dining tables at mealtime. Be sure to collect the boxes after each meal so they aren't destroyed. Your group members will eagerly look forward to every meal as they anticipate opening their Surprise Boxes.

Secret Servants—Write the name of each young person on a slip of paper. Place one name in each of the Surprise Boxes. (Make sure not to give anyone his or her own name.) Introduce the Secret Servants exercise by giving each group member his or her own Surprise Box. Have group members open their boxes privately. Each young person will be a secret servant to whoever's name is in the box. Secret servants will give small gifts or surprises, encourage and do favors for that person the rest of the weekend—without being discovered. This exercise makes each person feel special, and strengthens friendships within the group. Collect the Surprise Boxes for later.

Bible Surprise Session #1: Expecting the Unexpected—In each of the Surprise Boxes put *one* of the following items: a pipe cleaner, a foot-long piece of string, a sheet of construction paper (folded to fit), a small pair of scissors, a paper clip, a crayon, a lump of modeling clay or a foot-long ribbon. Place the Surprise Boxes on a table.

Divide the group into teams this way: Have each group member find and open his or her Surprise Box. The group members then form teams of eight by finding people who have different items from theirs, so that each team ends up with a complete set of the eight items. (If a team has fewer than eight members, give them the items they lack.)

In the small groups, give each young person a 3×5 card and a pencil. Display a sheet of newsprint with this incomplete sentence: "You may be surprised to learn this about me, but . . . " Have everyone complete the sentence on the back of their 3×5 cards. Remind them they don't have to reveal any embarrassing secrets. Examples of what kids might share include: a relative with an unusual occupation, something strange about their homes or a recent success such as a good report card.

After group members each complete their card, they should pass it to a designated person in their small group, who will then shuffle the cards and pass them back out. Each group member takes a turn reading the newsprint statement and then completing it by reading the card out loud. Group members try to guess whose card it is. To emphasize the "surprise" aspect, everyone in the small group should gasp loudly after guessing.

Give group members each an Expecting the Unexpected handout. Have them read the Bible passage and discuss the questions.

After about 10 minutes, give each small group a clothes hanger and tell them to use the items from the Surprise Boxes to build a "surprise-mobile," a symbol of Abraham and Sarah's surprise. As they complete and explain their surprise-mobiles, hang the mobiles across the front of the meeting room.

Expecting the Unexpected

Read Genesis 18:1-15, 21:1-7; then answer the following questions:
- Why did Sarah laugh at the angels' prediction that she would bear a son? How would you have reacted if you were in her situation?
- How do you think Sarah reacted when she found out she was pregnant?
- Which of these statements best describes your response toward surprises? Choose one and explain why you chose it.

_____ I look forward to the surprises God brings into my life.

_____ I adjust to surprises, but I wish I didn't have to.

_____ I don't like surprises at all. I prefer predictability.

Close with a "surprise prayer." Gather the group members into a circle. Once everyone has closed their eyes and become silent, pop a balloon. Regardless of the group's reaction, keep your head bowed and eyes closed and begin praying something like this: "God, we sometimes don't like surprises of any kind. But don't let that stop you from working in our lives."

Name That Tune—This is an easy game to play just before each meal or snack time. Make a cassette tape of several TV theme songs. Plan one song per meal or snack time. The first young person to name the theme's TV show wins. Offer a prize for each winner—a candy bar taped onto an old copy of TV Guide, for example.

Ice Cream Surprise—Promise everyone banana splits, but serve them in 8-foot-long chicken-feeding troughs or rain gutters. Fill them with scoops of different-flavored ice cream. Add bananas, nuts and toppings. Place the troughs or gutters on the floor and let the kids go at them, with one rule: hands behind the back. The scene provides a great photo opportunity.

War—Go outside for a rousing nighttime game of War. This version is adapted from the book *Play It!* (Zondervan).

Divide the group into two armies—red and black. Each army's soldiers wear black or red strips of cloth tied around their arms to identify themselves. Assign half of the playing area to each army.

The object of the game is to destroy the opponent's radar installation by bombing it. The radar installation is a powerful flashlight in a coffee can. Each army gets 25 bombs. A bomb is a small plastic bottle with a red or black jelly bean in it. Dropping a live bomb into a radar installation destroys it.

Soldiers defending the installation may seize bombs from their opponents and deactivate them by eating the jelly bean. They can then reactivate the bomb by putting one of their team's jelly beans into it.

Use felt tip pens for guns. One of every five players gets a gun. (The pens should be either red or black to match the team colors.) To shoot an opponent, the players must capture the opponent, hold him down and mark one finger of his left hand. The opponent then is out of the game for two minutes. Penalize a team if they mark more than just the finger. A player is dead (out of the game) when he's been shot four times.

Play for one hour. The team that's bombed the radar installations the most times is the winner.

Film—Close the evening with a film of your choice. Add a surprise: Show it backward! (*Up!*, a film about flying from Pyramid Film & Video, is a good choice.) Or show a film without the sound on. Let the kids guess the dialogue.

SATURDAY

Aerobics—Follow breakfast on Saturday and Sunday with a 15-minute aerobics workout, led by an experienced group member or adult leader. Use contemporary Christian music.

Bible Surprise Session #2: Slaying Giants—Give each group member a small slip of paper, a balloon and a pencil. Have each person write on the paper a fear they struggle with. Then have everyone fold the paper, stuff it into the balloon, blow up the balloon and tie the end.

On a sheet of newsprint, trace an outline of any group member's body. Tape the newsprint onto the wall and tape all the balloons onto the newsprint within the body outline.

Read 1 Samuel 17:1-50 to the group. Say: "Everyone was surprised when David killed Goliath. You have giants in your life—everyday fears. But you might be surprised to learn that, with God's help, you can defeat those giants. Just like David killed Goliath, we're going to kill some 'giants' today."

Have the group members get into pairs. Ask for volunteers to come up, one pair at a time, to throw a dart at the balloon-covered newsprint "giant." When one person pops a balloon, the partner picks up the slip of paper and reads the fear written on it. Have the entire group discuss with their partners how God could help "slay that giant." Ask people to share their suggestions. If a slip of paper contains a fear already discussed, ask for additional thoughts on the topic. Let group members take turns until all the balloons have been popped.

Close with a "victory prayer." Gather the entire group into a circle. Have them join hands and raise each others' arms in victory. With everyone's arms raised, pray: "God, help us to trust you to slay the giants in our lives. With your power, we can do it!"

Later, at lunch, place a small stone in each Surprise Box. Tell the kids: "Keep that small stone with you. When you face a fear, ask God how he can help you slay it, like he helped David slay Goliath."

Treasure Hunt—Conduct an outdoor treasure hunt. Choose 15 different locations around the camp to hide clues. Each clue cryptically describes a location in the camp. Put each clue in a plastic egg, and place them around the camp so that the clue in location #1 refers to location #2; the clue in location #2 refers to location #3; and so on. Spread the clues far apart.

Divide the group into teams. Allow one hour for the teams to finish the treasure hunt. When the last team finishes, announce first prize. For a surprise, award it to the last-place team!

Bible Surprise Session #3: Surprise! A Miracle!—Divide the group into four teams. Assign each team one of these passages: Matthew 9:18-26 (Jesus raising Jairus' daughter); Mark 6:30-44 (Jesus feeding 5,000); John 2:6-10 (Jesus changing water into wine); John 9:1-41 (Jesus healing a blind man).

Display these questions on newsprint:

● What happened in this passage that surprised everyone?

● How did people express their doubt that Jesus could perform a miracle?

● How did they express their surprise later?

Have each group prepare and perform a "silent movie" version of their miracle. Give each group a marker and five sheets of paper on which to write mini-dialogue like those shown in silent movies. For example, "Gadzooks! I can see!" for the blind man.

Concert—Feature your special musical guest in a one-hour concert Saturday night. The concert should be a worshipful, thought-provoking time and give the kids a chance to focus on their own relationship with Christ.

Saturday Night Spectacular—Encourage everyone to contribute skits for this talent show, including sponsors. (Require that participants clear their skits with you.)

Popcorn Surprise—Bring a large commercial popcorn popper to make Saturday's unexpected snack.

Fireside Sharing—Give your kids a chance to share what they've learned over the weekend. Ask the kids what has surprised them about God and about themselves. If the retreat center has a fireplace, sit together on the floor in front of it. Sing a praise song in between talk times.

SUNDAY

Bible Surprise Session #4: The Ultimate Surprise—Set out the Surprise Boxes. Before the worship service begins, have each young person find his or her Surprise Box and tape it onto the wall to form a large cross. Say: "These boxes symbolize that Christ's death on the cross has brought us together and made us one."

Play the tape recording of the instrumental version of "Via Dolorosa." Instruct the young people to face the cross they've constructed on the wall and stand with their arms straight out to the side. Have them hold their arms out while adult sponsors read the following Bible passages in this order: Luke 23:33-34; Luke 23:39-43; John 19:26-27; Matthew 27:45-46; John 19:28-30; Luke 23:46-47. The young people will become uncomfortable and even experience pain. Compare this pain to the pain Christ endured because he loves us so much.

Then have the young people, arms still outstretched, gather into a circle with their arms around each others' shoulders. Explain that the story didn't end at the Crucifixion; there was yet another surprise from God. Have young people take turns reading the following passages, taking their arms down to read their Bibles, if necessary: John 20:10-16; Matthew 28:5-10; Luke 24:28-31; John 20:19-23; John 20:26-29; Luke 24:50-53.

Close the worship service with communion. Have each young person come to the communion table with a friend, to partake of the elements together.

A Letter to Myself—Following communion, have the young people each write a letter to himself or herself. They should mention in the letters what the weekend meant to them, what they learned and what commitments they made. Have each group member place the letter in a self-addressed envelope.

Mail these reminder letters to the kids about four weeks after the retreat. Don't be surprised if the weekend makes a lasting impact.

30

This I Believe

By Dean Dammann

The concept of faith is hard to grasp, because it is based on belief of things "unseen." Teenagers, like all people, need time to discover the meaning of faith, and time to think of their own beliefs. This I Believe gives kids that time to discover and reflect on their faith.

This retreat will help participants:
- understand the concept and meaning of faith;
- reassess the content of their Christian faith; and
- share their faith with others.

Before the Retreat—Gather posterboard, magazines, glue, clay,

Retreat Schedule

Friday
7:00 p.m. Arrive at retreat site
7:30 p.m. Community-Building Activities
8:30 p.m. Refreshment break
9:00 p.m. Evening Worship
10:00 p.m. Free time
11:30 p.m. Lights out

Saturday
8:00 a.m. Breakfast
8:45 a.m. Morning Worship
9:30 a.m. Exploring Faith
10:30 a.m. Break
11:00 a.m. Being Sure
Noon Lunch
1:30 p.m. The Meaning of Faith

3:30 p.m. Free time
5:00 p.m. Dinner
6:30 p.m. What's Your God Like?
7:30 p.m. Expressing Our Faith
9:30 p.m. Evening Worship
10:30 p.m. Free time
11:30 p.m. Lights out

Sunday
8:00 a.m. Breakfast
9:00 a.m. Getting Ready for Worship
10:00 a.m. Break
10:30 a.m. Closing Worship
11:30 a.m. Pack and clean cabins
Noon Lunch, then leave for home

construction paper, yarn, scissors, pencils, Bibles, newsprint, markers, blindfolds, tug-of-war rope, copies of handouts, and one prize such as a piece of fruit or a bag of peanuts.

When you prepare the I Believe handout, include enough statements to fit each of your group members.

Read the retreat and write the designated discussion questions on newsprint.

Bring songbooks, and ask a person to be in charge of song-leading for the retreat. The songs listed in this retreat can be found in *Songs* (Songs and Creations, Inc.).

_____ Retreat Ingredients _____

FRIDAY

Community-Building Activities—Play some fun games to help kids get to know each other better. Give each person a pencil and an Interview Questions handout. Have the kids each choose a partner and interview each other with the questions.

Interview Questions

1. What are your likes?
2. What are your dislikes?
3. Who is the most important person in your life?
4. What do you look for in friends?
5. What are some of your hopes and dreams for the future?
6. Why do you belong to a church?
7. What are you looking for in life? (What are your purpose and goals?)
8. What do you want to happen during this retreat?

After each person has been interviewed, have each pair join two other couples. In these groups of six, ask each person to introduce his or her partner and tell information gathered from the interview.

Another community-building activity is for the total group. Have everyone sit in a circle, then give each person an I Believe handout. Tell the kids: "Survey the group while seated in a circle, and find a person who you believe best fits each description. Fill in a different name for each blank. Do not consult with another person or check out your belief until I tell you to."

I Believe

1. I believe _____ is the tallest person here.

2. I believe _____ is a straight-A student.

3. I believe _____ wears the biggest shoe.

4. I believe _____ is the only child in his or her family.

5. I believe _____ is the fastest runner.

6. I believe _____ knows how to sew.

7. I believe _____ can speak another language besides English.

8. I believe _____ has blue eyes.

9. I believe _____ is the shortest person here.

10. I believe _____ was born in (your city or community).

11. I believe _____ has the longest hair.

12. I believe _____ knows how to ski (snow or water).

After everyone has finished their game sheet, say: "Sometimes what we believe is not a fact. How many of your belief statements are true? You can move around now and talk to people to check out your list. A prize will be given to the one with the most accurate list."

Discover who had the most correct answers, award him or her the prize, then have the winner share the accurate statements with the total group.

Evening Worship—Gather in a circle, then introduce the theme "Be still and know that I am God" (Psalm 46:10). Open by singing a song such as "Peace Like a River."

Ask a young person to read Psalm 46 one line at a time. Have the other participants echo each line in a whisper.

For the meditation, go around the circle and have each person complete this sentence: "God has been a strength and help to me when . . . "

Close with a circle prayer. Ask each person to share something for which he or she wants to praise God. Have the kids begin with the words: "I will praise you Lord for . . . " (protection, everlasting life, good health, etc.). Then sing "They That Wait Upon the Lord."

SATURDAY

Morning Worship—Gather in a circle, then introduce the theme, "This I do believe." Ask someone to read John 20:24-29. Say that this passage is about Thomas, who doubted. Emphasize the verse where Jesus said, "Blessed are those who have not seen and yet believe" (John 20:29).

Discuss these questions:

● Faith is a fragile gift that God gives. Do you have to do anything to keep your faith? Explain.

● Do you have to see something in order to believe? Why or why not?

Go around the circle and have each person tell the first memory he or she has of learning about Jesus. When was it? How old were they? Close by singing songs such as "I Believe" and "Thank You."

Exploring Faith—Have everyone stand. Designate opposite sides of the room as A and B. Tell the kids: "Several times I'm going to ask the question 'Which is your faith more like?' Then I'll say two words of opposite meaning, and you'll need to move to either the A or B side of the room depending upon your choice." Solicit comments on their choices after each item. Use these lists of words:

"Which is your faith more like?"

A	B
rain	sunshine
skiing	mountain climbing
a balloon	a bowling ball
a pillow	a rock
knowing	searching
a baby	a teacher
a story	a song
a father	a TV newscaster
a river	a lake

Form groups of six people. Display the list of questions which you have printed on newsprint. Ask each person to choose a response to each of the questions. Discuss answers in the small groups.

1. Which best expresses your present feeling about faith?
   a. I think faith is a gift of God.
   b. I think you can prove your faith by attending church regularly.

c. I think you can have doubts about God and still have faith.

2. Which best describes your faith?
   a. I am not sure what I believe.
   b. I have the same basic beliefs as my parents.
   c. I have beliefs that are quite different than my parents.

3. Which best describes how you share your faith?
   a. I share my beliefs with friends and family members.
   b. I would like to tell a friend about my faith but don't know how to begin.
   c. I have never told another person what I believe about God.
   d. I have shared my personal faith with someone but feel that it was not appreciated.

Bring the small groups together and have them share their group's discussion. Encourage further discussion about why it is difficult to share one's faith in God.

Being Sure—Form new groups of six, then give each group a Bible, sheet of newsprint and marker. Post the following questions which you have written on newsprint. Tell the small groups to discuss the questions.

1. Do one of the following:
   a. Recall a time when you felt close to God. In a sentence or two describe the occasion.
   b. Select your favorite Bible verse or Bible story. Explain why it's your favorite.

2. Take turns reading Hebrews 11:1-13 aloud. Rephrase the first verse in your own words.

3. As a group, make a list on newsprint of all the actions (or results) of faith which are identified in Hebrews 11:2-13.

Have each small group present its newsprint list to the large group. Tape the lists onto the walls of the meeting room.

The Meaning of Faith—The following activities might be utilized to understand trust as an ingredient of faith. Divide the group into three smaller groups. Assign each group one of the following activities. After they have completed their activity, have them present or demonstrate it for the large group.

Activity A—Form pairs; blindfold one person in each pair. Have the "seeing" person lead the blindfolded person around in two ways:

by voice command, and by taking him or her by the hand.

Reverse roles. Discuss as a small group whether there was trust expressed in doing this activity. Was there more, or less trust needed in voice-leading over hand-leading? Explain.

The small group that does this activity could present it by having the large group experience the Trust Fall. Have the total group form two circles: a center circle and an outside circle. Everyone faces the center; each person in the center has a partner standing directly behind him or her. Ask each person in the center circle to relax and fall backward, while the partner catches him or her. Reverse roles. Discuss whether everyone trusted their partners to catch them.

Activity B—Form equal teams for a tug of war. Mark the center line and indicate that the winner will be the team that pulls the first person of the opposing team across the line in three out of five attempts. Say that there is one difference in this game from a usual tug of war. Each group can decide to let go of the rope rather than pull, to surprise the other team. Neither team will know the other's decision.

After a few tug-attempts, discuss what this activity said about trust in each other. Ask them to share how this activity relates to putting our trust in God.

The group members can share their experiences with the total group by demonstrating what happened or by structuring the same experience for any number of additional teams.

Activity C—This group will explore the outdoors for objects to symbolize their faith. For example, a seed could represent new life.

Explain to the group: "Since faith is often trust in something which we can't see, we create symbols to visualize and make real what we believe in. Examples are the cross and the fish symbol.

"Divide in pairs and take a nature walk to find items which symbolize your faith in God. Then reconvene with your small group and discuss the symbols."

The small group assigned to this activity can share its symbols with the total group, and ask the rest of the kids to find their own symbols.

What's Your God Like?—Form groups of six. Give each group a sheet of newsprint, marker, pencil, Bible and a How Would You Describe God? handout. Have them complete the handout in their small groups.

When all the groups are finished, let each one explain its mini-creed and how it relates to the passage they studied. Post the mini-creeds on the walls.

Expressing Our Faith—This activity is planned to assist participants in expressing their personal Christian faith. Ideas they de-

How Would You Describe God?

1. Let each person choose three of the following that best describe how he or she sees God.

. . . a doctor
. . . an old man
. . . a parent
. . . a king
. . . a movie director

. . . a policeman
. . . a teacher
. . . a judge
. . . an artist
. . . a Salvation Army officer

2. As a group, choose one of the following scripture passages. Read it silently. What does this section tell you about God and what he has done for you?

Psalm 31
Psalm 47
Psalm 121
John 1:20-34
Colossians 1:12-23

Ephesians 1:3-14
Romans 5:12-21
Romans 8:1-4
Romans 8:31-39

3. As a group, develop a mini-creed based on this section. Write your mini-creed on newsprint. (A creed is a statement of belief.)

velop from this session can be shared in the Sunday morning worship.

Distribute a piece of paper and a pencil to each of the young people. Have them write several sentences on what they personally believe about God the Father, God the Son and God the Holy Spirit.

After they have completed this, ask them to utilize their creative abilities to express what they believe. Some suggested art forms might be: a written creed, a song or poem, a drawing, a banner, a sculpture, a symbol, a drama. Supply materials such as clay, newsprint, posterboard, magazines, glue, markers, construction paper, yarn and scissors.

Evening Worship—Go outside for this one. Tell the kids: "We're going to have a 30-minute worship—in total silence. When we go outside, simply soak in the beauty of God's creation. Remember, no talking."

SUNDAY

Getting Ready for Worship—Ask all participants to help develop an order of worship. Ideas:
- Display and discuss each person's art creation.
- If people made banners, have a procession with them.
- Have a demonstration of a "trust" exercise.
- Share written creeds, songs, poems.
- Share thoughts on Hebrews 11:1-13.
- Sing songs learned during the retreat.

Agree on the order of worship and write it on newsprint so all can follow along. This planning session will probably take one hour. Afterward, give everyone 30 minutes to collect necessary items for the worship, then gather for the service. The closing worship will seal the enriching experiences the kids have had throughout the weekend.